SENATORIAL POLITICS AND FOREIGN POLICY

SENATORIAL POLITICS & FOREIGN POLICY

MALCOLM E. JEWELL

GREENWOOD PRESS, PUBLISHERS
WESTPORT, CONNECTICUT

Library of Congress Cataloging in Publication Data

Jewell, Malcolm Edwin, 1928–
    Senatorial politics & foreign policy.

    Reprint of the ed. published by the University of
Kentucky Press, Lexington.
        1.   United States—Foreign relations—1945–
2. Political parties—United States. 3.   United
States—Politics and government—1945–   I.   Title.
ₜJK1081.J4 1974ₔ   327.73   74-11587
ISBN 0-8371-7678-6

Originally published in 1962 by the University of Kentucky
Press, Lexington

Reprinted with the permission of the University Press of Kentucky

Reprinted in 1974 by Greenwood Press,
a division of Williamhouse-Regency Inc.

Library of Congress Catalog Card Number 74-11587

ISBN 0-8371-7678-6

Printed in the United States of America

TO MY WIFE

ACKNOWLEDGMENTS

THE MATERIAL IN THIS BOOK IS DRAWN IN CONSIDERABLE PART FROM the press (particularly the *New York Times*), periodicals, documents, and books. But I have also relied on interviews, about sixty-five of them, with senators, staff assistants and committee staff members in the Senate, and Washington correspondents. Men in such responsible positions are naturally reluctant to be quoted, and during the interviews I committed myself not to attribute information to them individually. I have not cited them as sources in the footnotes. But I want to express my debt to them. Their comments and the factual information they supplied were invaluable for such a study. I deeply appreciate the time they took from always busy Washington schedules to assist me in this study. Half an hour or more in a senator's day is a valuable commodity, and those whom I interviewed were generous indeed with their time. Members of the policy committee staffs of both parties were particularly helpful in supplying information about a subject almost unmentioned in the printed sources.

Professor Ruth C. Silva of Pennsylvania State University was a most conscientious adviser and critic in the preparation of an earlier version of this study. She never let me forget that political science writing, no less than any other, should be readable. Colleagues who contributed information and advice on specific subjects covered in the book include Ralph K. Huitt and Hugh A. Bone.

My wife assisted in proofreading several versions of this study and typed an earlier version. It is customary for a writer to declare that his book could not have been written without the encouragement, patience, and assistance of his wife, and in this case it seems to me an unusually appropriate statement.

I want to thank the University of Kentucky Research Fund Committee for making available funds for typing the final draft and Mrs. John B. Imredy for her conscientiousness at the typewriter.

I am indebted to the Roper Public Opinion Research Center at Williams College for making available the results of public opinion polls and for permission to publish these results. The *Congressional Quarterly Almanac* is an invaluable research tool for political scientists, and I appreciate the permission to use the rollcall statistics therein.

Portions of two chapters of this study are based on material originally published in the *Journal of Politics*, Vol. XXI (1959), and the *Western Political Quarterly*, Vol. XII (1959), and are used here with permission.

It is always appropriate to point out that, though I have been dependent on many others for assistance, responsibility for any errors of fact or judgment is solely mine.

M.E.J.

CONTENTS

drive

It is especially in the conduct of their foreign relations that democracies appear to me decidedly inferior to other governments. . . . Foreign politics demand scarcely any of those qualities which are peculiar to a democracy; they require, on the contrary, the perfect use of almost all those in which it is deficient.—ALEXIS DE TOCQUEVILLE

If, at the present time, the limitation imposed by democratic political practices makes it difficult to conduct our foreign affairs in the national interest, this difficulty will increase, and not decrease, with the years.—DEAN ACHESON

1

INTRODUCTION

THE PROBLEM RAISED A CENTURY AND A QUARTER AGO BY THE author of *Democracy in America* seldom troubled the American people during the many years that they enjoyed an isolation protected by two broad oceans. In our generation, however, every new foreign crisis brings increased international responsibilities to this country and further emphasizes the difficulties of conducting foreign relations in a democracy. Any nation, but particularly the leader of an alliance, needs to have dependability and continuity in its foreign policy; yet in a democracy the opposition party may overturn established policies at any time. Diplomatic moves must often be planned and executed with a speed and secrecy that contradict the democratic principles of consultation and consent. For success in international power politics a nation is often dependent on a degree of domestic unity that seriously restricts the democratic opposition party. Perhaps most important, international problems have become too complicated for public understanding, and foreign policies have grown too costly and risky for public popularity—and yet in a democracy these policies need public understanding and approval if they are to succeed.

In the United States there are additional handicaps not found in all democratic governments. The decision-making process in this country resembles John Calhoun's "concurrent majority": A large number of groups both within and outside the government must, in practice, approve any major policy. The division of authority between the American President and Congress is particularly conducive to difficulties in the field of foreign affairs. For as Professor Edward S. Corwin says, "the Constitution . . . is an invitation to struggle for the privilege of directing American foreign policy."[1] Furthermore, the United States, just now emerging as a leader in international affairs, has not developed the traditions, attitudes, and political techniques that are most valuable in adapting democratic government to the tasks of formulating foreign policy.

In most of its postwar foreign policy decisions the United States has been spared deep-seated disagreement on fundamentals. Before World War II, however, the interventionist-isolationist split was a profound one accentuated by party differences. Since the war there has been a large measure of agreement in principle on our aid and alliance policies in Europe; but the less successful Asian policies have caused deep and bitter disagreements culminating in the frustration of the deadlocked Korean war. William S. White has called the last months of the Truman administration "perhaps the most enfevered months of modern times in a nation savagely divided on foreign policy."[2] As the stakes in international relations continue to increase, the possibilities of political conflict and deadlock grow.

[1] Edward S. Corwin, *The President: Office and Powers, 1787-1957* (4th rev. ed.; New York: New York University Press, 1957), p. 171.

[2] William S. White, "Two Parties and One Foreign Policy," *New York Times Magazine*, Aug. 7, 1955, p. 12.

POLITICAL PARTIES AND BIPARTISANSHIP

Political parties, scorned and feared by the founding fathers, have gradually won recognition as essential in producing both an organized majority and an effective opposition in our system of democracy. The two parties bring a measure of order and unity out of the many varied interests, regions, and viewpoints found in this nation. Furthermore, by providing a strong bond between the President and a majority or a large minority in Congress, the party system has been primarily responsible for making workable the system of divided authority between an independent executive and legislature.

But the value of the party system in the realm of foreign affairs is often questioned because it produces not only a majority but also a minority, often a strong and vocal one. In the words of one veteran observer of Congress, the political party "restlessly snipes at unanimity in foreign policy."[3] The need for unity in foreign policy is clear; foreign policy that must be implemented by treaty requires a two-thirds vote in the Senate. Frequently the administration lacks a party majority in one or both branches of the Congress; therefore, issues which have become sharply partisan are likely to be deadlocked. The election of a President of the opposing party can destroy the continuity so valuable in foreign policy if his party has fundamentally opposed the programs of his predecessor. Overshadowing these constitutional considerations is the fact that success in foreign policy depends largely on a nation's strength; and unity is a major element of this strength. The necessity of unity in a hot war is obvious; its value in a prolonged cold war is almost as great.

After World War II, both the Truman and Eisenhower administrations sought bipartisan support for some of their foreign policies, often through consultation and collaboration with opposition leaders in Congress. The argument for a bipartisan foreign policy has always been a simple one—the need for unity. Senator Arthur H. Vandenberg emphasized that "it permits our democracy to speak with a great degree of unity at critical mo-

---

[3] Ernest S. Griffith, *Congress—Its Contemporary Role* (2d rev. ed.; New York: New York University Press, 1956), p. 163.

ments when swift decision is vital and when we face totalitarian opponents who can command their own instant unity by police decree."[4] Despite the force of this argument, politicians and scholars have raised serious objections to the bipartisan principle in foreign affairs. It may weaken the party system and blur the lines of party responsibility. Bipartisanship may damage the opposition party. By capturing its leaders, the administration may silence the opposition, or at least those members most responsible and skillful in foreign affairs, and may intensify divisions within that party. Bipartisanship may lead to the hasty adopton of unwise policies or perhaps to an illogical and ineffective compromise between the desires of the administration and minority demands. It may prevent an intelligent and comprehensive debate of the issues involved and cause rigid adherence to policies, once established.[5]

In addition, the difficulties of effective bipartisan cooperation are widely recognized by both supporters and critics. Neither of the congressional parties regularly produces leaders who can commit their colleagues to an agreed policy. The problem of secrecy constantly plagues executive-legislative consultations on delicate diplomatic questions. In practice both congressional leaders and executive officials are often too busy for the frequent, detailed consultation that both believe to be necessary for bipartisan cooperation.

The debate over the merits of bipartisanship and partisanship in foreign policy often creates the impression of a choice between two absolutes. The realities of post-war politics, however, have ruled out either extreme and have necessitated a blend of the two systems. A purely partisan conduct of our foreign policy is impossible because the parties are not unified and disciplined and because control of government is sometimes divided between the parties. Even when the President's party controls Congress and when there is no treaty involved requiring two-

[4] Arthur H. Vandenberg, Jr., ed., *The Private Papers of Senator Vandenberg* (Boston: Houghton Mifflin Co., 1952), pp. 450-51.

[5] The best recent analysis of the advantages and disadvantages of bipartisanship is Cecil V. Crabb, Jr., *Bipartisan Foreign Policy: Myth or Reality?* (Evanston, Ill.: Row, Peterson and Co., 1957). See also George H. E. Smith, "Bipartisan Foreign Policy in Partisan Politics," *American Perspective*, IV (Spring, 1950), 157-69; James MacGregor Burns, "Bipartisanship—and Partisanship, Too," *New York Times Magazine*, Jan. 27, 1957, pp. 17, 70-71.

thirds support in the Senate, the administration has to seek votes from the minority because it cannot usually depend on unanimous support from the majority. That being the case, the administration naturally takes steps to assure some bipartisan support. From the viewpoint of the opposition, a partisan stand is equally impractical. One observer has pointed out that "since there are two parties and only one integrated foreign policy, that which may be developed by the Presidency, the policy may well be advocated by both parties."[6]

On the other hand, bipartisanship cannot be applied to every foreign policy. The opposition is not usually willing to cooperate in the reexamination or resurrection of a program that appears doomed to failure. Sudden crisis may leave little time for bipartisan consultation. An administration that lacks domestic political strength or that is engaged in bitter domestic struggles with the opposition may find the political atmosphere not conducive to bipartisan cooperation in foreign affairs. Some foreign policies are so interwoven with controversial domestic questions, such as the level of the budget, that bipartisan agreement is difficult or impossible.

In practice both the Truman and Eisenhower administrations have developed a blend of bipartisanship and partisanship, which H. Bradford Westerfield describes as "extra-partisanship": The President seeks "to associate in active collaboration with his administration's conduct of foreign relations enough influential members of the opposition party to prevent its lines from solidifying against basic administration foreign policies—while at the same time the President's position as leader of his own party is used to mobilize support for those policies, to the limited extent that it can safely be done without causing the opposition party to consolidate in counteraction."[7] Under these conditions bipartisan consultation has been most frequent when it was necessitated by events, above all by the fact of one party controlling the Presidency and the other the Congress. Senator Vandenberg has said: "It is to be noted that this bipartisan liaison is much

[6] George L. Grassmuck, *Sectional Biases in Congress on Foreign Policy* (John Hopkins University Studies in Historical and Political Science, ser. 68, no. 3; Baltimore: Johns Hopkins Press, 1951), p. 173 [481].

[7] H. Bradford Westerfield, *Foreign Policy and Party Politics: Pearl Harbor to Korea* (New Haven: Yale University Press, 1955), p. 16.

simpler (as in the 80th Congress) when each major party controls one end of the executive-legislative process involved in foreign affairs. . . . We both confront unavoidable and obvious responsibilities in such cases."[8]

Although extrapartisanship seems to have been developed in response to the political necessities of recent years, it has liabilities. From the administration's viewpoint, it is a fragile system, because the support for policies must be based on unreliable and shifting coalitions and because policies must often be seriously compromised to win bipartisan support. On the other hand, the opposition party finds it increasingly difficult to challenge the administration's policies and present clear alternatives in foreign affairs. In an age of permanent international crisis, the danger is simply that we may drift to disaster through a chain of uneasy compromises and misguided policies that are protected from effective criticism by the umbrella of bipartisan consultation. The question is whether the policy-forming process in this country can be improved to produce sounder policies that are more strongly supported after fuller discussion. Critics of the existing techniques for framing foreign policy have frequently suggested some strengthening of party machinery.[9] A stronger majority party organization in Congress, working closely with the President, would offer the possibility of a more dependable, coherent foreign policy and reduce the risk that vital programs of the administration would wither away in the congressional labyrinth. It would give the individual congressman greater protection from the demands of pressure groups and constituents and would perhaps provide an instrument through which the reluctant voters could be persuaded to accept the expensive and dangerous policies that the administration so frequently is forced to sponsor. A stronger opposition party in Congress might be better able to present alternatives to the administration's policies. Without becoming obstructionist, it might serve a watchdog role, to prevent the President's misuse of the increasingly broad powers being granted to him in the execution of foreign policy. Since the techniques of bipartisanship ob-

[8] Vandenberg, p. 562.
[9] See, for example, W. Y. Elliott and others, *United States Foreign Policy: Its Organization and Control* (New York: Columbia University Press, 1952).

viously cannot be completely abandoned, the question is whether the political party can contribute more to framing both administration and opposition policy within the framework of the existing extrapartisan system.

The most realistic way of appraising the prospects for partisan contributions to policymaking is to examine in detail how party organizations and leaders have functioned in the past. Most of the recent studies of foreign policy formation have stressed the use of bipartisan techniques, but policymaking in Washington is fundamentally a partisan process. The President and the powerful congressional leaders are primarily party leaders, who exercise party authority, understand current issues in political terms, and owe strong allegiance to their party. Few are the issues, domestic or foreign, that have no political implications when they arise in Congress. Even bipartisanship has never signified nonpartisanship but has meant cooperation among party leaders to achieve support for a policy from substantial groups in both parties. Neither the opportunities for bipartisanship nor the chances for strong parties can be understood when they are simply debated in a theoretical vacuum. We can gain insight about both through an examination of the political process in Congress applied to international problems.

THE POLITICAL PROCESS IN THE SENATE

Although the international responsibilities of the House of Representatives have greatly expanded in recent years, the Senate still remains the more important body. Here the "great debates" are carried on, and here alone are treaties ratified. Those members of Congress who speak with authority on international problems are almost invariably senators. Despite the growing importance of the House, members of that body still defer to senatorial leadership on a large proportion of foreign policy questions. Constitutional provisions and tradition have combined to give the Senate the preeminent role in foreign policy. Consequently this study is confined to the Senate. To attempt a survey of both branches would require sacrificing the depth of analysis necessary for an understanding of senatorial politics.

Bernard Cohen in his study of conflicts arising from the Japanese peace settlement observes that "American political party differences are strong enough so that they cannot all be hidden by the blanket of a bipartisan political process. In a system of undisciplined parties, bipartisanship does not preclude differences of opinion on a party basis."[10] So much has been said about bipartisan foreign policy that the importance of differences between the parties on foreign policy has been little understood. Despite some differences between the parties on matters of policy, there is evidence that party positions and voting records changed when a Democratic administration was replaced by a Republican one.

A rollcall analysis that produces evidence of party voting suggests questions about the nature of leadership in the Senate. Do members of a party vote together on an international question solely because of conviction and perhaps loyalty to the President, or are they influenced by the organizational or persuasive efforts of party leaders in the Senate? Leadership in the Senate is a highly personal affair. Are the leaders of the administration party primarily the President's representatives in the Senate or the Senate's ambassadors to the White House? What techniques or tools do they possess beyond their own intellectual prestige? Can the opposition leaders in the Senate unite their party behind foreign policy alternatives, or can they achieve unity only in support of the President's policy? If party leadership is not to be dependent on the accidents of personality, it must be institutionalized. What evidence is there that party policy committees and caucuses are widely enough used and effective enough to be useful tools of party leadership? Does leadership in foreign policy rest primarily on the Foreign Relations Committee and on its talented leaders? How can this committee, a model of bipartisanship, provide party leadership as well?

If the political parties are to become more effective instruments for the creation of foreign policy, much of the initiative must rest with the President, who not only holds the initiative in foreign policy but is the recognized leader of his party. Can he be a party leader in foreign policy without losing bipartisan

---

[10] Bernard C. Cohen, *The Political Process and Foreign Policy: The Making of the Japanese Peace Settlement* (Princeton, N. J.: Princeton University Press, 1957), p. 200.

support? Presidential leadership in foreign policy rests in part on his powerful influence over public opinion. In turn, the willingness of senators to support presidential programs rests in part on the climate of public opinion that they sense. How is public opinion manifested? To what extent has foreign policy been an issue in election campaigns? Will electoral controversies over foreign policy strengthen or weaken the President's position?

Bernard Cohen concludes: "The study of bipartisanship will make useful progress only when the normative element can be set aside long enough to accumulate more specific knowledge about the forms, the substance, and the results of the various political processes that the word describes."[11] The same questions apply to the role of parties in the formation of foreign policy. This study attempts to answer them by examining the political process in the United States Senate and the influence of two forces—the President and the public—on this process as it was demonstrated in the international issues that engaged the Senate's attention from 1947 through 1960. The final chapter presents some tentative answers with regard to one major question: Can the political parties contribute a greater measure of rationality and responsibility to the policymaking process in foreign affairs? In an age when our very existence may depend on the wisdom of our foreign policy, there are few questions more important.

[11] *Ibid.*, p. 235.

In both of the two great fluid periods of the twentieth century—the periods just before, during, and after the two World Wars—the Democrats were in the position of responsibility for the conduct of foreign affairs. . . . This, I think, had more to do with the hardening of attitudes than innate party characteristics. The Democratic attitude was formed by government in power, responsible for its acts, and with that innate knowledge of the new pressures and necessities which comes only from the conduct of affairs.

—DEAN ACHESON

2

THE DECLINE OF DEMOCRATIC INTERNATIONALISM

SAMUEL LUBELL HAS CALLED ELECTION RETURNS THE "WATER-marks which reveal the flow of history."[1] As the student of party politics must start by examining election returns, so the student of senatorial politics must first analyze rollcalls. It is true that some issues never reach a rollcall vote and that the votes alone leave questions of causation unanswered. Yet rollcalls are vital to our study because they alone provide unbiased, uncontrovertible evidence of decisions on foreign policy questions in the Senate. Because our foreign policy has so often been labeled bipartisan, it is important to emphasize the frequent contrasts in voting patterns of the two parties and to identify the most partisan issues. The change in both Democratic and Republican voting patterns with the advent of the Eisenhower administration was radical enough to require careful examination. This change may well provide the key to understanding the potential role of parties in foreign policy. Finally, the outstanding sources of disunity in the two parties—notably regionalism—deserve examination.

The analysis of Democratic and Republican records in this and the following chapter is based on a selection of rollcalls from 1947 through 1958. This twelve-year period is evenly divided between Democratic and Republican administrations and includes Congresses in both periods controlled by the opposition as well as by the administration party. The necessity of comparing party voting records during the various Congresses has dictated the selection of recurring issues rather than the inclusion of all rollcalls relevant to foreign policy. Most of the analysis is based on 179 rollcalls in three fields: foreign aid, reciprocal trade, and collective security. These are also the categories of rollcalls that best measure "internationalist" and "isolationist" voting, terms that may be usefully defined respectively as support for and opposition to foreign commitments of the United States.

The rollcalls on foreign aid provide a particularly good measure of party voting because the authorization and appropriation of funds must be renewed annually. There are two groups of foreign aid rollcalls in our compilation. The first (totaling 35) includes all those taken on the passage of authorization and appropriation bills and on the approval of Senate-House conference committee reports of such bills.[2] The second (totaling 76) includes all amendments to foreign aid bills designed to increase or reduce the funds to be authorized or appropriated for

---

[1] Samuel Lubell, *Revolt of the Moderates* (New York: Harper & Brothers, 1956), p. 261.

[2] In addition, there are included votes on a few substitute amendments that would have had the effect of killing the aid program. After 1950, all rollcalls were on the extension of existing programs rather than on new ones. In the rollcalls on conference reports, opposition votes were sometimes cast by senators who objected simply to certain features inserted by the conference committee.

foreign aid.[3] These two groups are treated separately because the records of the two parties and of regional groups of senators were different on the two categories. At times, particularly after a foreign aid program has been generally accepted, a key vote on an amendment cutting the aid funds has given a clearer picture of foreign aid sentiment than has the final vote on passage of the bill. On the other hand, there are many senators who have regularly supported foreign aid bills while voting for most amendments to reduce funds. The large number of other amendments offered to foreign aid bills are excluded from this compilation because they have varied considerably in substance from year to year and have seldom provided clear-cut tests of internationalist sentiment.[4]

In six of the twelve years under study Congress voted on extensions of the reciprocal trade program. There has been strong substantive continuity in the issues reaching a rollcall vote. In addition to the final passage of bills, votes have been recorded concerning how many years the program should be extended, how much discretion the President should be given, and whether special protection should be accorded certain products—all questions going to the heart of the program. The 30 rollcalls in this compilation include all except a few omitted because they did not distinguish clearly even the strongest supporters and opponents of the program.

In eight of the twelve years the Senate voted some expansion of American military commitments abroad: the NATO and SEATO pacts; mutual defense treaties with Japan, Korea, and Nationalist China; and resolutions authorizing the President to send troops to Europe, defend the area of Formosa, and resist Communist aggression in the Middle East. The 38 rollcalls on these questions have a substantive homogeneity because they were all concerned either with whether this country's military commit-

---

[3] Throughout this study, rollcalls on reducing aid and those on increasing aid have been lumped together. These are different questions, of course, and on the relatively few rollcalls concerning proposed increases the sentiment for economy was usually stronger than on rollcalls proposing reductions. For our purposes, the record of a party or a group of senators on the two types of rollcalls can be combined.

[4] Examples are amendments designed to prevent recipients from selling strategic materials to Communist countries and to encourage European political cooperation or to discourage cartels or socialism in Europe.

ments abroad should be extended or with how much discretion the President should be given in implementing new security commitments.[5]

Although these three major categories of rollcalls provide the best measure of both voting continuity and internationalism, a larger sample would provide a more comprehensive picture of party voting. A supplementary group of 104 rollcalls has been added to the compilations on those occasions when a larger sample seemed desirable. These include nearly all of the previously omitted amendments to bills in the three major categories[6] and votes on four other questions that stirred considerable controversy: the Truman-Attlee talks in 1950, the MacArthur hearings in 1951, the Japanese Peace Treaty in 1952, and the Bricker amendment in 1954.

A rough measure of partisanship in senatorial voting is the proportion of rollcalls on which a majority of Republicans took a position opposed to that of the majority of Democrats. This occurred on just over half of the 283 rollcalls in the comprehensive sample (excluding rollcalls on which either party was evenly divided). Partisan conflict dropped when Eisenhower entered the White House; the proportion of such rollcalls fell from 63 percent in the first six years to 32 percent in the latter period. The two parties (that is, a majority of the senators in each) agreed on most of the foreign aid bills and the collective security commitments. They disagreed half the time on the size of foreign aid funds and more often than that on other amendments to foreign aid bills. They disagreed on a majority of rollcalls concerning reciprocal trade and concerning the discretion granted President Truman to implement security commitments. In other words, there was bipartisan support for most of this country's fundamental commitments abroad, but considerable partisan

---

[5] In addition to the issues listed, there are included rollcalls on the Vandenberg resolution, which preceded American membership in NATO; measures to admit Greece, Turkey, and West Germany to NATO; and the Status of Forces Treaty. A few rollcalls on amendments to measures concerning collective security have been omitted because they did not deal with this topic.

[6] Those amendments not included in this broader category are ones on which the administration's position was not clear. In order to measure the support provided by each party for the administration, it was necessary to include only questions on which the administration had announced a position or on which its position was clear from the substance of the issue.

controversy over many important details of carrying out these commitments.[7]

THE DEMOCRATIC VOTING PATTERN

In a survey of voting on foreign policy issues during the Truman administration, one fact stands out: the consistently high degree of support given by Democratic senators to the administration's program. As Table 1 illustrates, this meant not only the support

TABLE 1—Foreign Policy Rollcalls by Percentage of Democratic Senatorial Support of the Truman and Eisenhower Administrations, 1947-1952 and 1953-1958 (283 Rollcalls)

Percentage of support	Truman, 1947-1952		Eisenhower, 1953-1958	
	Number	Percentage	Number	Percentage
90-100	81	47.4	11	9.8
80-89.9	41	24.0	16	14.3
70-79.9	25	14.6	14	12.5
60-69.9	9	5.2	24	21.4
50-59.9	10	5.8	14	12.5
40-49.9	1	0.6	13	11.6
30-39.9	2	1.2	12	10.7
20-29.9	2	1.2	2	1.8
10-19.9	0	0.0	3	2.7
0-9.9	0	0.0	3	2.7
Total	171	100.0	112	100.0

of a majority of Democratic senators on nearly all rollcalls, but also the support of 80 percent or more of the Democrats on 71 percent of the rollcalls. Moreover, Democratic support was greatest on those measures most important to the Truman administration. When the major foreign aid programs were passed the first time, three-quarters or more of the Democrats voted for them. There were seldom more than one or two Democrats voting against the extension of these programs thereafter. Most of the rollcalls on which Democratic majorities were small and the few on which a majority opposed the administration involved amendments to the foreign aid bills. The Democratic vote was

[7] The rollcalls compiled in the *Congressional Quarterly Almanac* (hereafter *CQA*) are the source of all statistics used in this book. They are used with the permission of Congressional Quarterly, Inc. In every case, only the votes actually cast for and against measures have been included, with pairs and announced positions excluded except where specifically mentioned.

nearly unanimous for the two major security commitments of the Truman administration, the North Atlantic Treaty and the Japanese Security Treaty. In a series of twelve rollcalls on these issues, there were a total of only 15 Democratic votes cast against the administration.[8] The Democrats were equally willing to grant President Truman authority to implement the NATO treaty by sending troops to Europe. On the key votes to approve this policy and to bar any military limitation on the troops or any binding restrictions on the President (through a joint resolution), Truman had the support of all but one or two Democrats. There was greater disagreement in Democratic ranks about framing the resolution to request that Congress be consulted about the assignment of further troops to Europe without unduly binding the President.[9] On the most important rollcalls involving reciprocal trade, almost complete unanimity prevailed in the Democratic party.

The Truman administration was defeated on only 31 of 171 rollcalls, including the 5 on which it lacked majority Democratic support. None of these were rollcalls on the passage of foreign aid or collective security measures or on amendments vital to any of these measures. The only important defeats suffered on reciprocal trade involved several attempts in 1948 to extend the program beyond one year. When the administration lost, it was usually because of the opposition of a large number of Republicans and a sizable minority of Democrats. Most of the losses involved amendments to foreign aid bills and, although some were damaging to the administration, they were far less important than defeats on the major bills would have been.

This Democratic record does not mean that President Truman's efforts to secure bipartisan backing for his foreign programs were unnecessary. The constitutional requirements for passing treaties, the need of large majorities on major legislation to reassure our European allies, and the Republican Senate majority in 1947 and 1948 were all factors necessitating bipartisanship. Moreover, the Democratic margin in the Senate was never great enough to

---

[8] *CQA*, 1948, p. 218; 1949, pp. 429-30; 1952, pp. 177, 182. There was virtually no Democratic support for reservations to the North Atlantic Treaty that would have required prior congressional authorization for armed assistance to NATO partners.

[9] *Ibid.*, 1951, pp. 257-58.

assure victory even if the party remained nearly united. There were nearly always two reasons for the administration's victory in a legislative battle: the high degree of Democratic unity and the success in winning at least a few and often many Republican votes.

The Democratic record during the Truman administration is important because it proves that political support for foreign programs can be built primarily on the massive unity of the administration's party. Conversely, it suggests that an administration cannot expect legislative success for its foreign programs unless it can depend on strong, consistent support from its own party in the Senate. The Truman administration had substantial numbers of Republican votes for its major programs. But it was the Democrats who not only provided the majority of votes for the Marshall Plan, foreign military assistance, Point Four, NATO, and the other important measures, but who also repeatedly defeated amendments (usually Republican-sponsored) that would have undermined these measures. With a few minor exceptions, a higher proportion of Democrats than of Republicans supported the Truman administration on all foreign policy rollcalls from 1947 through 1952.

A look at the right hand side of Table 1 reveals a different pattern of voting from 1953 through 1958. The Eisenhower administration had majority Democratic support on 71 percent of the rollcalls, a substantial proportion but much less than the 97 percent support that President Truman had enjoyed. Perhaps more important, 80 percent or more of the Democrats backed the Eisenhower administration on only 24 percent of the rollcalls (compared to 71 percent previously). During the Eisenhower administration a remarkably unified party became a divided one. If the Democratic senators had remained as united against the Eisenhower programs as they had been in support of the Truman programs, the explanation would be simple: The senators were motivated by a sense of loyalty to and confidence in one administration that disappeared with the advent of the next administration. In fact the picture is more complex. The Democrats gave President Eisenhower much more support for some of his policies than for others. Moreover, certain groups of Democrats voted nearly as often for Eisenhower's policies as they had for Truman's, while others voted very differently. We must look more closely at the variations that appeared during the Eisenhower administration.

The simplest way to demonstrate the differences in voting on various issues is to record the percentage favorable to the administration of all votes cast by Democratic senators on all rollcalls concerning the issue. During the Truman administration this figure had been 89 or 90 percent for each of three categories: collective security, foreign aid measures, and reciprocal trade. During the Eisenhower administration this figure slipped to 80 percent for collective security, 74 percent for foreign aid, and 69 percent for reciprocal trade. In the case of the other category, amendments determining the size of foreign aid funds, support dropped from 77 to 54 percent.[10]

The Democratic commitment to collective security weakened only slightly during the Eisenhower administration. Until the debate on the 1957 Middle East resolution, the Democrats supported the administration on every rollcall involving security and did so nearly unanimously on the key rollcalls. There was only a two-to-one Democratic margin for the Middle East resolution and there was a slight majority for one amendment to it opposed by the administration.[11] The Democrats voted for foreign aid (but by decreasing margins) on every rollcall except one involving an amendment to eliminate financial aid from the Middle East resolution. The Democrats continued to vote for reciprocal trade measures by lopsided majorities but were much more closely divided than before on amendments affecting the President's discretion. The greatest change was in the Democratic senators' attitude toward the size of the foreign aid program. The only time the Democrats voted against the Truman administration (out of 33 rollcalls) on this question was in 1951 when they opposed an amendment to restore one billion dollars eliminated in committee. But they voted against the Eisenhower ad-

[10] These percentages provide only a convenient general impression of voting support and obscure many details. Support of 70 percent on ten rollcalls, for example, could mean 70 percent support on each rollcall, or 100 percent support on seven and none on the other three, or many other things. The percentages are based on the total votes cast; nonvoting or paired senators are ignored.

[11] *CQA*, 1957, pp. 286-87.

ministration on 17 out of 43 rollcalls involving the size of the foreign aid program.[12]

To understand better the inconsistencies in the Democratic record, we must explore the regional variations in the Democratic ranks, outlined in Table 2.[13] During the Truman administration the regional variations were relatively minor (Table 3). The only region falling below 85 percent support was the South, where the average was pulled down by the vote on a single category—foreign aid spending amendments. Democrats from the Northeast and Midwest (containing most of the industrial states) supported both administrations overwhelmingly. In any geopolitical map of the Democratic party these would be the regions of internationalism. During the Eisenhower administration there was a distinct change in the voting pattern of Democratic senators from the other four regions, most notably in the South and the Mountain States. The trend away from internationalism in the South deserves particular attention because southern senators cast about 45 percent of all Democratic votes

12 In 1959 and 1960 Democratic support for foreign aid measures remained nearly stable, averaging 70 percent. Support for higher aid totals dropped to 42 percent, and a majority of Democrats favored cuts on about half of the rollcalls.

13 A study of regionalism in the Senate may be less accurate than a similar study in the House because of the distortion that may result from one or two maverick senators. The regions used by other political scientists have varied with the purpose of the writer. The following criteria have been used in establishing seven regions: (1) to follow other regional breakdowns wherever possible; (2) to group together states whose senators behaved alike in voting on international issues and separate those states whose senators have contrasting records; (3) to establish contiguous, compact regions, small enough to emphasize regional voting differences but large enough to provide a statistically significant number of senatorial votes in each party in each region except for one-party regions.

The seven regions are: (1) The Northeast—the six New England states, New York, New Jersey, and Pennsylvania; (2) The Midwest—Illinois, Indiana, Iowa, Michigan, Minnesota, Ohio, and Wisconsin; (3) The Plains States—Kansas, Nebraska, and North and South Dakota; (4) The Border States—Delaware, Kentucky, Maryland, Missouri, Oklahoma, and West Virginia; (5) The South—Alabama, Arkansas, Florida, Georgia, Louisiana, Mississippi, North and South Carolina, Tennessee, Texas, and Virginia; (6) The Mountain States—Arizona, Colorado, Idaho, Montana, Nevada, New Mexico, Utah, and Wyoming; and (7) The West Coast—California, Oregon, and Washington.

In other studies, Iowa, Minnesota, and Wisconsin are often considered Plains States, or else the Plains States and Midwest are combined. The different method used here is designed to sharpen voting differences.

on foreign policy in each administration and because they cast 58 percent of all Democratic votes against the Eisenhower pro-

TABLE 2—Democratic Senatorial Support by Region of the Truman and Eisenhower Administrations' Foreign Policy, 1947-1952 and 1953-1958 (Percentage of 179 Rollcalls)

Region	Truman, 1947-1952	Eisenhower, 1953-1958
Northeast	99	90
Midwest	91	89
Border States	90	69
South	79*	54
Mountain States	85	59
West Coast	98	69

* If votes on the size of foreign aid spending were excluded, the southern figure for 1947-1952 would be 88 percent.

TABLE 3—Democratic Senatorial Support by Region of the Truman Administration's Foreign Policy, by Various Categories of Issues, 1947-1952 (Percentage of 97 Rollcalls)

Region	Foreign Aid Measures	Foreign Aid Spending	Security Measures	Reciprocal Trade
Northeast	100	99	97	100
Midwest	95	83	95	98
Border States	97	90	93	82
South	84	63	87	93
Mountain States	88	85	84	85
West Coast	100	97	100	97
All Regions	90	77	89	90

TABLE 4—Democratic Senatorial Support by Region of the Eisenhower Administration's Foreign Policy, by Various Groups of Issues, 1953-1958 (Percentage of 82 Rollcalls)

Region	Foreign Aid Measures	Foreign Aid Spending	Security Measures	Reciprocal Trade
Northeast	100	89	87	86
Midwest	100	87	82	93
Border States	83	62	87	61
South	59	40	79	70
Mountain States	80	47	80	51
West Coast	91	67	65	64
All Regions	75	54	80	69

grams. While the percentage shift in southern voting is no greater than that in several other regions, the South was primarily responsible for the altered record of the Democratic senators.

Table 4 presents more precise information on the nature of

the regional shifts. Democrats in the Northeast and Midwest supported all Eisenhower programs by large margins. There were no significant regional variations on collective security between administrations except on the West Coast, where the low figure results from Senator Wayne Morse's opposition to nearly all security programs. The South was the only region in which a significant proportion of senators opposed foreign aid bills. The South and Mountain States contained the largest proportion who voted for reducing foreign aid. During the Truman administration the South had provided the lowest proportion of Democratic votes for foreign aid measures (84 percent) and by far the lowest proportion of votes against reductions in aid funds (63 percent). In the Border States, West Coast, and especially the Mountain States, Democratic support for maintaining high spending levels declined despite continued large majorities for foreign aid measures. Since Democrats in these three regions had provided the Truman administration with larger majorities on spending amendments than southerners had, their voting pattern underwent a greater shift during the Republican administration even though the percentages did not drop so low as in the South.[14] The figures for reciprocal trade present a different picture: Southern support for the Eisenhower administration (70 percent) was higher than that of the other three regions; the Mountain States, where Democrats were almost equally divided, ranked lowest.

The first conclusion to be drawn from the Democratic record during the Eisenhower administration is that, with a couple of exceptions, there was some decrease in the willingness of senators from each region to vote for each major category of foreign programs. Even the most internationalist Democrats seemed to feel less constrained to guarantee support for Eisenhower than they had for Truman. The variations in the voting pattern are more important. They indicate that Democratic internationalism was more consistent, and less dependent on loyalty to one administration, in the field of collective security than in the areas of foreign aid and reciprocal trade. The figures indicate that

<hr>

[14] During 1959 and 1960, southerners continued to provide a higher proportion of votes against foreign aid and for reductions in the program than Democrats from other regions. Democrats from the Northeast and Midwest continued to give the strongest support for foreign aid.

the trend away from internationalism was greatest in the southern and western sections of the party. The Democratic senators' remarkably strong loyalty to the Truman administration obscured the motivations for internationalist voting by a variety of senators on a variety of issues. The voting record in recent years makes possible a closer look at the changing motivations of Democratic senators.

The South has long been regarded as the bulwark of internationalism in the Democratic party, and yet during the Eisenhower administration the largest number of senators whose voting records changed were southerners. For these reasons we shall focus our search for the causes of declining internationalism on the South, without neglecting the attitudes of Democratic senators in other regions. One possible cause would be the reluctance of Democrats to grant a Republican President such broad discretionary powers in foreign affairs as they had given President Truman. A second cause might be a belief by some senators that international economic policies of this country are increasingly damaging the economy of their states, an argument that has been applied particularly to the South. A third might be opposition to continuing the heavy drain on the national budget by prolonging large-scale foreign aid, a view motivated primarily by what we shall call fiscal conservatism. Finally, since we have already recognized the Democrats' decreasing sense of obligation to support a Republican administration's programs, we must consider whether certain of these programs seem to have taken on greater Republican coloration than others.

MILITARY SECURITY AND PRESIDENTIAL POWER

The first question—the discretion that should be granted to the President—is associated almost entirely with the issue of collective security. On several occasions during the Truman administration the Democrats stood firm against attempts to curb the President's authority through reservations to collective security treaties or through amendments to the troops for Europe resolution. In 1955, when President Eisenhower asked advance congressional approval for whatever policies he found necessary to protect the vaguely defined area of Formosa, many Democrats had grave misgivings about the consequences of such a step. Yet only two Democrats voted against the Formosa resolution and no more than twelve voted for a series of amendments to the resolution designed to define more precisely the area of presidential authority. The Democratic voting pattern was similar on the related defense treaty with Nationalist China.

In 1957, when President Eisenhower asked for a similar broad grant of authority to provide military assistance to any victim of Communist aggression in the Middle East, the Democrats became sharply divided. One-third of the Democratic senators (11 southerners and 5 others) opposed the resolution. Just over half of the Democrats (including the same number of southerners) supported an unsuccessful amendment that would have tied the President's hands by requiring him to notify Congress before sending armed forces to the Middle East or, if this were impossible, to submit his action for congressional approval. These votes on the Middle East resolution were certainly out of step with traditional policies of the Senate Democrats; the result likely would have been very different had a Democrat been in the White House. But the Democratic split apparently represented less a growing distrust of presidential power than the sober belief that the administration had failed to present a strong enough case for the authority it was seeking in the Middle East. Southern opposition was caused partly by the fact that the resolution provided funds for Middle Eastern countries both for military and developmental purposes. Fourteen out of nineteen southerners voted for Senator Richard Russell's unsuccessful amendment to eliminate this aid provision.[15]

Democratic voting on the Bricker amendment, considered by the Senate in 1954, might appear to indicate that the Democrats had abandoned their devotion to strong presidential authority in foreign affairs. The amendment would have placed executive agreements under the control of Congress and would have limited the treaty making power to those areas that fall within the delegated powers of Congress. The Bricker amendment was subject to a variety of interpretations, but it would clearly have imposed considerable limits on the authority of the President, as well as the Senate, in foreign affairs. No rollcall was taken on the version

[15] CQA, 1955, pp. 115-16; 1957, pp. 286-87.

of the Bricker amendment that would have imposed the greatest curbs on the conduct of foreign affairs. In rollcalls on other versions, the southern senators represented the hard core of Democratic support for the principle of the Bricker amendment. On the final vote on the Bricker amendment—which had been completely rewritten by Senator Walter F. George—eighteen southerners voted affirmatively, one was paired for it, and three opposed. The remaining Democrats voted against it 13-10.[16] These votes can be misinterpreted, however, if it is not realized that many southerners viewed the issue primarily as one of states' rights. Many of them were primarily interested in trying to prevent the use of treaties to effect domestic reforms, particularly in the area of civil rights. The southern Democratic vote appears to have been as much a conservative vote as an isolationist vote. Moreover, Senator George's substitute was viewed by some normally internationalist Democrats (northern and southern) as a relatively harmless compromise far preferable to more damaging versions of the Bricker amendment.

The southern vote for the Bricker amendment must also be explained in terms of personal support for two distinguished southern senators, Russell and George. Russell's advocacy of severe limits on the treatymaking power appears to have inspired a strong stand by the most conservative or isolationist southerners. George, with a long record of internationalism, seems to have won moderate and internationalist southerners to his compromise by making it appear to be above reproach.

By and large, Democratic votes against the broad grants of authority sought by President Eisenhower in the collective security field reflected doubts about the wisdom of specific policies rather than suspicions of presidential power. Many years of responsibility for the conduct of foreign policy have bred in the Democratic party a strong respect for the authority of the President in this field.

FOREIGN AID

The changing economic situation of the South has been used most often by analysts to explain the declining internationalism

[16] *Ibid.*, 1954, p. 294.

of senators from that region. With increased industrialization the South is less dependent on exports of cotton and tobacco. While this factor might primarily affect voting on reciprocal trade measures, it could influence voting on amendments to foreign aid bills intended to limit imports and even voting on the basic issue of foreign aid. Senator Herman Talmadge of Georgia, a vigorous opponent of foreign aid, has argued: "While unfair competition is closing the doors of numerous American industries, we continue to send our technicians and machines to foreign lands to provide the know-how to produce goods that will destroy markets for our own, due to the vast differential between slave wages and free wages."[17] If southern senators generally accepted this line of argument, they would presumably vote against foreign aid to protect the new industries of their states. But industrialization has not proceeded rapidly enough in the South to account for the considerable drop in southern votes for foreign aid during the Eisenhower administration.

A more pertinent economic reason for the recent shift in the voting pattern might be the changing nature of the foreign aid program. As the program's geographic emphasis has shifted from Europe to the underdeveloped areas, southerners have seen a threat to cotton exports in irrigation programs and other agricultural measures that might cause increased cotton production abroad. Cotton is still important enough in some southern states to make the threat of competition carry weight with the voters. Strong substantiation of such reasoning came in 1956, when southern senators opposed the administration's plan to help Egypt build the Aswan Dam, a project likely to expand cotton production. Senator Walter F. George, then at the height of his influence, expressed strong opposition to the project. The Senate Appropriations Committee, containing seven southerners, wrote into its report on the foreign aid bill a requirement that no funds be spent for this project without advance approval by the committee. Shortly thereafter John Foster Dulles abruptly withdrew the American offer of aid to Egypt. While other groups both in Congress and in the State Department had strong reasons for opposing the grant to Egypt, southern concern over cotton

[17] Quoted by Marquis Childs in the *Washington Post and Times Herald,* July 2, 1957.

exports was undoubtedly one factor in the decision to withdraw aid.

Yet, southern support for the aid program has not been consistently lower on rollcalls dealing specifically with economic aid to underdeveloped areas than on those dealing with other aspects of aid. The Point Four Program, inaugurated in 1950, was the only aid bill during the Truman administration opposed by a majority of southern senators.[18] In 1955, when slightly over half of the southern senators voted for several cuts in military and defense support spending, fifteen out of nineteen voted against an increase in the Fund for Asian Economic Development, but twelve out of nineteen opposed eliminating the Fund. In 1957, twelve out of twenty southern Democrats voted for a severe cutback in the Development Loan Fund, virtually the same number that voted several times for large cuts in military and defense support aid. Although seventeen out of nineteen southern Democrats in 1955 approved a $10 million cut in aid to India already suggested by the Appropriations Committee, only five out of nineteen agreed to a $40 million cut in aid to India the next year, and a slight majority supported the amendment in 1958 pledging American aid to India's development program. During the Eisenhower administration, southern senators have repeatedly voted—often overwhelmingly—to make large cuts in military and defense support aid.[19]

Probably some southern senators are becoming increasingly hostile to the principle of foreign aid itself because of the belief that the program as a whole damages the southern economy. Yet, in a period when northern Democratic senators have been voicing repeated demands for greater emphasis on economic development programs rather than military aid, those southern senators friendly to the principle of aid have not dissented. Moreover, the rollcalls do not reveal that the development of Asian and African countries has less southern support than military assistance has. Further reasons must be sought for southern voting trends in the Senate.

One explanation for decreasing southern support for foreign

[18] Southern senators voted against Point Four by a margin of 11-8. *CQA*, 1950, p. 267.
[19] *Ibid.*, 1955, pp. 127, 132; 1956, p. 175; 1957, pp. 300-301, 313; 1958, p. 437.

aid might be the election, in recent years, of senators who were not committed to the major postwar aid programs and who might be identified as isolationists. As a rule, however, isolationism has not been a campaign theme of successful southern candidates for the Senate. It is true that Herman Talmadge of Georgia campaigned successfully in 1956 on a platform of opposition to aid and trade and fulfilled his campaign promises in the subsequent rollcall voting. Some other candidates have followed this tactic and failed at the polls. The evidence does not suggest that a new generation of southern senators is committed to isolationism by campaign promises or by strong trends in southern public opinion.

Fiscal conservatism, a factor that has distinguished southern from northern Democrats in their attitude toward domestic issues, may now be a factor in the issue of foreign aid, which represents an annual tax burden of several billion dollars. Because it is difficult to cut domestic expenditures without first cutting those for foreign aid, reductions in the aid program have had a growing appeal to conservative senators—men like Harry F. Byrd and Walter F. George. ("Conservative" is used here simply in a fiscal sense to describe those who attach a high priority to the reduction of governmental spending, taxes, and the public debt, who give more than lipservice to the slogan of "economy.") Although the distinction may not always be clear or measurable in rollcalls, there is an important difference between opposition to the principle of foreign aid and opposition to the high levels of foreign aid consistently sought by the administration. Concern over the cost of foreign aid, inspired by fiscal conservatism, would appear to be the explanation for a senator's consistently voting for foreign aid and for reductions in aid spending. It would also logically explain a senator's following this pattern for several years and then finally voting against foreign aid itself.

Although a few southern Democrats voted against new foreign aid programs introduced by the Truman administration, they supported the annual extensions of these programs virtually unanimously through 1954. Yet from 1947 through 1954 southern Democratic support for higher funds on spending amendments dropped from 78 to 43 percent, presumably because of growing concern over the burden placed on the national budget by an annual foreign aid expenditure of several billion dollars. The sharp drop in southern Democratic support for aid bills that began in 1955 probably reflected primarily a protest against the scope of the Eisenhower program rather than a vote in principle against foreign aid.

Those veteran southern senators who continued to vote for most of President Eisenhower's aid measures were nearly all men who voted for higher funds on a majority of spending amendments during both administrations. Among veteran southerners the opposition to Eisenhower's aid program came primarily from those who supported most of Truman's aid program but who more often than not voted for reductions in it, generally men with relatively conservative records on domestic issues. This latter group consistently voted for amendments to foreign aid bills intended to increase the proportion of funds designated as loans rather than grants—another symptom of fiscal conservatism. Most Democrats who continued to vote for foreign aid were opponents of these amendments.

The explanation for the changing attitude of other Democratic senators toward foreign aid is somewhat similar. Foreign aid would not seem to present any direct economic threat to the Mountain States and some of the Border States, where this change was most evident. In these regions the change came primarily on amendments affecting the size of the aid program. This strongly suggests a desire for economy rather than a dissent from the principle of foreign aid. Most of the nonsouthern Democrats voting frequently to reduce foreign aid during the Eisenhower years, however, cannot be classified as conservatives on domestic issues; moreover, most of them are men who voted regularly to supply maximum funds for aid during the Truman administration.[20] Some of them simply wanted more funds available for domestic purposes, and some were influenced by growing constituent antipathy to the aid program, while some believed that the foreign needs had decreased.[21] Another cause of dis-

[20] Examples are Robert S. Kerr of Oklahoma, Mike Mansfield of Montana, Dennis Chavez and Clinton P. Anderson of New Mexico, and Warren Magnuson of Washington.

[21] One senator, explaining to the writer his growing opposition to foreign aid, pointed to an architect's drawing of a post office scheduled for a major city in his state, construction of which had been barred by an executive order while foreign aid spending continued.

satisfaction was clearly some disagreement with the direction the program had been taking in recent years. Numerous Democratic senators stated both publicly and privately their concern that a disproportionate share of aid funds had gone for military purposes. A large proportion of the spending amendments on which rollcalls were recorded during the Eisenhower administration involved proposed cuts in military spending. Several Democratic senators voted for most of these cuts while supporting other aspects of the program more fully. Frequent votes to reduce the foreign aid program were cast for a variety of reasons by nonsouthern as well as southern Democrats, by liberals as well as conservatives, and usually by Democrats who would not be judged as isolationists on the basis of their votes on other international issues.

RECIPROCAL TRADE LEGISLATION

The strongest opposition to reciprocal trade legislation may be anticipated in states having industries suffering from foreign competition, particularly if these are new industries not yet strongly established. The textile and apparel industries of the South have not only been growing in recent years but have faced rapidly increasing competition from Japanese industries. There is some correlation between the states whose senators have recently grown hostile to reciprocal trade and states in which textile and apparel industries are important. In 1954 South Carolina, North Carolina, and Georgia were the only three southern states in which the textile and apparel industries employed over 10 percent of the civilian labor force and the three with the greatest increase in these industries since 1947.[22] All senators from these three states supported the Truman administration on every rollcall involving reciprocal trade. These were the only southern states, however, having senators who opposed the Eisenhower administration's stand on more than half of the rollcalls dealing with reciprocal trade. While support for reciprocal trade in these three states dropped from 100 to 34 percent, in

---

[22] Bureau of the Census, *United States Census of Manufactures, 1954*, Vol. II, Part 1, pp. 22-23; Bureau of the Census, *Statistical Abstract of the United States, 1958*, p. 207.

the eight southern states where textiles are less important the drop was only from 90 to 83 percent after 1952, not enough to suggest that voting on this issue was significantly affected by the change in administrations.[23]

The voting shift by senators from the three textile states is apparently not an accidental byproduct of changes in personnel. Although several strong supporters of reciprocal trade left the Senate and were succeeded by men less favorable to it,[24] Richard B. Russell of Georgia and Olin D. Johnston of South Carolina, who served throughout the twelve-year period, abandoned their strong voting support for reciprocal trade after 1952.

In the case of a few amendments designed to benefit specific commodities, the economic motivation for voting was even clearer.[25] In 1956 two amendments were introduced to the foreign aid bill designed to limit imports of cotton and cotton textiles. The southern vote on the two amendments was identical. Voting for the limits on imports were all six senators from the three states in which textile and apparel firms employ the largest proportion of the working force (North Carolina, South Carolina, and Georgia) and five other senators from major textile or cotton-growing states (Alabama, Mississippi, and Arkansas).[26]

During the Eisenhower administration, as Table 4 indicates, there was more opposition to the reciprocal trade program among Democrats from the Mountain States, Border States, and West

[23] For purposes of comparison, an analysis of two House rollcalls was made: one in 1955 on a motion to return the reciprocal trade bill to committee in order to curb the President's tariff-cutting powers and one in 1958 on passage of the reciprocal trade bill. Only 58 percent of the Southerners opposed the motion in 1955 and 75 percent voted for the trade bill in 1958. In 1955, South Carolina, Georgia, and North Carolina were the three southern states with the largest proportions of members opposing reciprocal trade and in 1958 these were three of the four states in that category. This gives added support to the theory that the shift in southern voting on foreign trade has largely resulted from the problems faced by the textile industry. *CQA*, 1955, pp. 138-39; 1958, pp. 388-89.

[24] Walter F. George, Clyde Hoey, Frank Graham, and Burnet R. Maybank were replaced by Herman Talmadge, Sam Ervin, W. Kerr Scott, and J. Strom Thurmond.

[25] Amendments to foreign aid bills designed to promote the export of surplus agricultural products drew a mixed response in the South. Those that seemed likely to apply primarily to northern crops gained the fewest votes. Three of the four southern states whose senators most often voted for agricultural amendments were Mississippi, Arkansas, and South Carolina, the three having the largest percentage of the labor force employed in agriculture in 1950.

[26] Senator George A. Smathers of Florida cast the only other southern vote for limiting imports. *CQA*, 1956, pp. 173-74.

Coast than among those from the South. During the Truman administration some of this opposition was already evident in the Mountain and Border states. As in the South, the opposition in these three regions can be pinpointed to states in which significant segments of industry face serious foreign competition. Because mining and petroleum are outstanding examples of such industries, Democratic opposition to reciprocal trade assumed a more distinctly regional character in the Mountain States than it did in the South or in other regions during the Eisenhower administration. Democratic senators in Wyoming and Nevada voted to restrict or oppose the trade program on a majority of rollcalls from 1953 through 1958, while those from New Mexico, Montana, and Colorado voted that way on over one-third of the rollcalls. These five states include some of the largest producers of copper, lead, zinc, and petroleum, all industries concerned about substantial foreign competition; and several of these states produce wool, which also faces competition from imports. Democratic senators from Oklahoma, who were evenly divided on rollcalls involving trade during both administrations, were concerned about protecting petroleum, lead, and zinc industries as well as glass manufacturing. West Virginia's Democratic senators on several occasions voted against foreign trade. That state has a high proportion of industries claiming protection: coal (competing with imported petroleum), glassware, pottery, and textiles. In Washington and Oregon the fruitgrowers and fishing industry were among those clamoring for protection and apparently helping to produce some of the votes against reciprocal trade among Democrats from those states.

The states whose Democratic senators have frequently voted to curtail or abolish the reciprocal trade program are not in all cases those states containing major industries affected seriously by foreign competition. Some Democratic senators have continued to vote for the full, unrestricted trade program despite the demands for protection from important industries in their states. But in all of those states where Democratic senators have broken with traditional party policy of consistent support for reciprocal trade, there are important industries seeking protection. On the other hand the loyalty of Democrats from the Northeast and Midwest to the trade program is clearly related to the dominant position in most of those states of established manufacturing industries able to compete well with foreign industries.[27]

DEMOCRATS AND THE CHANGE OF ADMINISTRATIONS

Dean Acheson has argued that the Democratic party's internationalism results primarily from its control of the administration and its responsibility for conducting foreign policy during the major wars and critical postwar periods in this century. Conversely, the Republicans have lacked until recently both the responsibility and the continuing, detailed familiarity with foreign problems that engender internationalism.[28] While often differing with both Franklin D. Roosevelt and Harry S. Truman over domestic policy, senators appeared to have had confidence in the foreign policy of both Democratic administrations and to have felt a sense of responsibility and loyalty to them in this area. Despite the emphasis placed on bipartisan foreign policy by the Eisenhower administration and by Senators Walter F. George and Lyndon B. Johnson, both southern and northern Democratic senators apparently felt a smaller obligation to support President Eisenhower's foreign policies.

There is a significant interrelationship between Democratic senators' views on international issues and their attitude toward the administration. Most Democrats supported most of Truman's programs because of convictions that grew out of the traditional internationalism of Democratic administrations. On some occasions Democrats voted for Truman's programs, despite serious misgivings or pressure from constituents, in order to avoid undermining a Democratic President's position on foreign policy. During the Eisenhower administration these misgivings were unhampered by party loyalty. But there remained a strong sense of loyalty to those policies most traditionally associated with the Democratic party, coupled with a strong respect for the President's authority in foreign policy.

[27] See the similar conclusions of Richard A. Watson, "The Tariff Revolution: A Study of Shifting Party Attitudes," *Journal of Politics*, XVIII (Nov., 1956), 678-701.

[28] Dean Acheson, *A Democrat Looks at His Party* (New York: Harper & Brothers, 1955), pp. 64-67.

The principle of support for collective security has been widely accepted by Democrats since Woodrow Wilson's battle for the League of Nations, and it was natural that Democratic senators should support the collective security programs of both Truman and Eisenhower. The Democratic party has also been traditionally committed to low tariffs, and the principle of reciprocal trade is closely associated with Franklin D. Roosevelt and Cordell Hull.[29] Consequently, it is not surprising that the Democrats claimed greater devotion to President Eisenhower's reciprocal trade program than Republicans did and occasionally prodded Eisenhower to take a bolder stand in defense of his program. Except for senators from states where industry was suffering from foreign competition, most Democratic senators were consistent supporters of reciprocal trade.[30]

Large-scale foreign aid is a relatively new issue and lacks the long history of Democratic endorsement enjoyed by the policies of a low tariff and collective security. Moreover, it is a costly program contrary to the conservative fiscal beliefs of many Democrats, particularly southerners. Never in the postwar period does it appear to have had the enthusiastic southern endorsement given to reciprocal trade and collective security. Few southern senators, however, wanted to repudiate programs that had become established policies—and outstanding achievements—of the Democratic party. The southerners as well as many other Dem-

[29]A study of nine key rollcalls in the House of Representatives on tariff measures from 1929 through 1953 showed this to be an issue on which party lines were closely drawn. Of all the votes cast on these rollcalls, only one out of every fifteen did not fall into the pattern of Democratic opposition to the tariff and support for reciprocal trade and Republican backing for the tariff and opposition to reciprocal trade. Three-fifths of the nonconforming votes were cast by Democrats. The margin of victory usually approximated the margin of the majority party in the House. Howard R. Smith and John F. Hart, "The American Tariff Map," *Geographical Review,* XLV (1955), 337. In a study of seven congressional sessions from 1933 through 1945, V. O. Key found that on nine rollcalls on which the parties took opposite sides an average of 95 percent of southern Democrats, 84 percent of northern Democrats, and only 13 percent of the Republicans in the Senate supported reciprocal trade. *Southern Politics in State and Nation* (New York: Alfred A. Knopf, 1949), p. 353.

[30] In 1954 President Eisenhower urged Congress to adopt the recommendations of the Randall Commission in reciprocal trade legislation but agreed to the Republican congressional demand for a one-year extension of the existing law while the recommendations were studied. The Democrats sought to amend the bill to incorporate the commission's recommendations immediately. Although all of the Republicans opposed this in the Senate, just six Democrats (one a southerner) voted against it.

ocrats continued to vote for foreign aid in the Eisenhower years of 1953 and 1954 probably because they still thought of it as a Democratic program. Over a period of time not only the sponsorship of the aid program changed but also its emphasis and content. Moreover, the Republican administration gradually began to stress the need for a long-term program—an idea that had little appeal to those senators most concerned about the cost of foreign aid.

Southern senators appear to make the greatest distinction between traditional Democratic programs and other measures. The South has long been regarded as the bulwark of internationalism, its senators have longer seniority than many others, and in lean years the Democratic record has been primarily a southern record in the Senate. Democrats from the northern industrial states, most of whom came to the Senate after World War II, have backed the entire range of foreign programs with consistently only slight reductions in support during the Republican administration. In the West, Democratic senators have subordinated tradition to the demands for tariff protection.

This pattern of voting in the 1947-1958 period has an interesting parallel in the pattern of Democratic voting in the Senate from 1921 through 1941. George L. Grassmuck studied voting in both houses of Congress on several topics that are comparable to postwar issues.[31] The question of membership in or cooperation with the World Court and the League of Nations is somewhat similar to the more recent controversies over collective security. There is a closer parallel between the neutrality legislation from 1935 through 1941 and recent security measures; moreover, both involved the grant of discretionary power to the President. There has also been some continuity in foreign fiscal policy. The war debts settlements of the 1920s and the Export-Import Bank late in the 1930s are comparable to economic aid, and the Lend-Lease program resembles military aid.

Approximately three-quarters of the Democrats voted for

---

[31] Although Grassmuck in *Sectional Biases in Congress on Foreign Policy*, studied both branches of Congress, comparisons are made here only with his figures for the Senate. Using slightly different regions, Grassmuck included Iowa, Minnesota, and Wisconsin in the Plains States and Delaware in the Northeast. His regional comparisons were handicapped by a paucity of Democratic senators in the Midwest, Plains States, and West Coast from 1921 through 1932, and a shortage of Republicans from the Mountain and Border states after 1932.

membership in international organizations during both Republican and Democratic administrations between the wars and favored relaxation of neutrality legislation before World War II. Variations among regions and those within each region between administrations were comparatively small in the case of regions with substantial Democratic strength. The Democratic record on foreign debts and aid is very different. Senate Democratic support for war debt settlement proposals and foreign aid measures rose from 42 percent during Republican administrations to 85 percent during Roosevelt's regime. The contrast was greatest in the South, where the percentage rose from 36 to 92. Among northeastern Democrats the support for the financial measures was more consistently high. The similarity of this pattern to that in recent years is not simply that the Democrats, and particularly those from the South, supported foreign economic programs less consistently than other types of foreign commitments. During the 1920-1932 period the Democrats were endorsing the Wilsonian principle of international cooperation and voting for measures that involved the authority and prestige of a Democratic President even though the immediate sponsors were Harding, Coolidge, and Hoover. Actually, in key votes on joining the World Court, the Democrats provided more united support in 1926 than in 1935, when the Wilsonian tradition had begun to fade. The Democrats gave stronger support to these foreign policy measures than Republican senators did.

The comparison with voting records of the 1920s and 1930s is useful because it adds perspective to and reinforces the conclusions from our analysis of the 1947-1958 period: The Democrats have not been consistently a party of internationalism but have supported international programs much more strongly during Democratic administrations. Democratic support has been consistently higher, however, even during Republican administrations, for policies traditionally associated with the Democratic party—most notably collective security. In voting on foreign policy, southern Democrats have been more influenced than others in the party by a sense of loyalty to Democratic Presidents and traditional party policies. Northeastern Democrats have been more consistently internationalist.

I believe that if the Republican party is going to stay in power it must support the President. As a result, I sometimes "hold my nose"—as the saying goes—and go along with the Administration, though I might personally prefer to vote the other way.
—Republican senator quoted by DONALD R. MATTHEWS

3

THE REPUBLICAN RECORD

THE REPUBLICAN VOTING RECORD ILLUSTRATES, EVEN MORE vividly than the Democratic record, the transformation that can occur when partisan responsibility for foreign policy changes. As shown in Table 5, a majority of Republican senators supported the Truman administration on only 37 percent of the rollcalls; the party was almost united in opposition on a substantial number of the remainder. During the Eisenhower administration, majority support rose to 83 percent. There are some striking differences between the Democratic and Republican records, notably the greater resistance to internationalism in Republican ranks. A majority of Republicans voted for Truman's programs only about half as frequently as a majority of Democrats backed Eisenhower. The Republican support for Eisenhower fell somewhat short of Democratic support for Truman. Yet these contrasts simply emphasize the importance of loyalty to the administration as a factor in voting on foreign policy. Although the Republicans had a long isolationist tradition, although many of them deeply distrusted the Democratic authors of programs inherited by President Eisenhower, and although many of them disliked Eisenhower's internationalist views, Republican senators

TABLE 5—Foreign Policy Rollcalls by Percentage of Republican Senatorial Support of the Truman and Eisenhower Administrations, 1947-1952 and 1953-1958 (283 Rollcalls)

Percentage of Support	Truman, 1947-1952		Eisenhower, 1953-1958	
	Number	Percentage	Number	Percentage
90-100	10	5.8	22	19.6
80-89.9	8	4.7	12	10.7
70-79.9	15	8.8	22	19.6
60-69.9	14	8.2	28	25.0
50-59.9	17	9.9	9	8.0
40-49.9	15	8.8	5	4.5
30-39.9	17	9.9	6	5.4
20-29.9	31	18.2	1	0.9
10-19.9	17	9.9	0	0.0
0-9.9	27	15.8	7	6.3
Total	171	100.0	112	100.0

reversed their stand on a wide variety of issues to provide strong support for the Republican President, particularly on the most important elements of his program.

President Eisenhower had broader bipartisan support for his foreign programs than Harry Truman usually enjoyed. This is because Eisenhower gained Republican votes faster than he lost Democratic votes. Commentators have emphasized those occasions when Eisenhower's programs drew more votes from Democratic than Republican ranks. It seems more remarkable and more significant for our study that Eisenhower had a majority of Republican votes more often than a majority of Democratic votes. His defeats more often resulted from defection by a majority of the opposition than by a majority of his own party. As the Eisenhower administration progressed, Republican voting support grew and Democratic support fell.

Eisenhower had to secure bipartisan support for the same

reasons that Truman did: the need of large majorities to satisfy the Constitution or our allies and the absence of a Republican majority after 1954. Eisenhower had less support from his own party and gained more votes from the opposition than Truman did. Yet each President discovered his own party to be the more dependable source of votes, and each became increasingly dependent on his own party as his administration progressed.

THE REPUBLICANS OUT OF OFFICE

The Republican record during the Truman administration was not uniform. During the early years, while the major economic and military programs for Europe were being launched with the active support of Senator Arthur H. Vandenberg, the Republicans provided substantial support despite the rigid opposition of an isolationist wing. In later years, during the annual struggles over implementation of these measures, there was growing opposition from the party, now led by Robert A. Taft and increasingly hostile to the policies being carried out in Asia.

Republican backing for the Truman administration was strongest and most consistent on the major issues of collective security. In 1948 only two Republicans voted against the Vandenberg resolution on collective security. Both the North Atlantic Treaty and the Japanese Security Treaty had nearly three-to-one Republican majorities. The party was divided, however, on the reservations and resolutions concerning the relative authority to be permitted the President and retained by Congress in implementing collective security measures. Only about one-fourth of the Republicans favored a reservation to the NATO pact in 1949 reserving for Congress sole authority to send armed assistance to the NATO allies; when similar reservations were proposed to an expanded NATO pact in 1951 and to the Japanese Security Treaty in 1952, only 10 and 12 of 47 Republicans, respectively, were opposed. The prolonged controversy over sending troops to Europe found the Republicans sharply divided not only on the question of limiting the President's authority but on the wisdom of sending troops. Nearly one-third of the Republican senators favored the sending of troops and opposed placing binding restrictions on the President through a joint resolution. The remainder, who thought that the President should be required by law to get congressional approval for any further troop assignments to Europe, were divided when the joint resolution was defeated; a minority voted for the simple resolution and a majority opposed it because it lacked binding authority and in some cases because they flatly opposed sending troops.[1]

The Republican votes cast for the North Atlantic Treaty were vitally important. A bitter partisan contest in the Senate would have drained from the treaty most of its value as an assurance to our European allies. In the face of Soviet expansion in eastern Europe and dangerously strong Communist parties in western Europe, Republican senators did not dare to risk the consequences of defeating the treaty. Two years later, Republican indecision on the troops for Europe issue was costly to the administration because the prolonged debate on both the military and political questions shook the confidence of our allies in the reliability of American commitments. The changed attitude of Republican senators resulted primarily from decreasing confidence in the President, resentment over his unilateral decision to send troops to Korea, and frustration with the unsuccessful Korean war. The military commitment in Europe was never seriously challenged by many Republican senators; enough of them voted against restrictive amendments to prevent serious handicapping of the European program. Yet in the later years of the Democratic administration, the implementation of military as well as economic policy in Europe became a partisan question, affected by partisanship over Asian issues.

The Asian controversy began with the collapse of Chiang Kai-shek's forces and the Communist conquest of mainland China. Republicans blamed the Truman administration for initially encouraging Chiang to reach a compromise with Communist Chinese leaders during 1946 and then for refusing to provide substantial military assistance to Chiang in late 1948 and 1949 in an attempt to prevent the rout of his forces. After Chiang Kai-shek withdrew to Formosa, many Republicans criticized the Truman administration for refusing to help defend that island until the start of the Korean war. Some Republicans charged that the administration had in effect invited the Korean

---

[1] CQA, 1948, p. 218; 1949, pp. 429-30; 1951, pp. 257-58; 1952, pp. 177, 182.

attack by the weakness of its stand against Communist expansion in Asia. After Chinese troops entered the war at the end of 1950, there was mounting Republican criticism of President Truman for sending American forces to Korea without congressional approval. The Asian controversy was climaxed by the President's dismissal of General Douglas MacArthur in April, 1951, which precipitated a partisan debate on whether to expand, limit, or terminate the Korean war. Ultimately the Korean war became the major issue of the 1952 election.[2]

Although these Asian issues frequently dominated the headlines throughout Truman's second administration and created an atmosphere of controversy undermining bipartisan support for all his foreign programs, very few of them reached the point of a rollcall. Controversies on aid to Chiang Kai-shek were settled in committee without being carried to the floor. The Senate did unanimously pass in 1951 a resolution opposing Communist China's admission to the United Nations, and there was a series of rollcalls along party lines involving Republican efforts to open hearings on the MacArthur dismissal to all senators.[3] The only other important Asian issue to reach the rollcall stage was the Japanese Peace Treaty ratified in 1952. Although the fact that John Foster Dulles had negotiated the treaty helped to create a three-to-one Republican margin for it, the Republicans supported most of the proposed reservations to the pact, sometimes by substantial margins.[4] The peace treaty, however, like the Japanese Security Treaty, was largely removed from the partisan controversy over China and Korea.

The Republicans were more opposed to the major components of President Truman's foreign aid program than to the collective security treaties. The Greek-Turkish aid program in 1947 and the Marshall Plan in 1948 were launched with the backing of substantial Republican majorities. In later years, Republican doubts about the changing emphasis of the aid program and its continued high cost, together with declining confidence in the administration, diminished the ranks of Republican supporters.

[2] For analyses of Republican policy toward China, see Crabb, *Bipartisan Foreign Policy*, Ch. 5; Westerfield, *Foreign Policy and Party Politics*, Chs. 12, 16.
[3] Senator Pat McCarran, Democrat of Nevada, was the only senator crossing party lines on these rollcalls. *CQA*, 1951, p. 259.
[4] *Ibid.*, 1952, p. 177.

During 1947 and 1948, 76 percent of the Republican votes cast on foreign aid measures were favorable; in succeeding two-year periods the figures fell to 60 and 51 percent. Republicans voted for the first general military assistance program in 1949 by a narrow 19-14 margin. The next year they opposed the Point Four Program for technical assistance, 25-8 and almost defeated it.[5]

During the later years of the Truman administration, when the concept of continuing foreign aid itself had become well established, questions tended to center on the size of the appropriations. During 1947 and 1948, 70 percent of all Republican votes cast on spending amendments were in favor of increases or in opposition to reductions. This figure fell to 36 percent and 21 percent in the successive two-year periods. During the second Truman administration a majority of Republicans voted for reductions on 23 out of 28 rollcalls involving spending amendments. Not only did the proportion of Republicans voting for economy grow steadily during these years, but the size of reductions they supported likewise grew. The strength of Republican economy sentiment suggests that most of the votes cast against the extension of existing aid programs were primarily protests against the size and scope of these programs.

It was on the question of reciprocal trade that Republican senators most consistently opposed the Truman administration. On eighteen rollcalls involving various aspects of trade, only 24 percent of all votes cast by Republicans were favorable to the administration. Substantial numbers of Republicans voted to extend the trade program on several occasions and voted against amendments to give special preference to certain products. But the party opposed the administration almost unanimously on the most important amendments affecting the President's authority to reduce tariffs and the length of time for extending the program.

THE EISENHOWER YEARS

The Eisenhower administration brought about an increase in Republican voting support that extended to all the major cate-

[5] *Ibid.*, 1947, p. 270; 1948, p. 216; 1949, p. 431; 1950, p. 267.

gories of foreign programs. Collective security continued to be the issue on which the administration received most consistent backing, but even here the voting pattern changed considerably. The minority of Republican senators opposing major security programs almost shrank from sight. The larger number—and frequently a majority—of Republicans who voted to restrict President Truman's power voted almost to a man to give Eisenhower freedom in implementing the collective security program. This voting pattern did not immediately arise when Eisenhower entered the White House. In 1953 the Republicans voted 37-9 for the Status of Forces Treaty after defeating Senator John Bricker's crippling reservation 27-15. These margins of support were adequate but did not appear to foreshadow any major change in Republican voting on security. On ten rollcalls during 1954 and 1955, however, there were never more than two Republican votes cast against the administration's security proposals. On most of these there was only one dissenter: William Langer, the North Dakota maverick, consistent only in his isolationism. In addition to several relatively noncontroversial issues, these rollcalls included the Formosa resolution, the Chinese Mutual Defense Treaty, and amendments to these measures designed to restrict the President. In 1957, although seventeen Republicans voted to set an expiration date for the Middle East resolution, only four voted to require presidential notification of Congress before the dispatch of troops, and only three voted against the resolution. On this most controversial of Eisenhower's major security proposals, Republican support was much stronger than that provided by the Democrats.[6]

President Eisenhower never had the overwhelming Republican support for foreign aid that was provided on security issues. He was able rather quickly to regain and eventually to surpass the level of Republican voting support that President Truman had enjoyed in the early days of his administration. In the rollcalls on foreign aid measures, favorable Republican votes had fallen from 76 percent in 1947-1948 to 51 percent in 1951-1952. The figure rose to 76 percent in 1953-1954 and to 80 percent in 1957-1958. The percentage of votes for higher spending had fallen more precipitously in the comparable time periods, from

6 *Ibid.*, 1953, p. 257; 1954, p. 296; 1955, pp. 115, 116, 121; 1957, pp. 286-87.

70 to 21 percent. It rose to 64 percent and eventually to 73 percent during the Eisenhower administration. There was a Republican majority for every one of Eisenhower's foreign aid measures. During the first six Eisenhower years there were 43 rollcalls involving the total to be spent for foreign aid; on only 5 of these did a Republican majority vote for lower funds. Three of these five defections involved rollcalls to suspend aid to Yugoslavia in 1956. Except for Yugoslav aid, the Republicans surpassed the Democrats in voting for aid and aid spending during the Eisenhower administration.[7]

The Eisenhower administration had a greater impact on Republican voting concerning aid than on that involving collective security. By the end of the Truman administration the Republicans had clearly grown more disillusioned with the foreign aid program than with collective security. The reversal in the Republican record on aid spending that began in 1953 was more complete than changes in other aspects of the record. Yet this Republican record occurred during a period when many senators thought that foreign aid was losing its popular support. The voting change did not represent renewed enthusiasm for foreign aid; it was a continuing vote of confidence in the Republican administration.

During the Eisenhower administration the proportion of Republican votes cast for the reciprocal trade program more than doubled. Yet the Republican record on this issue contrasts with the records on security and aid; it remained a highly partisan issue during both administrations. It was the only issue on which more Democrats than Republicans supported the Eisenhower administration. A large, but not increasing, majority of Republicans continued to vote for the final passage of trade bills. The significant differences occurred on major amendments. In 1954 most Democrats but no Republicans voted for a three-year extension of the measure along the lines recommended by the Randall Commission and originally endorsed by Eisenhower before he yielded to Republican pressure. In 1955 two attempts by Senator Paul Douglas to eliminate protective features of the measure met

---

[7] The percentages of Republican support for foreign aid remained high in 1959 and 1960: 81 percent on aid measures and 76 percent on spending amendments. A majority of Republicans supported the President on all rollcalls in both of these categories.

unanimous Republican (and considerable Democratic) opposition. In 1958 both parties were badly divided on several amendments involving protectionism and presidential discretion.[8] The change in Republican voting on reciprocal trade was important to the Eisenhower administration and in fact became essential as Democratic support began to wither. But, in contrast to the aid and security measures, the President had to depend more on Democratic than Republican votes to secure satisfactory reciprocal trade measures.

A DIVIDED PARTY

Regional differences on foreign policy have been even deeper in the Republican party than in Democratic ranks. Several conclusions stand out from an appraisal of Tables 6, 7, and 8. Among Republicans, internationalism has been consistently strong in the Northeast and nearly as strong on the West Coast.[9] The simplest description of regional differences in the party is the contrast between these two coastal regions and the four interior regions. During the Truman administration coastal Republicans provided majorities for all categories of international programs except reciprocal trade. No other region provided such majorities on any issue (except the Midwest on foreign aid measures). Coastal support for the Eisenhower administration on all issues except trade was remarkable. Coastal Republicans cast 377 votes for and only 3 votes against foreign aid measures and collective security, a record not even matched by Democrats from these areas during the Truman administration. Coastal Republican support for the full amount of aid sought by Eisenhower was an impressive 90 percent.

Figures for Republican voting in the four interior regions cannot be combined without overlooking significant variations. During the Truman administration there was more internationalist voting in the Midwest than in the other three regions. During the Eisenhower administration senators from the Midwest and Border States ranked approximately halfway between those from the coastal regions and those from the Plains and Mountain

8 CQA, 1954, p. 296: 1955, p. 123; 1958, p. 454.
9 See note 13, chapter 2, for a list of the states in each region.

states.   This meant a considerable change in the voting of senators from the Midwest and a complete reversal in the voting of

TABLE 6—Republican Senatorial Support by Region of the
Truman and Eisenhower Administrations' Foreign Policy,
1947-1952 and 1953-1958 (Percentage of 179 Rollcalls)

Region	Truman, 1947-1952	Eisenhower, 1953-1958
Northeast	67	90
Midwest	42	73
Plains States	27	44
Border States	26	71
Mountain States	22	51
West Coast	57	94

TABLE 7—Republican Senatorial Support by Region of the
Truman Administration's Foreign Policy, by Various Categories of Issues, 1947-1952 (Percentage of 97 Rollcalls)

Region	Foreign Aid Measures	Foreign Aid Spending	Security Measures	Reciprocal Trade
Northeast	87	59	76	43
Midwest	61	38	43	24
Plains States	47	21	29	13
Border States	42	18	29	18
Mountain States	45	14	22	5
West Coast	77	61	56	23
All Regions	63	38	47	24

TABLE 8—Republican Senatorial Support by Region of the
Eisenhower Administration's Foreign Policy, by Various
Groups of Issues, 1953-1958 (Percentage of 82 Rollcalls)

Region	Foreign Aid Measures	Foreign Aid Spending	Security Measures	Reciprocal Trade
Northeast	100	91	99	69
Midwest	77	69	90	62
Plains States	46	32	81	39
Border States	89	62	87	66
Mountain States	49	45	85	35
West Coast	100	89	97	69
All Regions	76	65	90	56

those from the Border States. The change was evident on all
categories of issues. Republicans from the Plains and Mountain
states, who voted nearly alike, were among the least internationalist during the Truman administration. Their response to the

change of administrations was less enthusiastic and varied with the issues. Republicans from these latter two regions, who so frequently voted against Truman's security proposals, voted almost as consistently as other Republicans for Eisenhower's security program. In both administrations the Plains and Mountain states were the sources of greatest Republican opposition to the trade program; the contrast with other regions was much sharper after 1952. Yet there was a substantial increase in voting for the trade program in these two regions. There was least change on the question of foreign aid. Although Republicans from the Plains and Mountain states no longer voted overwhelmingly for reductions in aid, the proportion voting against aid measures remained about the same.

The growing Republican internationalism might be explained in part by the defeat or retirement of veteran isolationists. The regional variations, however, do not seem to be explained by the election of new Republican senators; moreover, in all of the regions with changing voting patterns there were Republicans serving during both administrations who changed their voting pattern.

A comparison with regionalism in the Democratic party (Table 2) reveals striking similarities. In both parties the Northeast has been the most consistently internationalist region, where a high proportion of senators have supported the foreign programs of both administrations. The West Coast and Midwest rank next, although the order varies between the two parties. Despite the major difference in party records, the effect of changing administrations, and the regional variations already noted, the outstanding intraparty difference on foreign policy is a conflict between the major urban-industrial states and the more rural ones. The least internationalist regions in both parties are those where only one party elected senators during the Truman and Eisenhower administrations—the South and the Plains States. There are vast differences between these two regions in geography, degree of two-party competition, and attitude toward foreign policy. Nevertheless, in their respective parties these are the centers of isolationism.

A major explanation for the shift in Republican voting patterns after 1952 is the greater Republican loyalty to and confidence in President Eisenhower and his policies, a response that the Truman administration had elicited with decreasing success from 1947 through 1952. The variations in this change from region to region and issue to issue invite further speculation. Was President Eisenhower's voting support, initially at least, primarily from the "Eisenhower Republicans" who had favored him over Taft in 1952? Did the Republicans give greater support to security proposals because they were more clearly identified as Eisenhower programs than aid and trade measures?

TABLE 9—First Ballot Votes Cast for Eisenhower, Taft, and Other Candidates at the 1952 Republican Convention*

Region	Eisenhower No.	Eisenhower Pct.	Taft No.	Taft Pct.	Others No.	Others Pct.
Northeast	276	87.9	35	11.1	3	1.0
Midwest	63	22.7	190	68.3	25	9.0
Plains States	28	41.2	37	54.4	3	4.4
Border States	50	43.8	58	50.9	6	5.3
South	98	50.8	93	48.2	2	1.0
Mountain States	37	34.9	68	64.2	1	0.9
West Coast	38	33.9	4	3.6	70	62.5

* This is the vote before some states switched their votes. Based on the state-by-state tabulations in Paul T. David, Malcolm Moos, and Ralph M. Goldman, *Presidential Nomination Politics in 1952*, Vol. I, *The National Story* (Baltimore: Johns Hopkins Press, 1954), pp. 95-97.

Can Republican resistance to aid and trade be linked to fiscal conservatism and local economic interests? In short, do the conclusions we can draw from an analysis of the Republican record confirm or refine those drawn in the previous chapter from the Democratic record?

President Eisenhower's strongest support in the voting on international issues came from senators representing "Eisenhower territory." A comparison between Table 6 and Table 9, illustrating Eisenhower's strength in the 1952 Republican convention, makes this clear.[10] Individual senators who had supported Eisenhower during the 1952 campaign for the nomination were often among his most dependable supporters in the

[10] It should be noted that most of the votes for other candidates shown in Table 9 were cast for men whose internationalist views were similar to Eisenhower's. For a chart showing the regional strength of Taft forces on seven major issues at the convention, see Westerfield, p. 41.

voting on foreign policy, and even those who had not been among his early allies in 1952 tended to vote for his policies with greater consistency if their states had been pro-Eisenhower at the convention. Cause and effect are too scrambled to permit any simple conclusion that these senators voted for Eisenhower's programs because of personal support for him. Obviously many Republicans endorsed Eisenhower rather than Taft precisely because they preferred Eisenhower's internationalism to what they considered isolationism on the part of Taft. Disagreement on international issues was the sharpest policy difference between the two candidates.[11] Senators who had been won to Eisenhower's cause because of his internationalist views would naturally vote for his foreign programs and would presumably have voted similarly even if Taft had been elected and had chosen to propose some of the same programs.

The significant facts to bear in mind when analyzing regional Republican variations are that Eisenhower was the candidate representing one wing of the party and that the issues creating party differences in the rollcalls under study were precisely those creating the split between Eisenhower and Taft. There were two parallel forces pulling the Republicans apart: the different attitudes toward Eisenhower and the different views on foreign policy. Yet Eisenhower gradually became a President of all the party, one who could depend on the votes of most Republicans on many issues of foreign policy.

REASONS FOR THE REPUBLICAN RECORD

Why did Republican senators vote in greater numbers for President Eisenhower's security proposals than for his other foreign programs? First, the threat of Communist aggression lent an air of urgency to the security measures introduced by both Truman and Eisenhower. Many Republicans who sincerely doubted the value of economic programs believed that security commitments were essential to prevent a further expansion of Soviet and Communist Chinese power. The pattern of Repub-

11 "[Eisenhower] rather vaguely remarked that he 'guessed he had become a candidate' because Robert A. Taft was an isolationist." Joseph and Stewart Alsop, *The Reporter's Trade* (New York: Reynal and Co., 1958), p. 40.

lican support for collective security had become established before 1953. In the immediate postwar period, Republicans had taken the lead in urging a tougher policy toward the Soviet Union. Because of this stand, they recognized that opposition to NATO would make them vulnerable to the charge of inconsistency. President Eisenhower's requests for congressional authority to act in the Formosa area and in the Middle East were presented in an atmosphere of crisis. Senators of both parties felt that congressional refusal to agree would be construed abroad as an invitation to Communist forces to advance.

Second, in the case of Eisenhower's security proposals, particularly his emergency requests for authority to block Communist aggression, the President's prestige was directly at stake. Republican senators naturally identified these measures more closely with Eisenhower than they did the aid and trade policies that Eisenhower inherited from Truman. This helps to explain why Republicans, who had repeatedly sought to curb Truman's discretionary power, voted to grant Eisenhower the widest latitude in implementing collective security measures. They did not have confidence in Truman's Asian policies, blaming the administration for the fall of China and for the deadlocked Korean war. They did have confidence in President Eisenhower and particularly in his military judgment.

One further reason why Republican support for collective security increased after 1952 was that several of the hardcore isolationists left the Senate before the major Eisenhower security proposals were introduced. Ten of the eleven Republicans who voted against the North Atlantic Treaty were the most consistent opponents of security measures. Half of these left the Senate before 1955.[12] Of those who remained, only William Langer of North Dakota usually voted against security; the others voted for parts of Eisenhower's collective security program.

The vote on the proposed Bricker amendment to the Constitution tested Republican attitudes both toward the President and toward the maintenance of American commitments abroad. Since the rollcalls occurred in 1954, the party was still badly

---

12 Those who left the Senate were Guy Cordon, Henry Dworshak, James Kem, Robert A. Taft, and Kenneth Wherry; those who remained through much or all of the Eisenhower administration were William Jenner, William Langer, George Malone, Arthur Watkins, and Milton Young.

split even though the Republican President's prestige was at stake. The Republican senators initially voted nearly unanimously for a compromise acceptable to the administration. In later rollcalls, almost two-thirds of the Republicans voted for revised versions offered by Senators Bricker and George, versions unacceptable to the President. Regional differences were clearest on the rollcall concerning final passage of the revised (and unacceptable) constitutional amendment. Voting against it were nine out of thirteen recorded Republicans from the Northeast, and five of fourteen from the Midwest and Border States, and none of the nineteen voting from the other regions.[13]

The comparatively low Republican support for foreign aid follows the same pattern set by some Democrats toward the end of the Truman administration; it derives mainly from fiscal conservatives who object to the high cost of the program. During the first six years of the Eisenhower administration, there were sixteen Republicans who voted for reductions on a majority of rollcalls involving the size of aid spending; twelve of them also voted against foreign aid measures on a majority of rollcalls. Three of the sixteen came from the Midwest, seven from the Plains, one from a Border State, and five from the Mountain States.[14] Four of the sixteen might be classified as hardcore isolationists because of their frequent opposition to collective security measures, but were not all conservative on domestic issues. All of the remainder had a conservative record, often a deeply conservative record, on domestic issues. There were other Republicans, equally conservative on domestic issues, however, who voted regularly for Eisenhower's aid program. One test used in Chapter 2 may be applied here. Two rollcalls were taken, in 1954 and 1955, on amendments to increase the proportion of aid funds to be granted as loans, not grants. Twenty-seven of the forty Republican votes for these amend-

---

[13] *CQA*, 1954, p. 294.
[14] The sixteen were: John W. Bricker, William Jenner, and Joseph McCarthy from the Midwest; Francis Case, Carl Curtis, Roman Hruska, William Langer, Karl Mundt, Andrew Schoeppel, and Milton Young from the Plains States; John Williams from the Border States; and Frank Barrett, Henry Dworshak, Barry Goldwater, George Malone, and Herman Welker from the Mountain States. All except Case, Mundt, Schoeppel, and Williams voted against aid measures on a majority of rollcalls. Eight of these—Curtis, Hruska, Langer, Schoeppel, Young, Williams, Dworshak, and Goldwater—cast virtually all the Republican votes against foreign aid measures and most of those for reductions in 1959 and 1960.

ments were cast by the sixteen senators voting more often for reductions in aid after 1952; the remainder were cast by domestic conservatives.[15]

Many Republicans had greater confidence in the administration of the aid program under Eisenhower than under Truman.[16] Many felt it important to vote for the aid bills, undiminished in size, to which a Republican President was giving his unqualified support. Yet there were sharp differences in the reactions of Republicans to the change in administrations. While coastal Republicans gave Eisenhower nearly everything he requested for the aid program, Republicans from the Plains and Mountain states were willing to loosen the purse strings only slightly. Republicans from the latter regions voted against Eisenhower's foreign aid measures in almost exactly the same proportion as they had voted against Truman's aid requests.

Those Republican senators who had approved the principle of foreign aid advanced by Truman but only had doubts about its size and administration were consistent backers of Eisenhower. Those who viewed foreign aid as an extravagant Democratic spending program and distrusted Eisenhower's commitment to it continued to vote for major reductions or the elimination of the program. The opposition to foreign aid among Republicans was more fundamental than among Democrats, more concentrated geographically, and at times was an expression of unmitigated isolationism.

Reciprocal trade, unlike foreign aid and collective security, has long been a matter of partisan controversy. Yet the Republican differences over the trade question resemble those concerning security and particularly foreign aid. The Republican split was most clearly indicated after 1952, when the Republican administration became the sponsor of trade bills. As Tables 7 and 8 show, Republicans from the Plains and Mountain states differed sharply from other Republicans. Eleven of the fourteen

[15] CQA, 1954, p. 295; 1955, p. 126.

[16] This was a constant theme of Republican senators interviewed by the writer. An indication of increasing Republican confidence in the administration was the changing attitude toward bills banning or limiting aid to nations selling strategic goods to certain Communist nations. Both administrations opposed most such bills. Only 15 percent of Republican votes cast on this issue were favorable to the Truman administration; the figure increased to 62 percent after Eisenhower took office.

Republicans who cast a majority of votes against reciprocal trade during the Eisenhower administration came from these two regions.[17] Eleven of these fourteen were senators who had also voted for reductions in foreign aid on a majority of rollcalls during the Eisenhower administration and included most of those who often opposed collective security during Eisenhower's administration.

The local economic interests, which usually motivated Democratic opposition to the trade program, played a part in Republican voting. Republican critics of reciprocal trade from the Mountain States of Arizona, Idaho, Nevada, and Wyoming were concerned about protecting the copper, lead, zinc, petroleum, lumber, and wool industries, for example. In the Plains States, the producers of petroleum, lead, and zinc were seeking protection from foreign competition. The two Republican senators from West Virginia, who served during the Eisenhower administration, although voting for foreign aid, responded to the pressure for tariff protection in that state.

It is difficult to compare protectionist voting in the two parties because there were no Democrats in the Plains States and no Republicans in the South. After 1952, while some Democrats voted against both aid and trade, Democratic opposition to the trade program usually reflected localized economic interests. Although there were economic explanations possible for most Republican votes against trade, such opposition was usually part of a pattern of isolationism—resistance to most of the foreign economic and military policies of both Republican and Democratic administrations. The Eisenhower administration created a new voting alignment on this issue. New divisions in both parties became evident. The strongest support for reciprocal trade now comes from the northern industrial states, where business today has less need of protection and greater opportunities for export than in the past. Opposition to the trade program is centered in those southern and western states where senators are seeking to protect new industries (such as textiles), mining and petroleum industries, and a few agricul-

---

[17] The fourteen were: Jenner from the Midwest; Hugh Butler, Case, Curtis, Langer, Schoeppel, and Young from the Plains States; John Hoblitzell, and Chapman Revercomb from the Border States; and Barrett, Dworshak, Goldwater, Malone, and Welker from the Mountain States.

tural products. At a time when three-quarters of American exports are manufactured goods and half of the imports are raw materials, the traditional alignments on the tariff issue are changing. The changing economy has made the Northeast and Midwest not only the centers of support for collective security and foreign aid programs in both parties but also the source of bipartisan support for reciprocal trade.[18]

The Republican record during the Eisenhower administration offers new proof that a party's stand on foreign policy is heavily dependent on control of the White House. The Roosevelt administration in 1933 had brought a complete reversal of Republican voting on international issues. Twenty years later, the change was less only because the party's record had become much more internationalist since World War II. Regional differences followed the same pattern as they did earlier, but in many respects the Eisenhower administration brought, not greater unity, but greater regional differences to the Republican party.[19] All elements of the party rallied around a Republican President when he requested security treaties or resolutions permitting him to use military force in emergencies. On the other hand, when he sought legislation to extend the Democratic-established aid and trade programs, the depth of foreign policy differences in the Republican party became more evident than ever.

The voting records of the two Senate parties on foreign policy not only show a clear contrast but also demonstrate that the responsibilities of office give a party a new outlook on foreign policy. A Republican senator's loyalty to President Eisenhower makes possible but not inevitable a change in that senator's voting record. To what extent do the parties' voting records result from the organized efforts of party leadership? Anyone familiar with the Senate will doubt that party unity on any issue beyond the broad limits already suggested can be primarily the result of organizational efforts. Yet there are enough examples of remarkable party unity and sudden changes in voting patterns on specific issues to suggest that the mechanics of party leadership in the Senate deserve further examination.

[18] See Watson, "The Tariff Revolution," *Journal of Politics*, XVIII (Nov., 1956), 678-701.
[19] See Grassmuck, *Sectional Biases in Congress on Foreign Policy.*

Everyone knows something of leaders and leadership of various sorts, but no one knows very much. Leadership, especially in the political realm, unavoidably or by design often is suffused by an atmosphere of the mystic and the magical, and these mysteries have been little penetrated by systematic observation.—DAVID B. TRUMAN

The Senate always has had two duly chosen leaders, one for the majority and one for the minority. But the questions as to how and when (and sometimes whether) they really lead are open to a variety of answers. In this business there is no constant. The ways of the place are passing strange and the personalities and purposes of the various leaders are highly individual and highly at variance.
—WILLIAM S. WHITE

4

PARTY LEADERS

THE POLITICAL INSTITUTIONS OF THE SENATE CAN BE UNDERstood only in terms of the men who operate them. The student of leadership in the Senate must be constantly aware not only that he is dealing with intangibles but that the far greater part of his concern is hidden from scrutiny. The importance of personal influence rather than institutional techniques results from the relatively small membership of the Senate, the diffusion of power among a number of veteran senators, and the absence of party sanctions. Party leaders in the Senate have varied widely in their concept of the role they should play. William S. White has asserted that, except in times of emergency or during the political dominance of a man with Franklin Roosevelt's stature, the administration's leader in the Senate will be more responsible to the senatorial party than to the President.[1] In practice the leaders of the Senate do not view their role with such simple consistency.

Who is a party leader? The floor leader is not necessarily the most powerful figure in his party and may be overshadowed by senators holding other party posts or committee chairmanships. The Democrats concentrate formal leadership in one man, who serves as floor leader and chairman of both the Policy Committee and party Conference. When Lyndon Johnson held these posts, there was no doubt that he was the party leader, though when Ernest McFarland held the same posts, some observers thought that other Democrats exercised considerably more party authority. The Republicans divide formal leadership among three senators: the floor leader and the chairmen of the Policy Committee and of the Conference. Senator Robert Taft was clearly his party's leader whether he served as floor leader or chairman of the Policy Committee; among his successors, the floor leader has served as *primus inter pares*. The role of the party whip is not only ill defined, as Professor Truman has pointed out, but appears to vary substantially between the two parties.[2] The Democratic whips have more often been able to serve in practice as assistant leaders because of a close kinship of views with the floor leader. Cooperation between the Republican floor leader and whip has frequently been difficult because of wide differences of opinion (Kenneth Wherry and Leverett Saltonstall, for example). The Republican whip's post has sometimes been given to a member of a faction defeated in a contest for floor leader.

Professor Truman has well defined the difficulties of describing the floor leader: "A search for the substance and sources of power in the position, however, is frustrating, not because they do not exist but because they are tremendously varied and often inaccessible. One cannot draw up for this post a neat list of authori-

[1] William S. White, *Citadel: The Story of the U.S. Senate* (New York: Harper & Brothers, 1957), p. 96.
[2] David B. Truman, *The Congressional Party* (New York: John Wiley and Sons, 1959), pp. 117-22.

ties and prerogatives that describes its power adequately if not exhaustively, as one can for a place in a tightly structured hierarchy. The sum total of influence in the role as played by any individual senator depends upon the skill with which he combines and employs the fragments of power that are available to him." Truman proceeds to identify some of the more important powers: influence over committee assignments, the ability to facilitate passage of pet bills, responsibility for scheduling legislation, a frequent role in the planning of tactics, and (for the administration party) frequent contact with the President.[3]

The difficulties of identifying party leaders and defining their roles and techniques dictate caution to anyone trying to construct valid generalizations about senatorial leadership. It is possible, however, to measure the scope of the leaders' concern over foreign affairs and describe the variations in their techniques. It is impossible to prove that given leaders were responsible for specific degrees of party unity in rollcall voting, but some cautious conclusions can be drawn about the success of their efforts toward such unity. One further step is to assess the attempts to institutionalize party leadership. Can a strong leader establish traditions and create machinery that may help less skillful successors? Although personal techniques may be the most effective today, the political party is unlikely to play an increasing role in framing foreign policy if political leadership depends entirely on the accidents of personality.

Despite the variations in purpose, technique, and viewpoint, party leaders in the postwar period have one pertinent common denominator: They have had a relatively small influence on the development of foreign policy. Leaders of the administration party have seldom challenged the President on issues of foreign policy; in the Senate they have often played an important but unobtrusive role in support of the party's leader on the Foreign Relations Committee. When a leader such as William Knowland has differed with the President on an important international question, he has usually lost the support of his party. The most important opposition leaders in recent years, Robert Taft and Lyndon Johnson, had less impact on foreign policy than on

[3] *Ibid.*, pp. 104-105.

domestic affairs. The reasons lie partly in their lack of interest and specialized knowledge concerning world problems. More significant is the handicap any senatorial leader faces in competing with the President in the field of foreign policy.

DEMOCRATIC LEADERS DURING THE TRUMAN ADMINISTRATION

The post of Democratic floor leader from 1947 through 1952 was held for successive two-year periods by Alben Barkley (as minority leader) and Scott Lucas and Ernest McFarland (as majority leaders). Senate Democratic leadership during this period presents a paradox: The strength of party support for President Truman's foreign programs was much more impressive than the caliber of party leadership. Moreover, none of the three Democratic leaders appears to have engaged in extensive efforts to organize party support for the President; each played a role in foreign affairs subsidiary to that of Tom Connally, Democratic chairman of the Foreign Relations Committee.

Barkley, Lucas, and McFarland were all dependable internationalists who were willing to follow the administration's lead with little question. This quality of Truman's lieutenants in the Senate was so characteristic that its value was often overlooked until it became scarce during the Eisenhower administration. Barkley and Lucas supported the administration on virtually every foreign policy rollcall during this period. McFarland's record of support was not quite so consistent until he became floor leader in 1951.

Senator Barkley is the only one of the three who gained a reputation as a skillful leader in the Senate. He brought certain obvious advantages to this task: long seniority, a Border-State background, a sense of humor, and an understanding of how to handle men. He was able to retain the respect of the more conservative Democrats while pressing for the enactment of New Deal measures. Barkley had close personal friendships with both President Truman and Dean Acheson, especially important assets during his term as Vice President. Barkley's success as a leader seems to have rested particularly on those intangible and personal qualities that are highly valued in the Senate but are most difficult to describe on paper.

Despite his undoubted skill, there is little evidence that Alben Barkley played an active role in framing compromises or persuading Democratic senators to vote for the administration's foreign program. Nor was Barkley a frequent speaker in foreign policy debates. He left most of the leadership in this field to Tom Connally, with whom he had a close working relationship. During the Republican Eightieth Congress, a greater share of responsibility for foreign policy leadership fell to Senator Arthur Vandenberg, chairman of the Foreign Relations Committee. Vandenberg's steps to make foreign aid measures, for example, more palatable to Republican senators helped to solidify Democratic support and reduced the need for persuasive efforts by either Connally or Barkley. This is not to say that it was never necessary to explain a foreign program to a Democratic senator, allay his doubts, or assure his attendance during rollcalls. By conviction, however, most Democratic senators were sympathetic to the Truman Doctrine and the Marshall Plan and welcomed firm measures to stem the Communist tide in Europe. Barkley's skill was not a significant factor in the Democratic record because it was so seldom needed when foreign issues were pending in the Senate.

During their brief terms, neither Scott Lucas nor Ernest McFarland became strong majority leaders. Both were handicapped by increasing divisions in the Democratic party and a steady decline in the rapport between President Truman and southern Democrats. Lucas' close identification with the President and the northern wing of the party reduced his effectiveness in making accommodations with the southern senators.[4] Senator McFarland, on the other hand, was too closely connected with the Southern Democrats to work most effectively with the President. Lacking experience for the majority leadership, he appeared indecisive.

The Democratic divisions on domestic issues did not extend to foreign policy, nor did antagonisms toward either Lucas or McFarland prevent the Democratic senators from maintaining a remarkably united front when international issues were at stake.

---

[4] Truman has shown, however, that Lucas' voting record indicated he tried to play the role of a middleman, particularly by abstaining on certain votes when southern Democrats opposed the President. *Ibid.*, pp. 106-10.

Can Lucas and McFarland, ineffective generals in the battles for civil rights and welfare legislation, be credited with the victories on foreign battlefields? Both men as majority leaders carried heavier responsibilities than Barkley, and both had to overcome increasing Republican opposition to Truman's foreign programs. Both worked closely and in almost perfect harmony with Chairman Connally of the Foreign Relations Committee, with Connally maintaining primary responsibility for enacting the administration's foreign programs under a mutually satisfactory division of labor.

During the 1949 and 1950 debates on foreign aid, Lucas maneuvered adroitly to defeat crippling amendments by raising points of order, rallied the Democratic senators to prevent serious cuts in the aid program, and helped to develop compromises necessary to prevent defeat of the arms aid bill. When strong sentiment developed in support of a Spanish loan flatly opposed by the administration, Lucas negotiated a compromise (apparently without the President's backing) to assure that the funds for the loan would be in addition to those already scheduled for European aid. In 1949 Lucas held the party in line sufficiently to pass the reciprocal trade bill after defeating the Republican-sponsored "peril point" amendment.

During Senator McFarland's tenure as majority leader, the Democrats maintained sufficient unity to pass foreign aid bills with minimum reductions on the Senate floor, approve a troops-for-Europe resolution largely acceptable to the administration, and defeat Republican efforts to revise the ground rules for the MacArthur hearings—all controversial issues. Only on some of the less critical amendments to the troops-for-Europe resolution did Democratic unity seriously falter. There is little direct evidence concerning the scope and effectiveness of McFarland's activities with regard to these issues. Democratic backing for the administration did remain surprisingly firm in the face of the Korean war, the growing unpopularity of both Truman and Acheson, and mounting Republican attacks on foreign policy. McFarland must share some of the credit for translating this basic unity into actual votes.

The loyalty of Democratic leaders in the Senate to President Truman's foreign policy is a matter of record; their skill in guiding this program through the Senate was seldom critically tested because of the depth of internationalist convictions held by Democratic senators. The observer must conclude that Barkley, Lucas, and McFarland made a contribution to the Democratic record that was helpful but not of critical importance.

EISENHOWER'S LEADERS IN THE SENATE

Republican senatorial leadership during the Eisenhower administration differed sharply from the Democratic leadership that had preceded it. The difference was most pronounced on foreign policy because this was the issue that caused least friction between Truman and his leaders and most difficulty between Eisenhower and his leaders. At the 1952 Republican convention Eisenhower had been the choice of the eastern, internationalist wing of the party, which was a minority among senatorial Republicans. He was committed to foreign programs that Robert Taft and many Republican senators had been criticizing with increasing vigor. Eisenhower's distrust of Taft's views on foreign policy had been the strongest motivating factor in his decision to seek the nomination.[5] Knowland had deep convictions on foreign policy, which were increasingly to separate him from the President. Everett Dirksen and Styles Bridges were among the other Republican leaders who had been considered outside the internationalist wing of the party. Those Republican leaders most loyal to Eisenhower's foreign policies, such as Alexander Wiley and Leverett Saltonstall, were outnumbered and often ineffective.

It is intriguing to speculate on the kind of senatorial leader Taft would have become had he lived beyond the first six months of Eisenhower's administration. At the start, he showed a great sense of responsibility for the administration's success, willingness to employ his prestige and skill in behalf of the Eisenhower program, and determination to influence profoundly the shape of that program. Taft's biographer asserts that in this brief period "no President within twenty years—that is, neither Roosevelt nor Truman—had so effective a Senate leader as Eisenhower had

---

[5] George E. Allen, "My Friend the President," *Saturday Evening Post*, CCXXXII (April 9, 1960), 23-25, 50-54.

in Taft." He adds, however, that the President usually had to negotiate his programs with Taft substantially as a coequal.[6] By joining the Foreign Relations Committee in 1953, Senator Taft demonstrated his growing interest in foreign policy and his determination to influence the Republican record thereon before measures reached the Senate floor. William S. White quotes Taft as saying, "We have got to get a little stronger *conservative* voice on that committee."[7]

The controversy over the nomination of Charles E. Bohlen as Ambassador to Moscow in 1953 illustrated both Taft's skillful service to the administration and his desire to influence its policies. Although Taft clearly disliked the nomination because of Bohlen's alleged influence at the Yalta conference, he supported confirmation in the Foreign Relations Committee. When questions were raised about Bohlen's security clearance, Taft agreed to join Senator John J. Sparkman in reading an FBI file on Bohlen. Then, in a formidable speech on the Senate floor, he demolished the security argument and the opposition to confirmation. White has reported that Taft then passed the word to the White House: "No more Bohlens!"[8]

Taft took a firmer line on the Yalta resolution. President Eisenhower asked Congress to pass a resolution charging the Soviet Union with having perverted the wartime agreements and stating this country's unwillingness to acquiesce in the subjugation of free peoples. As Taft privately warned the President, most Republicans considered this totally inadequate and even an implied endorsement of the Yalta agreement. Taft took the lead in inserting a provision to make it clear that Congress was not passing judgment on the validity or invalidity of the wartime agreements. He headed the subcommittee that drafted the provision, fought successfully for its acceptance by the Foreign Relations Committee, and gained endorsement from the Policy Committee. The result of the deadlock was that no resolution passed.[9]

[6] William S. White, *The Taft Story* (New York: Harper & Brothers, 1954), p. 227.
[7] *Ibid.*, pp. 211-12.
[8] *Ibid.*, pp. 230-41.
[9] *Ibid.*, pp. 242-48. Robert J. Donovan, *Eisenhower: The Inside Story* (New York: Harper & Brothers, 1956), p. 49.

The level of spending for foreign commitments was the most serious issue in dispute between President Eisenhower and the Taft Republicans in the Senate. Early in the administration, Taft angrily criticized the President's budget, and particularly the high level of defense spending, at a private meeting with Eisenhower and top administration leaders.[10] In public he warned the President that foreign aid spending must be drastically cut in the face of congressional hostility. Although Taft spoke in a party caucus and voted on the floor against foreign aid cuts, on this issue Republican senators were badly divided and Taft could not command the degree of party unity evident on the Bohlen and Yalta issues. Had he lived, it seems likely that foreign aid would have become an increasingly divisive issue between Taft and Eisenhower.

William Knowland is remembered primarily in Washington as the Republican leader who so often challenged the policies of the Eisenhower administration. This does not necessarily mean that his concept of the floor leader's role differed radically from that of his predecessors. He was frequently an effective spokesman for President Eisenhower's programs in Congress, even though his responsibility for their passage was somewhat diminished when he became minority leader in 1955. When he differed with these programs, he sometimes sought to adjust the differences and on other occasions led the campaign for amendments unacceptable to the administration. Though his convictions occasionally led him to seek changes in bills, Knowland clearly recognized a degree of responsibility to the President on legislative questions. Knowland's most serious challenges involved not legislation, but diplomacy: such issues as a summit conference, the Indochina crisis, and policy toward Communist China, where he saw less need to temper his criticisms, private or public.

Knowland's interest in and convictions concerning foreign policy were more profound than those of any other party leader since the war. The term "isolationist," though often applied to Taft, could never be stretched to include Knowland. (Taft had chosen Knowland as his successor because he regarded Knowland as a safe, conservative Republican, not because of any identity

10 Donovan, pp. 108-11.

of views on foreign policy.)[11] Knowland supported the major foreign aid and collective security measures of the Truman administration (except for the Point Four Program). His frequent votes for limitations on spending programs seemed to reflect a growing distrust of the Truman administration rather than tinges of isolationism. He had greater respect for the President's authority in foreign affairs than Taft did. Knowland was best known during the Truman administration as a persistent advocate of firmer policies in Asia and critic of the administration's policies in that area. It was Knowland who repeatedly demanded steps to prevent Chiang Kai-shek's collapse on the mainland of China, an American commitment to defend Formosa, and later the adoption of policies in Korea urged by General Douglas MacArthur. In these efforts Knowland had the support of a gradually increasing proportion of Republicans. At the start of Eisenhower's administration this group was clearly a majority of the Republican senators, and Knowland was obviously its spokesman on Asian issues.

The controversy over the Bricker amendment perhaps best illustrates the role Knowland sometimes played as an agent of compromise as well as the difficulties he faced when it proved impossible to serve two masters. Knowland personally believed in the necessity of limiting executive encroachment on congressional prerogatives in foreign affairs. In his extensive efforts to make such an amendment possible, Knowland was expressing not only his own beliefs but those of a majority of Republican senators. On the other hand, he did not want the President to suffer a crushing defeat on the issue nor did he want the party to become divided. As a consequence of these conflicting loyalties, Knowland worked persistently and almost successfully for a compromise that the administration could accept.

Though he had been a cosponsor of the Bricker amendment, once the President's opposition had become clear, Knowland gave no public support to any version of the amendment unacceptable to the administration—that is, until the final rollcall. In July, 1953, Knowland introduced a compromise plan that had the President's public blessing. Early in the 1954 session he resumed the drafting of compromises and met frequently with

[11] White, *The Taft Story*, pp. 253-62.

Senator Bricker and administration leaders. Together with Senator Homer Ferguson he sponsored revisions of the Bricker amendment on the Senate floor and gained their approval with nearly unanimous Republican assistance. When Senator George introduced a further revision unacceptable to the President, Knowland spoke against it in vain; only one-third of the Republicans joined him in voting against it. When the final vote came on the frequently amended proposal, Senator Knowland left the majority leader's desk to speak as an individual senator and announced that, despite grave misgivings about the George revision, he would vote for it in the hope that the House would improve it before final passage. Knowland's failure illustrates the dilemma any leader would have faced in a party still deeply divided on foreign policy in 1954. His compromises served to postpone but not to prevent a showdown, and it is doubtful that he could have come so close to successful compromise had he been more completely identified with the President's viewpoint.

Knowland took a stand of outright opposition to only one major feature of Eisenhower's legislative program: aid to neutral and particularly Communist nations. On several occasions Knowland worked to reduce or place restrictions on aid to both India and Yugoslavia. In 1958 he succeeded in defeating Senator John F. Kennedy's amendment to the foreign aid bill, designed to give the President discretion to extend economic aid to Communist satellite countries.

Senator Knowland's efforts to persuade the Eisenhower administration to take a firmer stand in Asia did not represent merely a personal crusade. On this issue as well as in his opposition to aid for neutrals he frequently spoke for many congressional Republicans. For this reason the administration could not ignore him, nor could it seek to replace him as floor leader without risking humiliating defeat.[12] Some of his views on Asia were shared by Admiral Arthur W. Radford and by others on the Joint Chiefs of Staff as well as by Secretary of State John Foster Dulles. Knowland often expressed his opinions in public,

---

[12] Perhaps the breach between Eisenhower and Knowland was most serious in December, 1954, when Knowland voted against the censure of Senator Joseph McCarthy. At that time "Eisenhower Republicans" in the Senate were privately saying that Knowland should resign as floor leader but that an attempt to oust him would fail. *New York Times*, December 2, 1954, pp. 1, 23.

but there is little evidence that the President and Secretary of State consulted him except on those issues with legislative implications. The assertions Knowland may have made in private are unknown, but in public he claimed to speak only for himself and not for the Senate Republicans. He did not use his position as floor leader in attempts to organize his colleagues in opposition to the policies of the administration. He was willing to support measures in the Senate much more moderate than what he had publicly advocated.

In 1954 Knowland publicly threatened to resign as floor leader and devote his "full efforts" to canceling American membership in the United Nations if China were admitted. This incident offers insight into Knowland's views on the limits a leader might properly go in challenging the administration's policies. It can be said that Knowland's efforts helped to consolidate Republican opposition to American recognition or admission of Communist China to the U.N. and consequently established a major obstacle to any serious consideration of such policies by the President.[13]

The crisis provoked by the Communist threat to the islands off the coast of China made clear both the extent and limits of Knowland's influence on the administration. The Communist shelling of Quemoy in September, 1954, brought about a prolonged debate in the administration.[14] There was little disagreement over the necessity of reaffirming the American intention to defend Formosa itself or over the value of requiring a commitment by Chiang Kai-shek not to attack the mainland without the agreement of the United States. The critical question was whether the United States should commit itself to defend the offshore islands, as Knowland along with Admiral Radford and some other military leaders believed, or should exclude these islands from the defense perimeter. The President finally decided to exclude any reference to Quemoy and Matsu in the Formosa resolution submitted for congressional approval, leaving the question of defending these islands to the President's judgment concerning the scope and intention of any attack. The strength

13 Donovan, pp. 132-36.
14 Stewart Alsop, "How We Drifted Close to War," *Saturday Evening Post*, CCXXXI (December 13, 1958), 26-27, 86-88. Chalmers M. Roberts, "Strong Man from the South," *Saturday Evening Post*, CCXXVII (June 25, 1955), 30, 109-12. Donovan, pp. 300-10.

of the views represented by Knowland was one major reason why Quemoy and Matsu were not specifically excluded from the resolution, while the attitude of Democratic senators was a major reason preventing the specific inclusion of the islands.[15] Knowland was carefully consulted during the drafting of the resolution, though his proposal that the President appear before Congress in person was rejected. Knowland loyally defended the resolution on the Senate floor in January despite doubts about its limitations. Two months later he began insisting that the administration commit itself firmly and publicly to the defense of Quemoy and Matsu. He was unsuccessful in this effort, just as a number of Democrats—including Adlai Stevenson—failed to persuade the administration to abandon the offshore islands.[16] Even at its height, Knowland's influence (and that of his supporters) on diplomacy was a negative factor; it placed certain limits on the administration's flexibility, but it was never powerful enough to dictate a course of action.

Because of his deep interest in foreign affairs, Senator Knowland played a more active role and particularly a greater public role in international questions, both legislative and diplomatic, than most other recent party leaders. He completely overshadowed and appeared to virtually ignore Alexander Wiley, the ranking Republican on the Foreign Relations Committee. Knowland had unusual opportunities to influence foreign policy as a member of the Appropriations Committee for a prolonged period, the Armed Services Committee until 1953, and thereafter the Foreign Relations Committee. Knowland, like Taft, commanded support in the party because his views were respected and not because of any special skill in legislative negotiations. His influence would probably have been greater if he had been not only more flexible in his thinking but more adept at behind-the-scenes maneuvering. Knowland's greatest influence was over those Republicans who had been most critical of Truman's foreign policies. In the early Eisenhower years the President

---

[15] While the issue was being discussed, Knowland was making public speeches demanding a much firmer foreign policy and on one occasion calling for a congressional investigation of diplomatic and military policy.

[16] It has been reported, however, that at this time the administration failed in an effort to persuade Chiang Kai-shek to evacuate the islands. Alsop, *Saturday Evening Post*, CCXXXI, 88.

depended on Knowland to rally these senators behind the administration's program but paid a high price for this assistance because of Knowland's frequent revolts. Eisenhower was known to resent deeply Knowland's criticisms of his foreign policy. In later years Knowland's influence diminished for several reasons: a Democratic majority in Congress beginning in 1955, the declining popularity of the tough international policies he advocated, and (perhaps most important) Eisenhower's increasing ability to command Republican support in Congress for his foreign policies simply because he was the party's President. Finally, it may be concluded from Knowland's record that strong senatorial leadership may be a detriment and not automatically an asset to effective party unity on issues of foreign policy.

Among the other Republican party leaders in the Senate, Styles Bridges was usually regarded as most influential on questions of foreign policy during the Eisenhower administration. Throughout the period from 1947 through 1960 Senator Bridges was the ranking Republican on the Appropriations Committee and a member of the inner circle of party leadership, serving as floor leader in 1952 and becoming chairman of the Policy Committee in 1955. Bridges' record closely paralleled Knowland's. He supported the principles of foreign aid, criticized its administration by the Democrats, and voted for most of Eisenhower's aid requests. Like Knowland he was in the forefront of those demanding a firmer policy in Asia and criticizing aid to neutral and Communist satellite countries. Unlike Taft and Knowland, however, he voted against Ambassador Bohlen's confirmation in 1953. Bridges played a less prominent part than Knowland in foreign policy debates during the Eisenhower administration, but he stood for nearly all the same policies and represented the same wing of the party as did Knowland. He never appeared to share fully Knowland's internationalism or enthusiasm for foreign aid; consequently, Bridges' support of the Eisenhower foreign policy appeared to be more reluctant than Knowland's.

On those occasions when Bridges joined Knowland in opposition to some aspect of Eisenhower's foreign program, Bridges' stand was costly to the President. His opposition was less publicized and therefore less embarrassing to the President than

Knowland's, but Bridges' influence with conservative Republicans was just as great. On the other hand, Bridges' support of most foreign aid proposals was a major asset for the Eisenhower administration because of his strategic position as a senior party leader and ranking Republican on the Appropriations Committee. On some occasions in the committee Bridges voted for lower aid funds than a majority of the committee's members did, but on the floor he usually supported the committee's restoration of funds cut in the House. Because of his power, Bridges could have become a major obstacle to the foreign aid program; his support of it in most cases reflected his concept of the degree of loyalty owed by a party leader to the President.

Senator Dirksen, who succeeded Knowland as floor leader after being the party whip, has never been burdened with the deep convictions concerning foreign affairs characteristic of Knowland. As a consequence, he was a much more dependable leader for the Eisenhower administration. Though a vocal opponent of foreign aid as a senator during the last years of Truman's administration, Dirksen supported Eisenhower's aid program (and other foreign policies) with remarkable consistency. Although a junior member of the Appropriations Committee, he was given considerable responsibility for defending foreign aid appropriations during senatorial debates even before becoming floor leader. Unlike Knowland and Bridges, Dirksen supported the President's requests for aid to neutrals and to Yugoslavia, although in 1958 he helped to scuttle the amendment to facilitate aid to Communist satellites. Dirksen has never been as influential among conservative Republicans as Knowland or Bridges.

Leverett Saltonstall of Massachusetts has been a relatively ineffective party leader precisely because his support of internationalist policies has been too consistent for him to command respect among the less internationalist Republicans. Like Knowland and Bridges, Saltonstall has held high positions both in the party and on committees dealing with foreign affairs. He has been on the Policy Committee since 1947, was whip from 1949 through 1956, and chairman of the Conference thereafter. He has long service on both the Appropriations and Armed Services committees. On questions of foreign aid (to allies or neutrals), collective security, and the Bricker amendment, he supported most of Truman's proposals and virtually all of Eisenhower's. Such consistency by a man holding strategic posts was an obvious asset to the Eisenhower administration, but did not impress those Republicans who followed the lead of Knowland and Bridges, those who most needed conversion to the administration's viewpoint. Close observers of the Senate also think that though he is a competent senator, Saltonstall has lacked the political skill and ambition necessary to wrest the party leadership away from Knowland, Bridges, and Dirksen.[17]

REPUBLICAN OPPOSITION LEADERSHIP: TAFT & CO.

A leader of the opposition party in the Senate has more independence than the administration leader and consequently more opportunity to shape his party's policy. The two outstanding opposition leaders of recent years, Robert A. Taft and Lyndon B. Johnson, had a greater impact on domestic affairs, however, than on foreign policy. The term "Mr. Republican" so often applied to Taft was a measure of the respect he commanded from his party colleagues and of his ability to represent their viewpoints on a wide variety of domestic issues; the title was deceptive because it had limited application to international issues. From 1947 through 1952 Taft dominated the Republican leadership coalition from his post as chairman of the Policy Committee. He overshadowed the three floor leaders of that period: the aging Wallace H. White (in 1947 and 1948), Kenneth S. Wherry (1949 through 1951), and Styles Bridges (in 1952). With respect to foreign affairs, the scope of Taft's activity and influence varied not because of changes in the floor leader but because of Senator Vandenberg's role as Republican leader on the Foreign Relations Committee. When illness forced Vandenberg from the senatorial scene in 1950, Taft's role in foreign affairs began to change.

As long as Vandenberg was active in the Senate, he and Taft divided the *de facto* leadership of the party. Taft concentrated on domestic affairs, and Vandenberg devoted almost all of his attention to foreign policy. Vandenberg's son has described this

[17] When Saltonstall, the party whip since 1949, was promoted to conference chairman in 1957 and replaced by Wherry, some observers felt that he was being "kicked upstairs" and removed from the line of succession to the floor leadership.

as "a tacit and informal understanding" in which both "conscientiously sought to avoid direct conflict."[18] Only rarely did Taft directly challenge Vandenberg on international issues; when he was in disagreement, he usually avoided any open opposition. This tacitly recognized division of responsibility was a curious one not only because Taft disagreed with Vandenberg on certain important international questions but because he was deeply scornful of Vandenberg's conversion to internationalism and suspicious of the bipartisan approach to foreign policy. William S. White felt that Taft had "the greatest misgivings in letting Vandenberg have his head" in foreign policy and that it was "only by iron self-restraint" that Taft avoided public harassment of Vandenberg.[19]

There were at least four reasons why Taft was willing to leave leadership in foreign affairs to Vandenberg. The first was political: Vandenberg was potentially a powerful contender for the 1948 presidential nomination whom Taft, as another candidate, did not want to challenge. Second, Taft did not want to exacerbate intraparty differences on foreign policy by leading the opposition to Vandenberg in the Eightieth Congress, where the Republicans had finally achieved a majority. Third, Taft was trying to expand his alliance with southern Democrats on domestic issues and felt it prudent to avoid sweeping attacks on the Truman foreign policies accepted by most of them. The fourth reason, and perhaps the most important, was that Taft was not interested in, experienced with, or even well informed about international affairs.[20]

During this period Taft occupied a curious position. While the Republican internationalists looked upon him as an isolationist, the diehard isolationists felt he had abandoned their cause to further his own presidential ambitions. His greatest influence was on the sizable middle group of Republicans, who were often suspicious of Vandenberg's assurances regarding policy but felt it politically safe to vote for those programs endorsed by Taft.

The ambiguities of Taft's position can be illustrated in the

---

18 Vandenberg, *The Private Papers of Senator Vandenberg,* pp. 318-19.
19 White, *The Taft Story,* pp. 146-47.
20 See Westerfield, *Foreign Policy and Party Politics,* p. 271; White, *The Taft Story,* pp. 59-60.

case of foreign aid. Taft avoided assuming the leadership of those Republicans who wanted to defeat or cripple the aid programs, but on the floor of the Senate he provided the most reasoned and persuasive criticism of foreign aid. Taft argued fervently for reductions in the aid program, yet during the Vandenberg period he seldom had the support of a Republican majority in voting for cuts. On the other hand, his opposition to several large reductions may have helped minimize the number of Republican votes cast for them. Senator Taft felt that the aid program was justifiable only as a temporary measure to prevent Communist expansion; he criticized what he called the balance-of-payments approach to foreign aid, the long-term effort to close the dollar gap of recipient nations. He warned above all of the dangers resulting from the tax burden required to support foreign aid.

During this period Taft never used his authority as a party leader in an effort to delay or cripple foreign aid measures, but used this authority once to support Vandenberg. In 1948 Taft had introduced unsuccessfully an amendment to cut $1.3 billion from the Marshall Plan authorization. When the House sought to reduce the appropriation below the authorization figure, Taft supported the full amount and argued that the authorization represented a moral commitment that should be kept. When a Senate-House conference committee became deadlocked over the appropriation on the eve of the Republican national convention, Taft broke the deadlock by announcing that he would hold the Senate in session until a "satisfactory" total was agreed upon.

During 1948 Taft also yielded to Vandenberg on the issue of reciprocal trade. Vandenberg devised a compromise plan, which Taft criticized because of the discretion given to the President in accepting or rejecting recommendations of the Tariff Commission. Yet Taft voted for the Vandenberg plan in committee and endorsed it in the Senate, providing support that was probably essential in view of the closeness of the vote.

During the period of Vandenberg's leadership in foreign policy, the only major issues on which Taft actively opposed him were ratification of the North Atlantic Treaty and its implementation by military assistance. Taft opposed the NATO pact primarily because he felt it contained a firm moral obligation for arms aid to our European allies. He opposed such aid for two reasons: He believed it would seriously increase the danger of war by dividing the world into two armed camps, and he thought the United States could not afford large programs for both economic and military aid. Basic to Taft's attitude toward NATO, as his biographer has pointed out, were his abhorrence of war, his lack of familiarity with and understanding of military policy, and his habit of "putting price tags on military security."[21] His opposition also stemmed from his belief that this country must avoid any commitment to fight a land war in Europe, a belief that underlay his opposition to sending troops to Europe in 1951. Taft proposed a reservation to the treaty stating that the provisions in Article 3 for "effective self-help and mutual aid" would not commit any nation to furnish others with arms.

Despite Taft's stand, only one-quarter of the Republican senators voted against ratification of the North Atlantic Treaty and less than half supported his reservation to the treaty. Observers at the time expressed doubts that Taft had changed many votes, since most of the opposing votes were cast by diehard isolationists. Senator Vandenberg took a different view: "The Taft speech will lengthen the battle because it lends a certain respectability to the opposition, and some of those who wouldn't have dared stand up on their own will now join the anti parade. But I don't believe it will be serious. . . . I cannot ignore the fact that if Taft thought his negative vote would divide the Party, he would never have taken that responsibility."[22] Taft felt uncertain about his decision to oppose NATO, probably in deference to Vandenberg's leadership. He said he took that step "with the greatest discomfort" and "with great regret." Despite his speeches against NATO, Taft avoided leading any organized opposition to the pact. He avoided participation in the controversy over the military assistance bill until the last day of debate. Taft was not primarily responsible for the fact that a large minority of Republicans voted against the arms bill and over two-thirds voted for cuts in the program; numerous senatorial leaders in both parties criticized the scope and nature of the administration's program.

In the last three years of the Truman administration, Senator Taft played a more active role in international issues and was

21 White, *The Taft Story*, pp. 149-50.
22 Vandenberg, p. 498.

increasingly critical of the administration's policies. He was quoted as saying, "I am charged with moving in on foreign policy; the truth is that foreign policy has moved in on me."[23] One reason for Taft's increased interest was his decision to seek the Presidency in 1952 and his feeling that he must consequently become more prominent in foreign affairs. Moreover, Taft felt that the Truman administration had made a mockery of bipartisanship in foreign policy. The Korean war, the dismissal of General Douglas MacArthur, and the partisan controversy over Dean Acheson intensified Taft's hostility to the administration's policies. Probably the most important reason for Taft's increased activity and independence was Senator Vandenberg's illness in 1950 and death in April, 1951. Senator Alexander Wiley, who succeeded Vandenberg as ranking Republican on the Foreign Relations Committee, had no comparable following among Republican senators. Consequently, Taft did not have to defer to Wiley's views and in fact almost completely ignored Wiley while moving to fill the vacuum of foreign policy leadership left by Vandenberg's departure.

The "great debate" in 1951 over sending troops to Europe in support of the American commitment to NATO is the most significant example of Senator Taft's emergence in the area of foreign policy. More than any other Republican, Taft was responsible for launching the debate, and he greatly influenced its course and outcome. He presented the strongest arguments against sending any forces to Europe and in favor of congressional limitations on the President's authority to dispatch troops. Yet, in typical fashion, he finally compromised to support a resolution that endorsed four American divisions for Europe and that excluded most of the strict limitations on future presidential action that he had favored. Although a majority of Republicans voted with Taft on all but one of the long series of rollcalls on the issues, he could only count on the votes of a middle group of senators in the seriously divided party. A group of internationalist Republicans, varying in number from eight to fourteen on most rollcalls, repeatedly voted against Taft and (together with the Democrats) prevented the passage of a joint resolution that would have been binding on the President. There were nineteen Re-

23 White, *The Taft Story*, p. 148.

publicans who opposed final passage of the Senate resolution either because they opposed sending any troops or because the resolution did not have binding effect. On the other hand, some of the twenty-seven Republicans who voted for final passage were willing to bury serious doubts about the resolution because of Taft's strong insistence that this was a necessary step in asserting congressional authority. In a seriously divided party, Taft's personal ambivalence helped to prolong a controversy that was damaging this country's prestige and effectiveness abroad. Nevertheless, Taft's willingness to compromise and his ability to lead at least some Republicans in that direction helped to prevent any Senate action that would have been more damaging to American foreign policy.

There is no evidence that Taft used the powers of his party office or applied personal pressure on Republicans in order to gain votes. Had he been a more skillful compromiser, Taft might have been able to draft a resolution commanding wider Republican support. In fact, Taft as usual won votes primarily from those Republicans who respected his views. His influence in this controversy resulted from the fact that the criticisms he voiced were representative of many Republicans' views, though his eventual compromise was less widely supported.

Senator Taft became a frequent critic of the Truman administration's policies in Asia. He shared the view of many Republicans that greater emphasis should be placed on resisting the spread of Communism in Asia, though he was neither so aggressive nor so consistent as Senator Knowland in advocating bold policies to implement these principles. When President Truman dismissed General MacArthur as commander of the U.N. forces in Korea, Taft gave MacArthur his full personal support and that of the Republican party. He helped to direct the party strategy that led to MacArthur's address before Congress and a congressional investigation of Far Eastern policy. He served, along with Knowland and Bridges, as an adviser to MacArthur in the preparation of testimony for the hearings. He gave complete backing to the policies advocated by MacArthur, urged all-out war in Korea, and suggested that Congress go on record in opposition to any negotiated "appeasement peace" in Korea. Yet Taft never tried to bring about any further congressional action on Korea, perhaps because he realized that the administration could not be forced to act and perhaps because a number of Republican senators were less hostile to the growing possibilities of truce in Korea than Taft and Knowland were. Taft's frequently ambiguous position on one occasion led to virtual abdication of his responsibilities. While John Foster Dulles was negotiating the Japanese Peace Treaty, he frequently consulted Taft. But Taft avoided speaking for the treaty and left the Senate floor on a campaign trip during the ratification debate, leaving behind the typical announcement that he favored the treaty as well as most of the proposed reservations. Senators William Knowland and Alexander Smith shouldered the burden of defending the treaty during the debate.[24]

The Republican party that Taft led in the Senate was seriously divided on foreign policy. Taft's knowledge and experience, impressive in domestic affairs, were not great enough in foreign affairs to command broad support. Taft did not sway many internationalist Republicans until late in the Truman administration, when disillusion with Asian policies was profound, nor did he often speak for the small, diehard isolationist wing of the party. Taft's support, though grudging, of the administration's policies on frequent occasions probably had the net effect of increasing the votes cast for these policies by the middle group of Republicans. Taft's distrust of the bipartisan principle and of Truman and Acheson was too deep to permit him to play Vandenberg's role as a partner of the administration. Although, had he challenged Vandenberg's leadership, he might have divided the party and reshaped its postwar record on foreign policy, Taft lacked the qualities necessary to provide a focal point for Republican unity. Taft was not the master of personal negotiations designed to produce compromise; those senators who respected his intellectual position simply cast their votes with him. Taft held great political power in the Senate and carefully controlled party and committee assignments. The evidence does not suggest, however, that he used this power in significant efforts to create Republican support for his stands on foreign policy, except for his use of the Policy Committee, described in the next chapter.

[24] Cohen, *The Political Process and Foreign Policy*, pp. 240-44.

The dilemma Senator Taft would have faced had he been a consistent opponent of the Truman administration's foreign policy is illustrated by the example of Kenneth S. Wherry. Wherry was party whip and at times acting majority leader in 1947 and 1948 and minority leader from 1949 until his death late in 1951. Wherry was the strongest and most effective leader of the small Republican isolationist wing. He opposed the major foreign aid programs and collective security measures and was a leader in the attempt to prevent the sending of troops to Europe. While Wherry lacked Taft's stature in Republican ranks, he was a genial, popular senator, skilled in the informal practices of give-and-take that produce compromise. Wherry was not influential in foreign policy debates (outside the band of isolationists he led) for two reasons: his lack of knowledge and experience in foreign affairs and the rigidity of his extreme position on international questions. The leader who occupies middle ground in his party is the most likely to be effective. The most skillful, experienced, and popular man in the Senate will win few converts when he takes a rigid stand against the tides of events and opinion.

There is no evidence that Wherry used his power as minority leader to attempt to delay action on foreign measures or that he used this authority to pressure Republican senators into supporting him. Republican leadership was too widely dispersed, the tools of the floor leader were too ineffective, and Vandenberg's prestige was too great for Wherry to succeed in such an effort had he attempted it. During the period when the postwar foreign programs were being established, the isolationist group and Wherry, its *de facto* leader, seem to have felt rather fatalistically that they could do little to stem the tide of internationalism.

LYNDON JOHNSON: LEADER OF THE LOYAL OPPOSITION

Lyndon B. Johnson held the reins of Democratic leadership in the Senate throughout the Eisenhower administration. His participation in foreign affairs went through a cycle similar to Taft's. In his early years as floor leader he took a relatively small part in foreign policy questions. Like Taft, Johnson played a greater role in foreign affairs as he became a more experienced party leader with presidential ambitions. Unlike Taft, Johnson did not become more antagonistic to the administration's policies as he became more active, both because Johnson is an internationalist who could support the Eisenhower policies and because Johnson believes strongly in the President's primary responsibility for the direction of foreign policy.

Like Taft, too, Johnson began to play an active part in foreign policy only after the retirement of a powerful Democratic leader of the Foreign Relations Committee, Walter F. George. In 1953 and 1954 George was ranking Democrat on the committee, and in 1955 and 1956, as the committee chairman, George was the Democratic party's recognized leader in foreign policy. While Johnson remained in the background and let George speak for the party, the two held frequent consultations on policy and tactics. Because of his vastly greater experience in foreign affairs, George was the dominant member of this partnership. There was apparently little conflict between the two, and Johnson usually followed George's lead. It may be that Johnson derived some of his views on foreign policy and bipartisanship from his experience with George. An example of their cooperation was the foreign aid program; while George was speaking earnestly on the Senate floor in defense of a full-scale aid program, Johnson was reported by his aides to be working effectively behind the scenes to win Democratic votes for the program.[25]

The controversy over the Bricker amendment in 1953 and 1954 illustrates Johnson's lack of strong convictions on foreign policy and his techniques of compromise. Johnson opposed any amendment that he felt would seriously limit the President's authority. He was not an original sponsor of the Bricker amendment and never voted for its more stringent versions. On the other hand, he was not one of those senators who believed that any amendment would be dangerous. Johnson became convinced that the Bricker amendment could not be defeated in open combat but must be outflanked through a compromise, one which would also provide relief to Democrats under pressure to vote for some such measure. Though the Republican leaders had prepared a compromise acceptable to the President, Johnson worked with George to develop a Democratic compromise, one that proved unacceptable to the President.

[25] Based on interviews with members of Johnson's staff.

Johnson gave the George version of the Bricker amendment his full support, though he did not apply pressure on the Democrats to vote for it. In this case Johnson's approach was the antithesis of Taft's; what mattered was finding a solution to the Bricker controversy that would satisfy the most Democrats, whatever the substantive results.[26]

Lyndon Johnson first emerged as a prominent Democratic spokesman on foreign policy after George's retirement early in 1957, when the Middle East resolution came before the Senate. He was primarily responsible for remolding the administration's resolution to conform to the views of prominent Democrats and for guiding it through the Senate despite considerable Democratic opposition. At the same time, he urged the administration to block United Nations economic sanctions against Israel contemplated as an aftermath of the Suez invasion. There were press allegations that he delayed Senate approval until a compromise on the Israeli question had been achieved. Johnson was unable to serve as a foreign policy spokesman in the sense that George had, but he made it clear that if the party must speak with several voices, none would be more prominent than his. Johnson sympathized with, if he did not fully share, a wide variety of Democratic doubts about the administration's Middle Eastern policies and the proposed resolution. He persuaded the administration to accept changes in the resolution that were not crippling and then secured its passage. The effect of his actions was to serve notice that he must be consulted by the administration and that the Democratic party would not be so pliable on foreign policy as it had been in George's day.[27]

The other major foreign policy issues during the second Eisenhower administration involved the renewal of reciprocal trade and foreign aid programs. Johnson was credited by observers at the time with major responsibility for the passage of a four-year reciprocal trade bill in 1958 that was satisfactory to the administration. On this and other reciprocal trade measures he supported the administration more consistently than the

[26] This account of Johnson's role in the Bricker amendment controversy is based largely on interviews with senators and senatorial staff.

[27] See the comments of William S. White, *New York Times*, March 10, 1957, sec. iv, p. 3; Robert Albright, *Washington Post and Times Herald*, March 12, 1957; Roscoe Drummond, *New York Herald Tribune*, March 11, 1957. See also *Newsweek*, XLIX (March 11, 1957), 28-29.

Republican leaders. He likewise backed the administration during the annual battles over renewing the foreign aid program, while unsuccessfully helping the efforts of Democratic senators like William Fulbright and John Kennedy to make the aid program more flexible, strengthen its long-term developmental features, and permit aid to Communist satellite countries. In the fields of aid and trade, Johnson was seldom a prominent spokesman or an initiator of change but rather a tactician and floor manager.

The growing split in Democratic ranks on both the aid and trade issues raises questions about the effectiveness of Johnson's efforts. Some observers have argued that if Johnson had deeper convictions about these policies, he could and would have worked to produce greater unity in Democratic ranks. Such an assertion is difficult to substantiate. Democratic dissension came not only from neoisolationists but from internationalist senators deeply concerned about the Eisenhower administration's emphasis on military aid at the expense of developmental aid. On occasion, serious contradictions and vacillations in the administration's policy further handicapped Johnson. It can be said that, whenever possible, on issues of trade and aid Johnson was an agent of unity in the Democratic party and between the party and the Eisenhower administration.

Johnson differed from other floor leaders in recent years because of his skill in personal leadership, particularly in behind-the-scenes activities. Johnson roamed the Senate cloakrooms, seeking out Democrats with conflicting views and negotiating compromises with patience and persistence. He sometimes used intermediaries to approach senators at odds with him. In his role as mediator, he was seldom handicapped, as Knowland was, by dogmatic adherence to a personal viewpoint. As his personal prestige and assurance grew, Johnson became increasingly willing to use the powers of his office to compel support for the compromises he had fathered. These powers were informal and often hidden from view, but they certainly included the ability to promote or retard the favorite bills of senators. A skillful floor leader, as Johnson demonstrated, has considerable advantages over other senators. He has the initiative in legislative maneuvers and the right to be recognized first on the floor, he is able to make binding promises and threats, and he controls the party machinery and staff.[28] Accounts of Johnson's political brilliance often ignored the role of his staff, described by Stewart Alsop as "the biggest, the most efficient, the most ruthlessly overworked and the most loyal personal staff in the history of the Senate."[29] Whether designated secretary of the Senate, majority secretary, or members of the staff of the Policy Committee, Conference, or Democratic Campaign Committee, they were all in fact Johnson's personal staff.

Johnson also picked deputy leaders who were skilled in the arts of tactics and compromise and whose views were compatible enough with his to permit a close working relationship. Until his defeat in the 1956 election, Earle Clements was the deputy leader; for several years thereafter he served on Johnson's staff. Clements was succeeded as deputy by Mike Mansfield, who was adept at backstage negotiations and who commanded broad senatorial respect, particularly in foreign policy matters.

Johnson often belittled his own power, insisting that he could not force any senator to change his vote and that he was subject to the control of a majority in the party. He said that his only power was "the power to persuade." His failure to achieve greater Democratic unity on foreign aid bills illustrates this limitation; Johnson's greatest skill was his ability to find the formula for maximum agreement rather than a talent for bold leadership in new directions. But within these limitations, Johnson proved that a strong majority leader can assume greater control over the legislative process than most of his predecessors had thought possible.

THE MEANING OF PARTY LEADERSHIP

When is a leader in fact leading, and when is he merely reflecting and articulating the views of his party? It is difficult to

[28] Donald R. Matthews has pointed out the wide range of assistance that a party leader can provide for a senator, ranging from better office accommodations and information about legislation to better committee assignments and assistance in the passage of pet bills. A skillful leader is constantly placing other senators in debt to him through such favors, large and small. *U. S. Senators and Their World* (Chapel Hill: University of North Carolina Press, 1960), p. 127.

[29] Stewart Alsop, "Lyndon Johnson: How Does He Do It?" *Saturday Evening Post*, CCXXXI (Jan. 24, 1959), 13, 38.

judge and impossible to prove whether a leader is responsible for high party unity on one rollcall or to blame for disunity on the next. It is true that, on the foreign policy questions, Democratic unity was greater under Barkley, Lucas, and McFarland than under Lyndon Johnson, generally recognized as the most skillful Senate leader in recent years. Senator Taft's greatest successes occurred when circumstances had minimized the sharp divisions in the party and when his views coincided with the emerging consensus. If there are indeed times when the party leader's skill and influence make a difference, these occur when the party is neither deeply divided nor firmly united. The party leader is more likely to control tactical decisions, the timing of measures, the choice and wording of amendments, than to influence decisions on the basic issues. His tactics and persuasion may change a handful of votes rather than a majority. But the tactical decisions may have great influence on the final outcome, and a handful of votes may be the decisive ones on closely contested issues.

As long as the positions of party leadership are not institutionalized and the prerogatives of office remain vague, the sources of a leader's authority must lie primarily in his own experience and skill. The contrast between Taft and Wherry suggests that the effective party leader is one who takes a moderate position. A leader must not, by reason of his own dogmas, destroy his rapport with other senators. If the tide of opinion in his party is running in any visible direction, the most successful leader is the one who is moving with or ahead of the tide. Taft and Knowland were increasingly able to represent Republican opinion late in the Truman administration, but as the Eisenhower administration progressed, Knowland became gradually more isolated from his party in the Senate as well as from the President and thus no longer able to exert active leadership of his party.

Because the Senate respects the man whose interests, knowledge, and committee experience have equipped him to speak with some authority on a subject, party leaders gain an added measure of influence when dealing with subjects on which they are authorities, as Taft did on domestic economic issues. But, except for Knowland and Mansfield, no party leader has been an authority on foreign affairs, and for this reason, several of the leaders have often shared authority with the chairman or ranking party member on the Foreign Relations Committee. When the leader of the committee has been a powerful figure in his own right and when there has been basic agreement on issues, the working relationship has often been remarkably close, as in the case of Democratic leaders dealing with Connally and George. Johnson's role was heightened when there was no clearly recognized Democratic leader on the Foreign Relations Committee, and Republican party leaders have magnified their roles both because of Senator Wiley's weakness on the committee and because of their policy differences with him. The two administrations, though bound to recognize the power realties in Congress, exercised some discretion in consulting Vandenberg, George, Knowland, and Johnson, while ignoring Taft occasionally and Wiley often.

The leaders of an administration party have an opportunity, usually denied to the opposition, of influencing foreign programs in the early stages of formulation. Once those programs have been presented to Congress, however, the administration party generally has less freedom to criticize than the opposition does. The Democratic leaders accepted Truman's foreign programs with a minimum of advance participation and without criticism in the Senate. Republican leaders, notably Taft and Knowland, sought to have a much greater influence on the Eisenhower programs both before and after these reached the Senate. In a party as united as the Democrats were on foreign policy during Truman's administration, the senatorial leaders faced no conflict in determining their proper role. In a divided party, this conflict may become acute. At one extreme, both Leverett Saltonstall and Alexander Wiley were handicapped because many Republicans considered them mere puppets of the Eisenhower administration, while at the other, Senator Knowland began to discover that his influence was least when he challenged the President openly and forcefully on major questions of foreign policy.

The thin line that a successful administration leader must follow, particularly in a divided party, has been well described by David Truman: "The fundamental complexity and subtlety of the role lie in the fact that the elective leaders are, and probably must be, both the President's leaders and the party's leaders. However, . . . to be fully effective as leaders of the Congressional parties, they must above all be effective spokesmen for the President; or at least, excepting the most unusual circumstances, they must appear to be his spokesmen." These two roles "are not always cleanly compatible. At the same time it seems clear that they are generally interdependent, in the sense that representing the President provides a focus and part of the leverage for leadership of the Congressional party, and sympathetic reflection of the problems of legislative colleagues is an essential in advancing the President's program."[30]

The opposition leader in the Senate undertakes the problem of achieving unity in a frequently divided party uninhibited by political allegiance to the President, but confronted by the fact of presidential initiative and preeminence in foreign policy. In recommending a party policy, the opposition leader must choose among three courses: accepting the President's policy, modifying it, or proposing an alternative; but he must always contend with the fact that the President's authority is great in foreign policy, almost irresistible in a time of crisis. In recent years, the President has generally commanded at least a strong minority of support from the opposition party for his programs —particularly those presented with greatest urgency. As a result, the opposition leader finds himself in the anomalous position of commanding the greatest party unity on occasions when the party supports the President. A leader such as Taft, often deeply at variance with the Truman administration, usually sought to modify rather than negate the Truman policies; his choice was often dictated partly by the desire to maximize Republican unity.

Neither Robert Taft nor Lyndon Johnson were recognized as specialists in foreign policy. The question arises whether an opposition leader who combined the skills of Johnson with the experience in foreign policy possessed by Vandenberg or George could unite his party behind a policy boldly different from the administration's foreign policy. The answer must be negative. Senator Taft showed how this could be done on a domestic

[30] Truman, pp. 298, 302-303.

issue with the passage of the 1947 Taft-Hartley Labor Act; but foreign policy is a vastly different field. The opposition party leader has no hand in the making of diplomacy, no responsibility for the movement of troops, no sources of foreign intelligence. It is difficult to conceive of the American people turning to him for guidance in a crisis.

Lyndon Johnson described the problem in realistic terms: "We recognize clearly that the President has a special role to play in the field of foreign policy. . . . In the ultimate analysis, he is the man who must speak for our country in its dealings with other countries. This does not mean, however, that the sole role of the Senate is acquiescence or rejection of policies announced by the President. . . .

"The Congress has a responsibility to examine the facts; to weigh them in the light of past experience; to determine whether a policy is justified; to decide whether there are constructive alternatives; to unify the country by selecting alternatives if they are justified."[31]

Lyndon Johnson's term as party leader was less notable for its impact on the party's record in foreign policy than for the techniques he developed. Although many of Johnson's techniques were purely personal, some of the methods that he and other recent leaders have used set a precedent for others to follow. Johnson's greater use of staff assistance and his modification of the seniority principle in making committee appointments are practices likely to be continued because they provide improved tools for party leadership. There are not yet many such techniques that can become traditions. Those searching for evidence of institutionalization turn inevitably to the policy committees.

[31] *New York Times*, Jan. 30, 1957, p. 10.

*At the outset, the conclusion is inescapable that the policy committees are misnamed. They have never been "policy" bodies, in the sense of considering and investigating alternatives of public policy, and they have never put forth an overall congressional party program.—*HUGH A. BONE

5

THE POLICY COMMITTEES

THE POLICY COMMITTEE AND THE CAUCUS (OR CONFERENCE) of all members are the organs through which party leadership has been institutionalized in the Senate. The Democratic Conference has rarely met in recent years, while the Republican Conference has, in effect, become merged with the Policy Committee. Consequently, we can focus attention on the policy committees, created by the Senate in 1947 after the House had deleted a provision for committees in both branches from the 1946 Legislative Reorganization Act. Though the committees have a statutory base and have staffs financed by the federal budget, they are not uniform in size, functions, or philosophy. There have always been fundamental differences between the Republican and Democratic committees, and further differences are occasioned by the leaders' tactics and by the contrast between committees of the administration and opposition parties.[1]

The policy committee represents only a limited institutionalization of party leadership. It is largely a creature of its chairman, who decides how often it will meet, how broad its functions will be, and how extensively it will be used as an instrument of leadership. A strong leader may use it to further his purposes or may scorn it as a restriction on his freedom. A weak leader may rely on the committee for assistance without being skillful or powerful enough to make maximum use of it. Since the chairman of the Democratic Policy Committee is also the floor leader, he has greater opportunity but perhaps less incentive than the Republican chairman to make it into a strong institution. Democratic chairmen have been particularly sensitive to the danger that the committee might become a strong enough institution to limit their independence. Republican leadership posts are divided among several senators. During the Truman administration, Senator Taft chose to serve as chairman of the Policy Committee; he was influential enough to overshadow the successive floor leaders while developing the potential of the committee. His successors as chairman have been less prominent than the floor leader and have failed to make the committee a tool of personal leadership—in part because of the different requirements of an administration party.

As Taft said, when he resigned as chairman of the Policy Committee in 1953, "When our party controls the White House, most of the Republican policy is made there anyhow."[2] The policy committee, like the floor leader, may find some difficulty in retaining the confidence of both the President and the administration party in the Senate. It can function most effectively in a liaison capacity to overcome the differences between the two.

[1] The most comprehensive study of the committees to date is Hugh A. Bone, "An Introduction to the Senate Policy Committees," *American Political Science Review,* L (June, 1956), 339-59. Bone describes the service and research functions of the committees' staffs in addition to discussing the policy and liaison functions dealt with in the present chapter. The research functions, particularly of the Republican Committee staff, have continued to grow.

[2] White, *The Taft Story,* p. 215.

When the party is in opposition, the committee has greater independence and more opportunity to formulate policy. This opportunity is limited, however, by the frequent divisions in the party and the lack of means to impose discipline on even a small minority of senators. Whether representing the administration or opposition party, the policy committees have never sought to formulate an overall legislative policy, have seldom taken formal public stands on issues, and have played no disciplinary role. As a consequence they have not become the vehicle that many political scientists consider necessary to increase party unity, center responsibility, and bridge the gap between the President and his party in the Senate, partly because they have never included the chairmen or ranking minority members of all the standing committees. Moreover, they have seldom met with House leaders and almost never with the President to coordinate legislative plans. The major reason that the policy committees have never fulfilled the political scientists' ambitious expectations as instruments of party responsibility is that the senators—leaders and the rank-and-file—have never shared these expectations. The senators have not been willing to give the committees a chance to make any major change in the tradition of individualism and the multicentered power structure that characterize the upper chamber. While the committees have never been truly "policy" bodies, still they have had an impact on the formation of policy in the Senate.[3]

SENATOR TAFT AND THE REPUBLICAN POLICY COMMITTEE

From 1947 through 1952, as William S. White has said, "It became, and pretty correctly so, the custom to consider Taft *as* the policy committee."[4] Taft was largely responsible for develop-

[3] Much of the information on the policy committees in this chapter is based on interviews with senators and several staff members of the committees. These sources are not cited individually in footnotes. Although the minutes of the policy committees and caucuses are not open to scholars, Republican staff members checked the files to determine whether either group had discussed certain foreign policy issues of interest to the writer and also made available résumés of the 1953 and 1954 policy committee meetings, which were prepared for distribution to all Republican senators.

[4] White, *The Taft Story*, p. 61.

ing the committee into an institution of some significance more quickly than the Democrats developed their counterpart. When the Republicans gained a Senate majority in 1947, Taft recognized that the party needed an organized program with which to confront the Truman administration. He decided that the Policy Committee could provide the leadership and staff to achieve this goal.[5] Taft frequently dominated the committee by sheer intellectual weight. Appearing at a meeting armed with detailed reports on pending legislation, he would solicit opinions of the membership and then frequently win support for his views because he alone was thoroughly familiar with the facts. Moreover, a majority of the senators on the committee were conservatives, like Taft, although liberal elements in 1949 succeeded in having the committee enlarged and thereby secured a better reflection of their views.[6]

Taft's influence over the Policy Committee was least, particularly in the early years, in the field of foreign policy. Acknowledging Arthur Vandenberg's preeminence in this field, Taft frequently invited him to discuss foreign policy with the committee.[7] Vandenberg used the committee effectively as a forum in which to explain the administration's proposals and his own views on international affairs. The group was particularly representative of those Republicans (like Taft) who were cautious about Truman's foreign programs but were open to persuasion. Vandenberg also used the Republican Conference as a broader forum for presenting his views.

Vandenberg's meetings with the Policy Committee and Republican Conference may have helped to generate support for the foreign aid programs of 1947 and 1948, but these groups took no formal stand on the issues. The Policy Committee was divided and silent on the North Atlantic Treaty, though Senator

[5] Bone, p. 356. The Policy Committee replaced an informal steering committee, which Senator Taft, as chairman, had already used for several years as a device for tactical and policy planning. It is described in *Organization of Congress*, Hearings before the Joint Committee on the Organization of Congress, pursuant to H. Con. Res. 18, 79th Cong., 1st sess., p. 361.

[6] The Committee had five ex officio members: the chairman and the secretary of the Conference, the floor leader, the whip, and the chairman of the Policy Committee. The elected members increased from four in 1947 to six in 1949.

[7] Vandenberg was often a guest at meetings in 1947 and 1948; the next two years he was a member, although unable to attend after 1949 because of illness.

Wherry sought in vain to have it take a stand against ratification. Taft announced that the committee was skeptical of the 1949 military assistance bill and hoped it could be financed from the existing military budget. In this case, the skepticism was shared by Vandenberg.

After Vandenberg's retirement, Taft played a larger role in foreign policy and consequently used the Policy Committee increasingly as a vehicle to organize Republican opposition to some of the administration's foreign programs. Often the Republicans needed little urging from Taft or the committee to attack the administration, but the committee's recommendations appear to have facilitated a more unified party stand. A good example is the Point Four measure, which reached the Senate in 1950. Two members of the Policy Committee, Eugene D. Millikin and Leverett Saltonstall, introduced a substitute plan for a commission to study assistance for underdeveloped areas. The plan, apparently endorsed by the Policy Committee and explained at a meeting of the Conference, received all but five Republican votes on the Senate floor. After the substitute was defeated, only eight Republicans voted for the Point Four bill. When a conference committee added new provisions to the measure, Taft pointed out in criticism that these had never been discussed in the Policy Committee—an indication of the importance he attached to the committee's consideration of major measures. The Policy Committee then discussed the new version of Point Four—after it had passed.[8]

There are other examples of the Policy Committee's making recommendations on foreign aid that gained nearly unanimous party support. In 1951 its decision to oppose any restoration of cuts made by the Foreign Relations and the Armed Services committees was backed by all but one Republican in the floor vote. A discussion in the Policy Committee of a jurisdictional dispute over the 1952 foreign aid bill apparently led to a Republican vote of 37-2 in favor of letting the Armed Services

[8] *Congressional Record*, May 25, 1950, pp. 7714-16. Another occasion on which Taft complained that there had not been an opportunity for discussion in the Republican Policy Committee was in June, 1950, when congressional leaders were notified of the President's decision to send forces to Korea. *Ibid.*, June 28, 1950, p. 9320. (All references to the *Congressional Record* are to the bound volumes.)

Committee consider the bill after the Foreign Relations Committee had reported it. The members of the committee usually took a stand only when they judged there to be a strong consensus of opinion among their Republican colleagues; their decision appears to have caused a further closing of the ranks and usually a nearly unanimous vote. Occasionally the committee misjudged Republican views; often it avoided any stand because of a belief that at least a sizable Republican minority did not accept Taft's judgment on foreign aid.

During the controversy over the dismissal of General Douglas MacArthur in 1951, the Republican Policy Committee and Conference served to focus and publicize the virtually unanimous demands of the party for a sweeping congressional investigation of American policy in the Far East. The Conference, meeting first, unanimously recommended a full-scale investigation and delegated to the Policy Committee the task of drawing up an appropriate resolution. The Policy Committee proposed a somewhat more comprehensive investigation than the Democratic majority decided on. The Republicans sought in vain to include a House committee in the investigation or to add the Senate Appropriations Committee, which included two Republican leaders—Kenneth S. Wherry and Homer Ferguson. The Policy Committee also urged that the investigation be carried out through open hearings. The Democratic majority of the joint standing committee ignored the demand for expansion, however, and also voted for closed hearings, though it agreed to the Republican demand that other senators might attend as visitors. In a series of nearly straight party votes, the Democrats succeeded in postponing the secrecy issue for some time on the Senate floor and then defeated the proposal for open hearings despite its unanimous Republican support. While the Republican Policy Committee was unable to force its demands on the Democratic Senate leadership, it did intensify the pressure on Senator Russell's committee to conduct an impartial and comprehensive investigation. It may incidentally have minimized the impact of more extreme demands by individual Republicans —such as those for President Truman's impeachment.

The Policy Committee's indecisiveness in the face of strong

demands for Dean Acheson's resignation as Secretary of State in December, 1950, shows that it may be unable to act even on highly partisan issues if there is a substantial amount of disagreement in the party. Senator Taft convened the committee on December 5 to determine whether there should be a formal party endorsement of these demands, and Senator Irving M. Ives was assigned to draw up a resolution calling for Acheson's resignation. At a second meeting two days later, the committee was so divided on the question that it turned the burden of decision over to the Conference. While the senators hesitated, on December 15 the House Republican Conference almost unanimously supported a resolution calling for Acheson's resignation. Later in the day, the Senate Conference adopted the resolution by a vote of 23-5 but added Taft's amendment pledging full cooperation with the administration. One member of the Policy Committee, Senator Margaret Chase Smith, was among the five dissenters.

During the 1951 controversy over sending troops to Europe, the Policy Committee was too divided to take a stand on Senator Wherry's resolution providing that no ground troops should be assigned to NATO until Congress established a policy on the question. The committee was able to engage in tactical planning designed to assure that Congress had the maximum opportunity to consider the problem and express its views. Senator Taft announced that the Republicans might agree to send Wherry's resolution to the Foreign Relations Committee if there were assurance that some resolution would be reported. The Policy Committee debated the issue further both during and immediately after consideration of Senator Tom Connally's resolution by the Foreign Relations and Armed Services committees. It discussed without any apparent agreement a compromise clause drafted by the two standing committees to require congressional approval for the future assignment of troops abroad. The Policy Committee did decide to seek consideration of a concurrent resolution immediately after passage of the Senate resolution. Only two of the Republicans who voted against a concurrent resolution in the Senate wanted to prevent House action that might further curb the President; the other seven

Republican opponents disapproved the sending of troops in principle.[9]

The election of a Republican President for the first time in twenty years after a divisive contest for the nomination presented the party in the Senate, dominated by the Taft wing, with a serious challenge involving the maintenance of unity. Without sacrificing their own viewpoints, the Republican senators wanted to minimize friction with the Republican administration. One of the important devices for maintaining cooperation with President Eisenhower was a regular report to the Policy Committee by the Republican Senate leaders, usually on the day of their weekly meeting with the President. While this improvement in the channels of communication did not guarantee that Republican senators would agree with the President, it increased the possibilities of closer understanding, better information, and agreement. A meeting between the Policy Committee itself and the President, as advocated in the past, occurred only once, but the committee met occasionally with Vice President Nixon or with cabinet members.

The changing functions of the Republican Policy Committee led to pressure for its expansion. In 1953 Senator Homer E. Capehart urged unsuccessfully that the committee be reorganized to include all committee chairmen as well as the formal party leaders. This change would have been in keeping with many of the proposals of political scientists concerning policy committees. At the time, however, the proposal was viewed as a challenge to the Republican Senate leadership and a potential obstacle to close liaison between the Policy Committee and the

[9] Senator Taft, who stood in the center of his party during the troops controversy, favored sending four divisions under a joint resolution that would bind the President to consult Congress before sending any additional forces. Four members of the committee (Eugene D. Millikin, Milton R. Young, Owen Brewster, and Edward Martin) voted with Taft. Two members (Kenneth S. Wherry and Homer Ferguson) opposed sending troops, while four others (Leverett Saltonstall, H. Alexander Smith, Edward J. Thye, and William F. Knowland) opposed such rigid restrictions on the President. *CQA*, 1951, pp. 257-58.

White House. In 1955 the Committee was increased from twelve to twenty-three members to make it more representative, and all Republicans facing reelection were made committee members in order to give them added prestige. In 1957 the committee was cut to fourteen members, eight ex officio and six elected.[10]

The most important change in the committee's procedures occurred in 1956, when all Republican senators were invited to attend its meetings. This practice continued throughout the Eisenhower administration. The new plan was inaugurated in response to the demands of rank-and-file Senators, particularly the more liberal ones, for a chance to hear the reports of the leaders' meetings with the President. In practice, while attendance was not complete and varied with the issues under consideration, a sizable majority of Republican senators generally were present—including most of the ranking members of standing committees.

This innovation in procedure was indicative of the committee's changed functions during the Eisenhower administration. Republican policy was now made in the White House, and in the absence of any Republican senatorial leader frequently able and willing to challenge the President, the Policy Committee did not seek to compete.[11] The senators learned what the President wanted and what arguments he was presenting to defend his position; they discussed the issues, often extensively enough to give the leaders a consensus of opinion; they sometimes voted informally; but they avoided formal stands for or against measures or amendments. On some occasions when there were serious divisions among Republican senators or major differences between them and the White House, the Policy Committee sought to facilitate formation of a compromise.

In practice the Republican Policy Committee appeared to have taken over the functions of the Conference. During most of the 1956 session, the Conference did not hold meetings.[12] There-

[10] The three new ex officio members are the chairmen of the party's Campaign Committee, Committee on Committees, and Personnel Committee. In March, 1953, the Republicans decided to make the President pro tem of the Senate, when a Republican, also an ex officio member.

[11] Knowland served as chairman of the Policy Committee until July, 1953, when he became floor leader upon Taft's death. He was succeeded by Homer Ferguson, who served through 1954 and was succeeded by Styles Bridges.

[12] This was due in part to Conference Chairman Eugene D. Millikin's illness.

after the Conference met occasionally, and while it seemed to
have a slightly more formal status than the Policy Committee,
there was little practical distinction between the two bodies.
Since the Policy Committee had been opened to all Republican
senators and had duplicated the Conference, a new group with
smaller membership became necessary to perform the tactical
functions of the Policy Committee. It frequently became the
practice, after important legislation was discussed in an open
meeting of the committee, for a closed meeting to be held to
plan floor tactics such as the introduction of amendments and
the schedule of speakers. These informal meetings were generally attended by the top party leaders, those other members
of the Policy Committee most interested in the bill, and a few
other Republican senators particularly concerned with the measure—for example, members of the standing committee that had
reported it.

The Policy Committee's role as an agent of compromise is
well illustrated by its handling of the Bricker amendment, which
was a center of controversy in 1953 and early 1954. The committee played an important part in the long and patient efforts
of Republican Senate leaders—notably William F. Knowland—
to negotiate a compromise between the Bricker forces and the
administration. Although only a small group of Republican
leaders conducted the negotiations, the committee often discussed the question, offered some suggestions for a compromise,
served as a forum for the negotiations on occasion, and was constantly informed of talks held outside the committee. The
committee held twelve meetings on the Bricker amendment in
June and July, 1953. and in January and February, 1954.

On June 2, 1953, the Republican Conference directed the
party's leaders to inform the President that sentiment among
Senate Republicans was favorable to the amendment. This development emphasized the need for steps to prevent a serious
split in the ranks of Republican senators and between a majority
of them and the President. The Policy Committee invited Senator John W. Bricker and Attorney General Herbert Brownell
to discussions, which convinced the committee that further
negotiations were warranted. As the talks continued, Bricker
charged that the administration was pressuring the Policy Com-

mittee to delay his amendment. At a three-hour meeting on July 21, attended by Bricker, Brownell, and Secretary of State John Foster Dulles, a major attempt was made to reach agreement. A compromise was offered that appears to have been partially based on the committee's suggestions and that had the administration's support, but it was rejected by Bricker. With the negotiations stalemated, the Policy Committee postponed action until the next session of Congress. In January, 1954, the Policy Committee agreed to give the Bricker amendment high priority instead of sidetracking it but decided to take no stand on the issue. The committee was kept regularly informed of the negotiations with Senator Bricker that continued without success.

Two provisions of the compromise plan which was drafted under committee auspices in July, 1953, came to a vote in the Senate in February, 1954, and gained nearly unanimous Republican approval; no members of the Policy Committee opposed them. The members of the committee were badly divided, however, on whether or not to add more restrictive provisions to the compromise. When Senator Walter F. George proposed a substitute that required an act of Congress to make executive agreements effective as internal law, a substitute opposed by the administration, half of the Policy Committee members and almost two-thirds of the Republican senators voted for it. It is interesting that only three senators voted against the George substitute but for the final constitutional amendment as revised by George: William F. Knowland, Eugene D. Millikin, and Robert C. Hendrickson, all members of the Republican Policy Committee. They evidently felt committed to the Republican compromise instead of the George substitute but wanted some type of constitutional amendment to pass. The effect of the Policy Committee's actions was to increase the pressure on the administration to seek a compromise. The committee was unable, however, to devise or promote a compromise on which most Republicans could agree. Some Republicans wanted no amendment, while a larger number wanted a more far-reaching one.

Another measure on which the Policy Committee sought— with more success—to close the gap between the administration and Republican senators was the Status of Forces Treaty, which defined the legal position of American military forces stationed in Europe. In May, 1953, the Policy Committee postponed action on the treaty, apparently in response to the opposition of a number of Republicans. The next month it persuaded the Foreign Relations Committee to give Senator John Bricker a hearing on a reservation providing for exclusive American jurisdiction in all cases involving American military personnel accused of committing criminal offenses abroad. Senator Knowland discussed with the Policy Committee a compromise finally adopted by the Foreign Relations Committee, an interpretation designed to remove certain objections to the treaty without undermining it. In July the Policy Committee, apparently acting under pressure from the administration, agreed to schedule prompt senatorial consideration of the treaty.

The Policy Committee took a stand directly contrary to the administration's on another controversial issue, the Yalta resolution. After the Foreign Relations Committee by a straight party vote had added an amendment proposed by Senator Taft that had the effect of challenging the validity of wartime agreements, the Policy Committee unanimously supported the Taft version despite the known objections of President Eisenhower.

As the Eisenhower administration progressed, there were fewer examples of serious differences on foreign policy between the administration and Republican senators. The Policy Committee frequently discussed foreign aid and reciprocal trade, the issues most often reaching the Senate, but its activities were little publicized and were much less extensive than during the Bricker amendment controversy. The early success of the Policy Committee as a liaison agent was apparently one reason why the chasm to be bridged grew steadily less deep. During the first year of Eisenhower's term, when Republican differences on foreign aid were greatest, the Policy Committee held several discussions on the issue. One of the most important functions of the Policy Committee, particularly after all Republicans were invited to attend meetings, was to hear and discuss the President's requests and proposals relayed by congressional leaders who attended the weekly White House meetings. Since foreign aid was an issue on which President Eisenhower's views were strong and consistent, it seems probable that he used this channel effectively to impress on both Republican leaders and rank-and-file senators the need for large-scale aid programs.

The experience of the Republican Policy Committee during both the Truman and Eisenhower administrations suggests that this instrument must be flexible if it is to be at all effective, given its limitations. The committee is certain to reflect the personality, operating methods, and political strength of its chairman and perhaps other Republican leaders. Though it is more formal and in a sense more institutionalized than its Democratic counterpart, it is still difficult to conceive of the committee acting independently of its chairman or serving functions not initiated by him. Since the Policy Committee and the Republican leadership lack the sanctions necessary to compel party unity, the committee's most useful function during a Republican administration would seem to be that of compromise and communication with the White House. On the occasions when Senator Knowland as floor leader or Senator Bridges as chairman disagreed with aspects of the President's foreign programs, there is no evidence that they sought to induce the Policy Committee to endorse their views. On the other hand, the Policy Committee did not formally take the President's side in these disputes. During the Eisenhower administration the Policy Committee largely avoided taking public stands, particularly on issues dividing the party. The Policy Committee under Taft from 1947 through 1952 came closer to being a policy body than it has been since or than the Democratic Policy Committee has ever been. The primary ingredient necessary for such a recipe of action was a chairman determined to use the committee as a tool for translating his own policies into Republican policies. He succeeded only when a second ingredient was present: a high degree of Republican agreement, at least in general terms, on the issue at stake.

DEVELOPMENT OF THE DEMOCRATIC POLICY COMMITTEE

"The Democratic Policy Committee will meet—perhaps—once a week, and when it does the thing seems simply to happen and members will stroll in, usually late, with the air of a man dropping into another's office to have a drink and, having nothing better to do at the moment, to pass the time of day."[13] William S. White's graphic description highlights an important aspect of the Democratic Policy Committee: It lacks the formality and institutionalization that have characterized the Republican Policy Committee. The Democratic committee is smaller and more wary of publicity; it has a smaller professional staff, which is less concerned with producing political studies. As Professor Bone has pointed out, the Democratic Senate leadership is more experienced, contains more "old pros," has led a majority for most of the last quarter century, and therefore has preferred to rely on proven techniques to guide the party rather than to develop a highly institutionalized Policy Committee.[14]

While both policy committees are creatures of their chairmen, this seems especially true of the Democratic one. The slowness with which the Democratic Policy Committee developed after its establishment in 1947 resulted largely from Alben Barkley's belief that it would inhibit his leadership rather than become a valuable tool. Scott Lucas and Ernest McFarland held meetings more regularly, partly in an effort to strengthen their sometimes precarious leadership in the Senate; neither dominated the committee in the sense that Senator Taft dominated the Republican committee. Lyndon Johnson reshaped the Policy Committee to make it part of his farflung empire.

The Democratic Policy Committee has generally consisted of nine members: the floor leader (who serves as chairman), the deputy leader, the Conference secretary, and six others chosen by the floor leader.[15] The members serve on the committee as long as they are in the Senate, instead of rotating as do the senators on the Republican committee. As a result, its members are usually men with long experience in the Senate, who have gained the respect of their colleagues. In 1960 the committee contained five of the eight Democrats with the longest seniority in the Senate. When Senator Barkley first chose the Policy Committee in 1947, however, he deliberately omitted some of the older party leaders and committee chairmen, who would be difficult to control. He set a precedent followed by successors of

---

13 White, *Citadel*, p. 210.
14 Bone, pp. 356-58.
15 Since 1959 the Calendar Committee has met with the Democratic Policy Committee.

picking only those men who suited his choice.[16] From 1953 through 1960, eight of the nine members came from the South, the Border States, or the Mountain States; Theodore Francis Green of Rhode Island was the only member from the industrial section of the country. Because of its smaller size, lack of rotation, and geographic imbalance, the committee has been much less representative than the Republican one. Its membership has included liberal or centrist senators from these more conservative sections of the party, however, giving the committee a membership corresponding rather closely to the centers of power and influence in the Senate Democratic party.[17]

The student who tries to extract the Democratic Policy Committee's ground rules and list them in precise and orderly fashion runs the risk of distorting the true picture. The Democratic leaders have adapted the institution to fit their needs under changing conditions and to fit the rather aristocratic traditions of the party in the Senate. This aristocratic pattern has been heightened by the scarcity of caucuses. During the Truman administration, caucuses were seldom held, and during the Eisenhower administration, an annual cacus for organizational purposes became the rule. Both the limited size and functions of the Policy Committee and the absence of caucuses became the targets of liberal Democratic critics late in the Eisenhower administration.

During the Truman administration the Democratic Policy Committee did not fulfill the role of a liaison body with the President. Truman met with the committee only once, in January, 1951, in that case seeking to heal the wounds left by the struggle over Ernest McFarland's election as majority leader. Although the Democratic leaders did not regularly brief the Policy Committee on their meetings with President Truman, Senator McFarland occasionally made such a formal report. More often, he would mention the President's views while dis-

---

[16] Ralph K. Huitt, "Democratic Party Leadership in the Senate," *American Political Science Review*, LV (1961), 341-42.

[17] Lister Hill, Richard B. Russell, and (until his retirement in 1960) Theodore Francis Green have served on the committee since its origin in 1947. Lyndon B. Johnson and Robert S. Kerr joined in 1951. Thomas C. Hennings and James E. Murray served from 1953 to 1960. Carl Hayden joined in 1955 and Mike Mansfield in 1957.

cussing issues. He occasionally invited cabinet members or other government officials to the meetings. The liaison function may have been less necessary, at least in foreign policy matters, because of the wider measure of agreement between the administration and administration senators than Eisenhower subsequently enjoyed.

During 1947 and 1948 Senator Barkley did not hold regular sessions of the Policy Committee, partly because, as minority leader, he had no responsibility for scheduling legislation. The committee did consider the Greek-Turkish aid program and probably took the decision to schedule one of the rare party caucuses to permit discussion of the issue. The caucus, at which no vote was taken, revealed widespread support for the measure. The Policy Committee took the unusual step of endorsing the interim foreign aid bill preceding enactment of the Marshall Plan and at the same time complimented the Republicans on their cooperation. When the Marshall Plan itself came before the Senate, Barkley avoided any endorsement by the committee because, as he told the press, it was "a bipartisan matter and we didn't want to give it a partisan tinge."[18] This attitude may have caused Barkley and perhaps his successors to avoid endorsement by the committee of certain other foreign programs. Any type of formal party endorsement does carry the risk of alienating the support of the other party and undermining the bipartisanship so often necessary to enact foreign policy legislation.

From 1949 through 1952, while Senators Lucas and McFarland served successively as majority leaders, the Policy Committee met nearly every week. Since the party had a majority in the Senate, the Policy Committee asumed its role of advising the leader on the scheduling of legislation. This has become a function of the Democratic Committee more often than of the Republican one because of the usual Democratic majorities in the Senate. Though the Policy Committee has seldom adopted the House Rules Committee's practice of blocking important pieces of legislation, the priorities assigned to bills may be a matter of great consequence. In 1950, for example, the Policy Committee acceded to the President's request to postpone the

[18] *New York Times*, Feb. 5, 1948, pp. 1, 12.

contentious civil rights program until passage of the foreign aid bills. The previous year the question of priority had been referred to a caucus, and the Democrats had overruled Lucas by deciding to postpone a reciprocal trade bill until after an attempt had been made to revise the cloture rule, an attempt which led to a filibuster. Both Lucas and McFarland appear to have been guided considerably by the committee's advice in scheduling legislation. Since there was wide recognition among Democrats that the administration's foreign programs must be adopted, there was a minimum of controversy over scheduling these measures. On one occasion, in 1949, the Policy Committee settled a jurisdictional dispute over the military assistance bill by recommending that both the Foreign Relations and Armed Services committees consider it.

Lucas and McFarland relied heavily on the Policy Committee for tactical planning. This often involved seeking the members' judgment on senatorial sentiment and the prospects for passing administration measures without change. In 1949, for example, the committee agreed to accept certain cuts in foreign aid in order to concentrate on defeating various crippling amendments. The next year the committee unanimously concluded that there were enough votes to pass an amendment to the aid bill granting Spain a loan of $100 million despite the administration's opposition. The committee supported Lucas' compromise proposal to grant the loan from funds over and above those already scheduled for European aid. During McFarland's term the Policy Committee discussed foreign aid bills that were still being considered by the Foreign Relations or Appropriations committees and often gave those committees an estimate of the total amount likely to gain senatorial approval. After the bill had been reported, the Policy Committee would decide on the total which could be sought on the Senate floor without risk of defeat. The Policy Committee handled strategy during the troops-for-Europe controversy. It agreed to let the Senate debate the question, to send the restrictive Wherry resolution to a standing committee, and there to substitute the Connally resolution, which was unrestrictive and advisory. It also decided to give the Connally resolution highest priority on the Senate floor. The Policy Committee was able to plan tactics on these issues because its members and the Democratic senators as a whole were largely in agreement. Presumably the members could gauge the views of their senatorial colleagues better than the floor leader could alone; consequently the Policy Committee seems to have served a useful purpose during this period and contributed to the substantial Democratic majorities in support of the Truman program. Under Lucas and McFarland the Policy Committee seldom took formal votes or announced a public stand on an issue. The tactical decisions, sometimes revealed in the press, served as a partial substitute. On several occasions the Democratic Policy Committee or the caucus served a more political purpose of countering Republican attacks on the administration's foreign policy. In response to Republican demands that the administration commit this country to the defense of Formosa, a Democratic caucus was convened in January, 1950, to demonstrate support for the President. While no public pronouncement was issued, Senator Lucas announced that the consensus of the caucus had been to support fully the President's policy of nonintervention in Formosa. It was the Policy Committee that decided, with caucus approval, that Senator Joseph McCarthy's charges of Communist infiltration of the State Department should be investigated by a subcommittee of the Foreign Relations Committee, the Democratic members of which should be those also on the Policy Committee.[19] During the dispute over the MacArthur hearings in 1951, the Policy Committee planned tactics to counter the Republican demands for a joint Senate-House committee investigation. The Democratic Policy Committee's activities with regard to these most highly partisan questions were primarily tactical but implied united support for the President. In the absence of this unity, tactical planning would have been impossible.

LYNDON JOHNSON AND THE DEMOCRATIC POLICY COMMITTEE

The Democratic Policy Committee changed less in 1953 when it became the organ of the opposition party than its Republican counterpart did at the beginning of the Eisenhower administration. It continued to be a body concerned with tactics and the

19 Westerfield, *Foreign Policy and Party Politics*, p. 374.

measuring of Democratic sentiment. Though Lyndon Johnson could have used the committee to formulate a Democratic program, he chose instead to make it an agent of compromise to assist him in discovering which policies could win maximum support in the party and in winning votes for such policies. Unlike Taft, Johnson rarely announced the committee's stand on an issue. One exception was in 1953, when the Policy Committee formally and publicly endorsed President Eisenhower's resolution on the Yalta agreements and, thereby, accentuated the administration's differences with Republican senators seeking to revise the resolution. During the debate over the Middle East resolution, when Johnson was beginning to assume an increased role in international affairs, he gained unanimous public endorsement by the Policy Committee of a letter he had sent to the Secretary of State urging that this country oppose the imposition of U.N. economic sanctions on Israel. These were exceptions, however, to a Johnson policy of avoiding public stands by the committee.

During the last six years of the Eisenhower administration, Democratic control of the Senate meant responsibility for scheduling legislation. As in the past, the committee refrained from using its authority to keep legislation from reaching the floor, though in the closing days of a session it did have to choose which bills could be considered before adjournment. This latter situation, incidentally, was the only occasion on which votes were normally taken in the Policy Committee. Though it is difficult for the outsider to draw conclusions, Johnson appears to have assumed greater responsibility than his predecessors for scheduling legislation and to have given the committee a smaller role than before.

Senator Johnson exercised an authority over the Democratic Policy Committee equivalent to that of Taft over the Republican committee. He seldom used it to gain endorsement for a program, as Taft did, largely because Johnson was not often committed to specific policies. Johnson was also particularly conscious of the risk that bipartisan support might be lost through endorsement of a measure by the Policy Committee. Under Johnson, the Policy Committee held formal meetings nearly every week, but he frequently convened it informally or contacted its members individually for advice. The committee sometimes prepared compromises itself or mediated differences among other Democratic senators.

The Policy Committee's usefulness for Lyndon Johnson's purposes depended, of course, on the degree of unity in the party. The committee could not be expected to devise a compromise on civil rights, for example, acceptable to members with views as divergent as those of Thomas C. Hennings and Richard B. Russell. Though a large majority of the members favored the administration's aid and trade policies, Senator Russell became a bitter opponent of both. The controversy over the Bricker amendment illustrated both the committee's potentialities for fostering compromise and its limitations. The committee discussed the issue at considerable length and appears to have played a role in the genesis of Senator George's compromise, but it was too sharply divided on the plan for formal endorsement. Four members opposed any amendment, four favored the George amendment, and one—Senator Russell—was a vigorous supporter of the original Bricker amendment.[20]

Lyndon Johnson adapted the Policy Committee to serve his purposes as Democratic leader. Like his staff, the committee was a useful tool in developing Democratic support for Johnson's compromises.[21] A more formal Policy Committee issuing official party pronouncements might have been less valuable to Johnson or even a handicap. Yet by becoming merely a part of the Johnson organization, the Policy Committee failed to develop as a Democratic institution in the Senate comparable in stature to the Republican committee. Johnson's tactics, in fact, seemed deliberately designed to avoid such institutionalization. Johnson, like Alben Barkley before him, seemed to fear that the Policy Committee might become a threat to his authority as floor leader. The proper role of the Policy Committee—as well as the Con-

---

[20] In 1955, when Johnson was seeking to convince the administration that the reciprocal trade program needed modification if it were to pass Congress, he held two meetings of the Policy Committee, after both of which he reported the committee's judgment that there was substantial pressure in the Senate for changes in the bill.

[21] As Bone, p. 344, has pointed out: "In Democratic circles on the Hill the Democratic Policy Committee is often spoken of as the 'personal staff of Senator Johnson.'"

ference—was called into question in 1960 by those liberal Democrats who tried to make Johnson more responsible to the senatorial party.

PROPOSALS FOR REVISING THE
DEMOCRATIC PARTY MACHINERY

The liberal Democrats who challenged Johnson's leadership unsuccessfully during the 1960 session believed that in a period of
huge Democratic majorities in Congress, Johnson was making too
many compromises in an effort to maintain party unity and avoid
vetoes. The differences centered on domestic rather than foreign
issues, but the implications of the controversy for party leadership are significant enough to deserve consideration here. The
liberal Democrats were trying to eliminate a situation where, in
Senator William Proxmire's words, "the initiative as well as the
final decision is almost always resolved by the majority leader
himself on the basis of his own judgment of what is desirable and
what is possible."[22] There is a contradiction between the responsibility of the party leader to the party and the desire of
liberal Democrats to see the party take a more definite stand on
issues. Greater party democracy might lead to party disunity;
and a divided party is in no position to take a clear and forceful
public stand on any issue.

The liberals were not agreed on whether their objectives could
be better sought through reviving the conference or revitalizing
the Policy Committee. Early in January, when a group of liberals
succeeded in generating considerable support at a Democratic
caucus for regularly scheduled conference meetings, Johnson
headed off the challenge by promising to hold them whenever
any senator requested. A few days later when Senator Albert
Gore sought to increase the membership and functions of the
Policy Committee, he was defeated by a 51-12 vote in the conference.

Senator Gore wanted the Policy Committee to be given responsibility for formulating an overall legislative program, which
he emphasized was the intention of the LaFollette-Monroney
committee that first proposed policy committees in 1946. Mike

[22] *Congressional Record*, March 9, 1959, p. 3559.

Mansfield argued that the Policy Committee could not interfere with the functions of standing committees; Proxmire, one of the first and most vocal rebels, replied that the Policy Committee should provide general guidance to the Democratic members of committees. There is no doubt that strengthened policy committees would threaten the independence of standing committee chairmen as well as party leaders.[23]

Gore also sought to make the Policy Committee more representative by increasing its membership from nine to fifteen and by having members elected by the conference rather than appointed by Johnson. Senator Mansfield has argued that the Policy Committee is limited to seven members (plus two ex officio) by the original appropriations act establishing the committees; yet the Republicans have enlarged their committee on several occasions, and if legislation is actually needed, it could be easily passed.[24] Actually an increase in membership is important only if the committee's functions are increased. Beginning in 1959, Senator Johnson invited the three-man Calendar Committee to meet regularly with the Policy Committee, and its members participated in the meetings on an equal footing with regular members. The fact that the three members were all freshman senators was proof that the majority leader did not consider the Policy Committee an important policy body.[25]

The conference is probably a less effective vehicle for creating party policy than the Policy Committee. There is considerable validity to Senator Mansfield's description of caucuses as "a

23 A full account of the sporadic Democratic debate on the Policy Committee and Conference may be found in the *Congressional Record*, Feb. 23, 1959, pp. 2814-21; March 9, 1959, pp. 3559-85.

24 A letter to the writer from Senator Mansfield, March 24, 1959. Mansfield said that only the deputy leader and secretary of the Conference are technically ex officio members. They have "advisory functions," while the floor leader serves as chairman.

25 At the start of the 1961 session the Democrats agreed to a compromise plan under which the Policy and Steering committee members would be nominated by the floor leader and approved by the Conference. The agreement provided that the committee should be representative of geography and varying political viewpoints. Liberal Democrats who wanted a voice in filling two vacancies on the Policy Committee were critical because Johnson, in a *fait accompli*, had picked Senators John Pastore and Warren Magnuson in June, 1960, to replace Senators Green and Murray, who conveniently resigned early. In January, 1961, Senator Edmund Muskie was added to the Calendar Review Committee, making it a four-man group, and at that time some questions were raised about how large a role it should play in the deliberations of the Policy Committee.

waste of time." Mike Monroney, an author of the 1946 Legislative Reorganization Act which led to the establishment of policy committees, has pointed out that caucuses in the past have more often led to diffusion than unity in party policy. They have offered too much opportunity for impassioned oratory and bitter debate, which help to heighten party discord.[26] There is a constant fear that the substance of discussions will leak to the press. The conference is much too large for negotiation and the development of party strategy. It is one way of informing the floor leader about party viewpoints and perhaps even a way of putting pressure on the leader, but it is not a method of holding the leader responsible to the party. Senator Proxmire has suggested that the conference vote on major issues, not to bind the members but to bind the floor leader. Such a procedure might increase the rigidity of party divisions while seriously handicapping the party leader's maneuverability. The conference is an unwieldly body, too large and formal for adaptability to the changing needs of the party and likely to impose either too little or too much control over the party leadership.[27]

THE ROLE OF POLICY COMMITTEES

The crucial question that must be answered in regard to the policy committees is whether they have been able to bring greater unity to the parties in the Senate. The policy committees have never been able to unite either of the parties on deeply divisive issues and have never sought to impose conformity on a minority in a party. The greatest doubts about the committees' usefulness arise from the suspicion that they can lead only when the party is so united that leadership is unnecessary. Professor Truman concluded from a study of voting records in the Eighty-first Congress that "though the Committee *may* be providing voting cues, this is a minimal function and typically it is mirroring

[26] Huitt, p. 341, has pointed out the risks of a caucus: "Party members frequently stand together for different reasons, but talking about those reasons may open old wounds and drive them apart. Floor debate may do the same, but it is not so likely, since many members are usually absent and arguments are not made directly to each other."

[27] After Senator Johnson had agreed to schedule caucuses on request, only two were held on legislative issues during the 1960 session of Congress.

tendencies within the party."[28] He found that voting cohesion
in the committees was about as great as that in the parties, that
committee members would be in full agreement only when most
of the party was in agreement, and that "agreement within the
Committee reflected at least as often as it influenced the cohesion of the party."[29]

When a political party is seriously divided on an issue, the
policy committee probably can play no useful role unless it is
able to devise or assist in preparing a compromise measure, as
the Republican Policy Committee nearly succeeded in doing in
the case of the Bricker amendment. When there is a high level
of party unity, the policy committee's opportunity is greater; it
can reinforce this unity by acting as party spokesman and implement it by serving as the party's tactician. In the process it may
change a few votes, and when the political balance in the Senate
is close, a few votes may be decisive. The record of the two
policy committees in foreign policy, as reviewed in this chapter,
shows a number of such examples. When the policy committee,
recognizing considerable party agreement on an issue, publicly
or privately endorses a bill or an amendment and nearly all the
party's senators vote accordingly, it seems likely (though not
provable) that the committee's action has contributed to party
unity. Even when the party is split over some aspects of an
issue, it is possible that the policy committee can engender unity
on other aspects of it, as the Republican committee did during
the troops-for-Europe dispute. When it is not trying to overcome
profound differences in the party, the policy committee can
change some votes for several reasons: because its members are
influential in the Senate, because senators usually prefer if possible to remain loyal to the party, and because on some occasions
its actions may fill a vacuum in leadership.

There remains one vital question with regard to the policy
committees: Are they to be the instrument of the party or the
leader? When there are tactical decisions to be made, does the
leader accept the policy committee's judgment or call upon it
only to endorse his own views? In the administration party this
is a less crucial question because serious conflicts over tactics

[28] Truman, *The Congressional Party*, p. 129.
[29] *Ibid.*

may be referred to the White House. The President's judgment on foreign issues will normally carry particular weight with his party in the Senate. Though the committee has sometimes surveyed the views of the Senate and decided that a compromise unwelcome to the White House was necessary, the committee has never been used by the leadership of an administration party to challenge a major feature of the President's foreign program.[30]

Controversies over the proper role of the opposition policy committee stem from the lack of any clear responsibility for leadership of the opposition in the nation as a whole. The effort in 1960 to make Senator Johnson more responsible to the Policy Committee or the Conference was undertaken by liberals sympathetic to those national leaders in the party who disputed Johnson's claim to speak for the party. It is possible that in the Senate Republican party, with its formally divided leadership, the Policy Committee might be used by its chairman as a weapon in a power struggle with the floor leader. This has never happened, nor is it likely that the committee would be united in support of only one leader in a factional dispute. It would be possible to change the rules of the Democratic party, as Senator Gore attempted, to make the floor leader responsible to the Policy Committee. It is doubtful that the committee could serve effectively both as a check on the floor leader and as a vehicle for party unity. Successful legislative leadership demands a high degree of flexibility and finesse, qualities not likely to be present in the collective leadership of a divided party. In Professor Bone's judgment, the Democratic Policy Committee has greater potential than the Republican one because it is better adapted to the system of personal negotiation that characterizes senatorial leadership.[31] The most intimate observers of the Senate seem to be unanimous in emphasizing the importance of personal contacts and the difficulty of institutionalizing leadership in the Senate.

Yet in the last analysis a senatorial leader cannot unite the party singlehandedly. To succeed, he must keep in touch with the views of fellow senators and also give them a sense of participation in making party decisions. The staff may serve as an

[30] Bone, p. 351, has reported, however, that some Democrats felt the Democratic Policy Committee was occasionally used late in the Truman administration to strengthen Democratic opposition to certain of the President's domestic policies.
[31] Ibid., p. 357.

intelligence system, but the policy committee is better suited to serving both functions. A stronger policy committee, for the opposition party in particular, could distribute more broadly the responsibility for deciding what kinds of compromises are necessary and desirable. It would be better able than the floor leader both to judge what fellow senators would accept and to convince them to go along with an agreed position. The policy committee's potential for strengthening party unity has yet to be fully explored by leaders of the Senate.

More effective policy committees probably cannot be imposed on the Senate leadership. To be useful, they must be employed by the leaders rather than against them. Like other institutions of the Senate, they are more likely to develop informally through practice than formally through party resolutions. To be fully effective, the committees would have to represent in rough proportions the major geographic sections of the party and would have to include the senators who were most powerful either by virtue of personal strength or of major party or committee assignments. In the past the Democratic party has been handicapped in dealing with foreign policy, for example, by the fact that Foreign Relations Committee chairmen (except for Senator Green) were never members.

Fortunately for recent American foreign policy, the Committee on Foreign Relations stands high before the Senate, well able to look out for itself, in contrast to its counterpart in the House of Representatives.

—H. BRADFORD WESTERFIELD

6

THE FOREIGN RELATIONS COMMITTEE

POLITICAL POWER IS DECENTRALIZED IN CONGRESS LARGELY because of the strength of standing committees. In recent years perhaps the most powerful of these in the Senate has been the Foreign Relations Committee. Though the committee has been remarkably free from partisan conflict, its decisions have been instrumental in setting the record of both parties in the Senate on foreign policy. Most of the senators who have significantly influenced the Senate's deliberations on foreign policy have been leaders, not of the parties, but of this committee. The limitations of the party leaders and the institutions described earlier have frequently resulted partly from the influence of the Foreign Relations Committee and its leadership.

Since personalities so often are the key to explaning power relationships in the Senate, an examination of the Foreign Relations Committee may well start with its recent leaders. Though these men have not been elected party leaders, they have exercised political power as well as personal influence in the Senate. This power derives not only from personal skill and experience but also from the ability to speak for the party and for the Foreign Relations Committee. The records of men like Arthur Vandenberg and Walter George are a rich source of information on the meaning of political leadership in the Senate. Since the chairman's influence rests in part on the authority of the committee, it is important to probe the sources of that authority, the role of partisanship in the committee's decisions, and the relationship of the committee to other committees in the Senate that deal with foreign affairs.[1]

ADMINISTRATION LEADERS ON THE COMMITTEE

During the Truman and Eisenhower administrations, the ranking member of the Foreign Relations Committee from the administration party—whether chairman or not—was usually less influential than the opposition leader on the committee. Partly this was an accident of personality. In addition, the administration leader on the committee, like the administration floor leader, is under pressure to accept the President's program with a minimum of complaint. During the postwar period the chairmen of the Foreign Relations Committee have proved consistently willing to cooperate with the President; yet those chairmen who represented the opposition party have been able and willing to demand greater policy concessions than those bound to the President by ties of party loyalty. Consistent support of the President has sometimes reduced the influence of administration leaders on senators who respect independent judgment more than party loyalty.

We should not overstate the case. It would be rash to suggest

[1] For an excellent description of the sources of committee chairmen's power, see Matthews, *U.S. Senators and Their World*, pp. 159-62.

that Senator William Knowland would have given complete support to President Eisenhower's foreign policy had he been chairman of the Foreign Relations Committee. A member of the President's party who leads the Foreign Relations Committee faces the same problem as one who leads the party in the Senate: To attain maximum effectiveness he must represent faithfully both the President and the senatorial party. Democrat Tom Connally was a more successful chairman than Republican Alexander Wiley largely because Connally had much less difficulty than Wiley in serving two masters; the Democrats in 1949 were far more united on international issues than the Republicans in 1953.

Senator Tom Connally was a devoted internationalist and a loyal supporter of President Truman's foreign policies. From 1947 through 1952, first as ranking Democrat and then for four years as chairman of the committee, Connally had a record of complete support for Truman's foreign programs except for a few compromises that he felt were based on a more realistic appraisal of senatorial views. He sometimes criticized various aspects of bills without seeking revisions and on other occasions urged changes in details to make them more acceptable to the Senate. He was less inclined than Senator Vandenberg to seek revisions and occasionally criticized those sought by Vandenberg.

Connally's success is in large measure due to his close relations with his associates. His attitude toward the State Department has been well described as that of "a gruff old watchdog, snipping here and there at his State Department wards when he thought they were going astray, but all the while having their best interests at heart."[2] Connally was on close, though not intimate, terms with President Truman and the various men who served as Secretary of State, notably Dean Acheson. He had a close working relationship with the various Democratic floor leaders, who almost always agreed with him on the handling of foreign policy measures. We have previously described the arrangement giving him primary Democratic responsibility for management of foreign programs as a division of labor rather than the consequence of a struggle for power. Connally's

[2] Merle L. Gulick, "Tom Connally as a Founder of the United Nations" (Unpublished Ph.D. dissertation, Georgetown University, 1955), p. 151.

greatest talent lay in gauging the temper of the Senate and adapting the administration's program to senatorial views. Though the internationalist thinking among Democrats minimized the need for such adjustments, it did not eliminate the need for a man who knew when to be firm and when to seek compromise. When Connally reassumed the chairmanship of the Foreign Relations Committee in 1949, succeeding Vandenberg, his major responsibility was to secure approval of the North Atlantic Treaty and of its implementation through military aid. His handling of these measures illustrates his techniques as chairman. While the North Atlantic Treaty was being drafted, Connally participated with Vandenberg in talks with Secretary of State Dean Acheson in order to make sure that the treaty did not infringe on the congressional right to declare war and to remove any language from the treaty which might obstruct ratification. Though for a time it appeared that the senators' efforts might seriously damage the treaty, the draft that emerged was satisfactory to the administration. Having secured a satisfactory draft, Connally then resisted successfully every effort to attach reservations to the treaty in the Senate.

Connally correctly foresaw that opposition to the treaty would center on the military aid program to implement it. He tried to postpone discussion of the aid program and the release of information about its cost until after ratification of the treaty. This tactic conflicted with the administration's plan to bolster support for military aid by publicizing it in advance as an integral part of NATO and, thus, persuading the supporters of the treaty that they were also committed to vote for the aid bill. Connally yielded to the administration and announced his support for prompt passage of the aid program three weeks before Senate debate on the treaty. In his opening floor speech on the treaty he endorsed the aid measure and declared that the two programs were interrelated but not inseparable.

When the military aid program reached the Senate, Connally left to the Republican leaders primary responsibility for negotiating substantial revision with the administration. Nevertheless, he deferred hearings on the original bill, apparently advised the administration to change it, and agreed to certain cuts and postponements in spending in order to prevent more serious reductions. On the floor of the Senate he spoke vigorously and successfully against further cuts in arms aid beyond those already made in committee. Connally has testified, "I buttonholed the membership continually in an effort to change votes." He described the arms aid debate as the hardest fight since the passage of the Lend-Lease Act.[3] He was able to produce 36 Democratic votes for the arms assistance bill with only 10 opposed and to forge a similar Democratic majority against reductions in the program.

Connally was foremost among the Senate Democrats who supported the Truman administration in its opposition to supplying large-scale military aid to Nationalist China and later to Formosa. In 1949 he prevented hearings in the committee on a $1.5 billion economic and military aid bill for China sponsored by Senator Pat McCarran and flatly opposed by the administration; he refused to yield to an appeal by 50 senators, half of them Democrats, for hearings on the bill. Later in the year he delayed consideration of a $175 million military aid bill for China offered by Senator Knowland, held Democrats on the committee firmly in line against the proposal when it came to a vote, and then worked out a compromise with Senator Vandenberg giving the President authority to spend the funds in the "general area" of China. When the Truman administration decided in January, 1950, not to help Chiang Kai-shek defend Formosa, Connally publicly supported the decision and kept up a barrage of criticism against Republicans who sought to "plunge this country into war." Whatever the wisdom of the administration's policy, Connally's tactics saved the President from the embarrassment of serious Democratic dissension.[4]

Connally's firm support helped the President to avoid a defeat in the Senate on the troops-for-Europe issue in 1951. He proposed an advisory resolution in which the Senate could state its support for sending troops and its belief that future assignments of forces should be made in consultation with various congressional committees. This formed the basis for the resolution approved by the Senate after the addition of further re-

[3] Tom Connally, *My Name is Tom Connally* (New York: Thomas Y. Crowell Co., 1954), p. 339.
[4] Westerfield, *Foreign Policy and Party Politics*, pp. 347-50, 356-59, 365.

strictions on the President. Connally disliked the recommendation of the Foreign Relations and Armed Services committees to require congressional approval for future troop assignments to Europe. Nevertheless, he accepted it as the best compromise attainable and opposed with considerable success attempts on the Senate floor to add further restrictions. Though he was inconsistent and in one case out of step with Majority Leader McFarland on two amendments to remove restrictions on the President, his vacillation did no real damage because these amendments had no chance of success. Connally shares with McFarland some of the credit for the unusually large Democratic majorities in support of Truman on this issue.

In presenting foreign policy legislation to the Senate, Connally was always careful to emphasize that it had bipartisan endorsement by the Foreign Relations Committee, and he fully recognized the necessity of maintaining unity in the committee whenever possible. Nevertheless, in Senate debates and to a lesser extent in committee, Connally's attitude was sharply partisan. He was not only a partisan speaker but often a blunt and sarcastic one whose personal criticisms of other members stood out in sharp contrast to the Senate's traditional elaborate courtesy. This ingrained characteristic considerably limited Connally's influence in Republican ranks but did not prevent his extensive cooperation with Republican senators in shaping legislation on foreign affairs. As a veteran internationalist, Connally looked upon Vandenberg's comparatively recent conversion with some scorn; this feeling did not, however, undermine the close working relationship of the two senators on most issues.[5]

How should Connally's influence be evaluated, and what were its sources? One observer has concluded that "whatever leadership he was able to exercise in the Senate on foreign affairs derived from his personality and his long association with the work of that committee—not, as did Vandenberg's, from his standing as a fullfledged leader of his party."[6] Such authority as Connally's does not come automatically to a committee chair-

[5] The Connally-Vandenberg rivalry is mentioned in Vandenberg, *The Private Papers of Senator Vandenberg*, pp. 379, 505-506. It is also evident in a number of references to Vandenberg in Connally's autobiography.
[6] Westerfield, p. 119.

man. Connally was a veteran senator, a forceful personality, a chairman who exercised the full prerogatives of that office and commanded respect in the committee. It is true that he never achieved the stature in the senatorial party of southerners like Walter F. George and Richard B. Russell. The Democratic administration, however, worked closely with him, and since most Democratic senators respected the administration's views in this field, they were willing to follow his lead.

Tom Connally is generally not credited with playing a decisive role in the success of the Truman administration's programs in the Senate. This assessment is true in the sense that he faced relatively few obstacles in implementing the President's policies. His record indicates that a successful administration leader on the Foreign Relations Committee needs personal ability, support from the committee, acceptance by the administration, and substantial unity in the party.

As Republican leader of the Foreign Relations Committee during the Eisenhower administration, Alexander Wiley lacked each of the assets that Connally possessed and consequently lacked authority in the United States Senate. Wiley had been the ranking Republican on the Foreign Relations Committee since Vandenberg's death in April, 1951, and served as chairman in 1953 and 1954. He inherited from Vandenberg a firm belief in the principles and programs of internationalism. Despite criticism of some aspects of the Truman foreign policies, he voted for all the major economic and military measures of that administration, and he gave unswerving support to President Eisenhower on issues ranging from the Bricker amendment and the Yalta resolution to the Middle East resolution.

Wiley owed his position to seniority and lacked the talent for leadership, the parliamentary skills, industry, and persuasiveness that more influential senators have. These shortcomings are serious in a legislative body where an individual's talents are shrewdly appraised. The contrast in personal abilities of Connally and Wiley is not great enough, however, to explain the wide difference in influence. Wiley became chairman in 1953 at a time when the Republicans in the Senate were seriously divided on foreign policy. Those whose votes the President most needed were suspicious of Wiley's consistent internationalism; they looked instead to Knowland, Bridges, or Taft for leadership.

Wiley lacked influence also because he never held a place in the Republican hierarchy. His absence from the Policy Committee until 1955 was indicative of his standing in the party.[7] Perhaps most damaging to Wiley was the Eisenhower administration's failure to accord him the recognition normally due the ranking Republican on the Foreign Relations Committee. In this regard Eisenhower notably did not give Wiley the slightest encouragement or assistance in his 1956 Wisconsin primary contest against opponents who were sharply critical of the administration's foreign policy. The apparent magnitude of the political opposition to Wiley in Wisconsin was itself one of the factors undermining his senatorial authority. In the last years of the Eisenhower administration a broad measure of party unity was achieved on foreign policy, but Wiley remained a neglected figure and the administration lacked an authoritative senatorial spokesman in this field.

The controversy over the Bricker amendment best illustrates Wiley's peculiar role as chairman of the Foreign Relations Committee during the first two years of the Eisenhower administration. Wiley was the only Republican leader who flatly opposed every version of the Bricker amendment and firmly supported the President. Yet because this unequivocal position made him unrepresentative of most Republican senators, the administration ignored him during most of its prolonged negotiations with those senators who were seeking a compromise. He was not consulted on the Ferguson-Knowland compromise and, although absent during rollcalls, made clear his opposition. At a press conference the President refused to choose between the compromise efforts of Ferguson and Knowland and Wiley's position of flat opposition to compromise.[8] Wiley's lack of influence

[7] During the debate on the foreign aid bill in 1954, Senator Paul H. Douglas asked Wiley if the Republican Policy Committee was opposed to a reduction of one billion dollars proposed by Senator Russell B. Long. Wiley answered that he assumed it was but that he was not a member. *Congressional Record,* August 3, 1954, p. 13027.

[8] After Wiley told the Wisconsin Republican convention that the Bricker amendment was "the most dangerous thing that has ever been brought before Congress," the convention censured him for refusing to support the amendment. *New York Times,* June 14. 1953, p. 75. His stand greatly increased his difficulties in winning renomination in 1956.

on this issue resulted fundamentally from his want of stature and his previous failures to assert leadership. An important additional factor, however, was the administration's decision to accept the judgment of other Senate Republican leaders that the Bricker amendment could be defeated only through a compromise. In the process of reaching that decision, Wiley was not consulted; once it was reached, his stand against compromise destroyed his potential senatorial influence on the issue.

A MODEL OPPOSITION LEADER: SENATOR VANDENBERG

The two senators with the greatest influence on foreign policy in recent years, Arthur H. Vandenberg and Walter F. George, had much in common. Both were opposition leaders and consequently could bargain with the administration at times and not merely follow it. Both were picked by the administration as bipartisan collaborators because their parties had won congressional majorities at a time when the enactment of major foreign programs was essential. Both were needed because their backgrounds and sympathies gave them rapport with the various factions within their parties. Vandenberg and George, as internationalists, represented the majority wings of their respective parties. Yet each owed part of his influence to a reputation for independence and fiscal conservatism and even to an early history of isolationism that commanded respect among senators who dreaded the heavy burdens of this country's international responsibilities. Both men were prominent party leaders as well as senators commanding respect on both sides of the aisle.

Dean Acheson has summarized some of the reasons for Vandenberg's success as the Republican leader in foreign policy: "He had ability of the highest order. He was a master of advocacy and maneuver. He had the full respect and admiration of the Senate and the added strength of having been a severe critic of 'foreign entanglements.' But he did not have a particularly original or creative mind. His instincts were toward caution—to hold back, to examine the difficulties of the course proposed, and to restrain the enthusiasts.

"These were good qualities. They were ideal qualities for a leader of an opposition which had for a part of the time control

of the Congress. . . . He was free to do what he could do best—
criticize, question, examine—until he became convinced of the
necessity for a proposed program. He would then put his un-
mistakable mark on it, and finally give it the essential help of
his incomparable advocacy and fervor, the shrewd guidance
of his knowledge of the Congress."[9]

Vandenberg's publicized conversion from a leading isolationist to the foremost Republican internationalist in the Senate
made it easier for other Republicans to change their stand on
foreign policy. This fact and the caution with which he ap-
proached all proposed legislation strengthened his influence
among most Republican senators. Vandenberg was always careful to add Republican trademarks to the administration's programs. This tactic served to show that bipartisanship was not a
policy of "me too," while it also led to the removal or revision
of those sections of a bill most vulnerable to criticism. Like
any skillful leader in the Senate, Vandenberg could gauge the
temper of that body with great accuracy. More than most leaders,
he was skillful in devising compromises that were adapted to
the views of the Senate but did little damage to the substance
of the measure. James Reston has suggested that one of Vandenberg's greatest talents was his "capacity to *anticipate* opposition" in Congress in time to remove its causes.[10]

Vandenberg's first opportunity to display his skill as chairman of the Foreign Relations Committee came in March, 1947,
just two months after he had assumed the post, when President
Truman introduced his program for aid to Greece and Turkey.
After he had attended a White House briefing, Vandenberg
explained the program on two occasions to the Republican
Conference and took the unusual step of inviting all senators
to submit questions about the program for transmittal to the
State Department. He received some 400 questions, which were
consolidated into a document of 111 questions and answers.[11]

Vandenberg felt that the administration had made a "colossal

[9] Acheson, *A Democrat Looks at His Party*, pp. 104-105.
[10] James Reston, "The Case for Vandenberg," *Life*, XXIV (May 24, 1948), 101.
See also Richard H. Rovere, "The Unassailable Vandenberg," *Harper's*, CXCVI
(May, 1948), 394-403. Rovere suggests as a moral that "it is better to be wrong
before you are right than to be right all along."
[11] Vandenberg, p. 344. The *Private Papers* provide by far the best information on Vandenberg's role in the foreign policy issues under study.

blunder" by ignoring the United Nations in the Greek-Turkish aid measure. He recognized that this failure had caused serious misgivings among some internationalist senators while providing a powerful argument for isolationist opponents. He recognized further that this obstacle could be overcome without significant danger to the purposes of the aid measure. He rewrote the preamble of the bill to state that the U.N. had recognized the political and economic problems of Greece but was unable to provide aid to either Greece or Turkey. More important was his amendment stating that the program would end if the U.N. General Assembly or Security Council concluded that U.N. action made the program unnecessary or undesirable and stating further that in this event the United States would waive its veto power in the Security Council.[12]

These additions, though accepted unenthusiastically by Senator Connally and the administration, served their purpose. Vandenberg succeeded in defeating crippling amendments, and he gained passage of the bill with the support of over two-thirds of the Republicans as well as most of the Democrats. While he made it clear that support for the Greek-Turkish aid program involved no commitment to the broader aspects of the Truman Doctrine, Vandenberg emphasized his support for the principles enunciated by the President. He said that when free governments are facing threats of totalitarian aggression, "we do not necessarily react in the same way each time, but we propose to act."[13]

Vandenberg's experience in guiding the Greek-Turkish program through the Senate was a dress rehearsal for his performance in behalf of the European Recovery Program (ERP), launched by Secretary of State George C. Marshall in June, 1947. Vandenberg's initial reaction was cautious; he endorsed the principle of an overall rather than a piecemeal approach to foreign aid but did not commit himself to the program. Rather, he took the first in a series of steps to facilitate congressional approval: the calling for a bipartisan study of the required foreign assistance and the resources of the United States available for

12 *Ibid.*, pp. 345-46.
13 *Assistance to Greece and Turkey*, Hearings before the Committee on Foreign Relations, U.S. Senate, 80th Cong., 1st sess., on S. 938, pp. 13, 30-31.

the task. The three study groups which President Truman created prepared impressive documentation in support of the Marshall Plan.[14]

When legislation for ERP itself was introduced, Vandenberg took further steps to undermine opposition. A complicated dispute developed over the administration of the program. The State Department wanted to have direct control, many Republicans desired an independent agency, and the Appropriations committees of both houses feared that the independent board suggested by the Herter Committee would bypass them. Vandenberg solved this tangled question neatly by turning it over to the Brookings Institution; that widely respected research organization proposed a compromise acceptable to all sides. In his attempt to maintain maximum congressional support for ERP, Vandenberg rejected Truman's suggestion for an administrator, selected Paul Hoffman for the post, and then persuaded both Truman and Hoffman to accept the idea.[15]

Vandenberg recognized that the administration's request for a specific four-year authorization of $17 billion was an invitation to controversy and would probably be reduced by Congress. He considered any fixed four-year figure useless because it would not determine future congressional appropriations and could be only an "educated guess of highly doubtful validity." He persuaded the administration to remove the specific dollar request before congressional opponents were able to center their attack on that figure.[16]

A group of senators critical of ERP, who became known as "revisionists," held several meetings to draft changes and limitations to be inserted in the measure. Vandenberg's foresight in eliminating several sources of controversy enabled him to reject all but a few innocuous proposals. He realized that it was important to make minor changes in language in order to win broader support for the measure. On one occasion, when someone in the Foreign Relations Committee objected that the words "impact on our domestic economy" in the bill were too vague, Vandenberg replied, "I can tell nineteen different Senators on

14 Vandenberg, pp. 376-77.
15 Ibid., pp. 393-94.
16 Ibid., p. 385.

the floor of the Senate who are worried about something—your problem is taken care of by that clause in the bill."[17]

Vandenberg used the Foreign Relations Committee as a forum for a galaxy of distinguished witnesses to defend the Marshall Plan. On the floor of the Senate, he spoke effectively for the bill, answered criticisms, defeated objectionable amendments, and accepted those he considered innocuous. He devised an ingenious solution to the demands for economy. By reducing the term for the initial authorization from fifteen months to twelve, he was able to make a corresponding reduction in funds without any loss to the program and could argue that this would give the new Congress an earlier chance at reassessment in 1949. By this means he defeated Taft's amendment for a cut of approximately $1.3 billion in the authorization. When the House voted to stretch the appropriations to fifteen months without increasing the total, Vandenberg appeared before the Senate Appropriations Committee to denounce reductions achieved by "meat axe techniques" as a "cynical reversal" of congressional policies. After a long struggle between the two houses and with Taft's help, Vandenberg won his point.

Although it is difficult to believe that the Senate would have defeated ERP under any circumstances, it is easy to imagine that the scope of the measure might have been drastically curtailed either in 1948 or in succeeding years. Sentiment for such limitations was strong in 1948 and grew stronger each year that followed. Vandenberg's great accomplishment was enactment of the program substantially as requested by the administration with such firm support that it withstood most proposed reductions, especially in the Senate, for several years. His technique of accommodation in detail and form but defense of the essential was not unique in the Senate, but he used this technique with unusual skill and success.

The third major achievement of Senator Vandenberg during his two years as chairman was passage of the Vandenberg resolution in 1948. The resolution expressed the Senate's support for strengthening the United Nations by restricting use of the veto and for association of the United States by constitu-

---

[17] *Ibid.*, pp. 388-89.

tional processes in mutual security arrangements. It was no small achievement to win passage for this resolution with only four dissenting votes after a day of debate. Vandenberg had laid the groundwork by prolonged consultation on the text of the resolution with Under Secretary of State Robert A. Lovett. He had been careful to link the endorsement of collective security arrangements—the major purpose of the resolution—to the popular concept of strengthening the United Nations. He denied that his resolution represented a moral commitment to support any future regional pact or program of arms aid, and he avoided any debate on its probable consequences. The resolution was hurried through in the last days of the congressional session. The only disadvantage of these tactics was that they minimized the impact of the resolution and somewhat limited its utility as a stepping stone to the North Atlantic Treaty.[18]

Much of Vandenberg's success was due to personal characteristics: his legislative skill, his intelligent use of the tactics of compromise, and his cautious conversion to internationalist principles. Beyond this, he derived his power from his authority as chairman of the Foreign Relations Committee and recognized leader of the Republican party on matters of foreign policy. Vandenberg had served on the committee since 1929. He appreciated the importance of maintaining unity on the committee and sought with notable success to continue that practice.[19] He ran the committee, not arbitrarily, but with firmness and skill. Even more important, he was recognized by both his fellow Republicans and the administration as the Republican leader on foreign policy at a time when the support of the majority Republican party was essential to enact President Truman's bold new programs abroad. Vandenberg's understanding with Taft on a division of authority between the two of them has already been described; it reflected the views of a majority of Republican senators, who followed Taft on domestic questions and Vandenberg on international matters.[20] The Truman administra-

[18] *Ibid.*, pp. 404-408. Walter Millis, ed., *The Forrestal Diaries* (New York: Viking Press, 1951), pp. 422-24, 434.

[19] Senator Vandenberg stated proudly that during the Eightieth Congress the committee gave unanimous support to the administration's policies on "47 critical occasions." *Congressional Record*, January 5, 1949, p. 61.

[20] See chapter 4.

tion was willing and even eager to consult Vandenberg in advance on some foreign policy legislation. This enabled Vandenberg to speak with greater authority in the Senate and to influence the content of legislation at an earlier stage. Clearly Vandenberg enjoyed the role of a world statesman and was flattered by the attention given to him by the administration. Some critics felt that by making Vandenberg a well-publicized partner in bipartisan policymaking, the administration was damaging his influence among the less internationalist Republicans. There is no doubt that a man in Vandenberg's position walks a political tightrope; he was skillful enough and retained enough independence to avoid falling.

The China question, which eventually became a bitterly partisan issue, was the greatest potential threat to Vandenberg's position. He handled the issue cautiously and followed a tactic of disassociation and even ambivalence that enabled him to retain the confidence of both the administration and his fellow Republicans. Vandenberg repeatedly emphasized that the Republicans were not being consulted on policy toward China and bore no responsibility for it. Though he had doubts about the policy of trying to encourage a Chinese coalition government that included the Communists, Vandenberg did not want to challenge Secretary Marshall's judgment on the matter. When Chiang Kai-shek's military plight began to grow desperate, Vandenberg accepted the administration's judgment that Chiang could not be saved without massive military intervention by the United States and agreed that this would be unwise. He did not join Republicans, like Senator William Knowland and Congressman Walter Judd, who demanded large-scale American aid for China and who later insisted on military intervention to defend Formosa. His legislative role was one of devising compromises that provided for more aid than the administration wanted and less than many Republicans wanted. Had other Republican leaders pressed their demands for a different policy in China earlier and more urgently, Vandenberg might have found his middle position untenable. Likewise, had he lived to play an active role in the Senate during the MacArthur controversy, Vandenberg would have been forced to choose sides. Critics can argue that Vandenberg failed in his role as an opposition leader because he did not lead the fight for a policy capable of stemming the tide of Communism in China. But policymaking was not Vandenberg's forte; he had no answer for the Chinese problem and considered it of secondary importance. Vandenberg's purpose was twofold: to prevent partisan controversy over China from damaging bipartisan support for the economic and military programs in Europe and to disassociate the Republican party from the administration's China policy. In these efforts he was wholly successful.[21]

When the Democrats regained control of Congress in 1949, there was a perceptible drop in Senator Vandenberg's influence. He no longer was chairman of the Foreign Relations Committee, nor did he command the strategic position of foreign policy leader for a majority party. The administration recognized, however, the value of continued collaboration with Vandenberg, but it became a matter of less importance and less frequency. Vandenberg lost the chairmanship at the same time that Secretary of State Marshall and Under Secretary Lovett were resigning. Vandenberg never achieved the close, personal relationship with Dean Acheson that he had enjoyed with Marshall and Lovett.[22]

The change in Vandenberg's relationship to the administration had no effect on the ratification of the North Atlantic Treaty, the groundwork for which had already been laid. The military assistance measure posed more difficult problems, which were aggravated by the administration's failure to work closely with Vandenberg. There was little bipartisan consultation on the terms or timing of the arms aid measure. Vandenberg was disturbed by this. "He seemed to feel that liaison between the State Department and Congress was breaking down and that legislators were being rushed into important decisions."[23] He took the lead in negotiating major changes in the arms assistance bill, changes he considered essential to prevent the bill's emasculation or defeat at the hands of reluctant senators. Vandenberg's own criticisms probably increased Republican opposition, but in large part he was here simply reflecting Republican

21 Westerfield, pp. 247-50, 256-59, 262-66, 346-50, 356-59, 364, 372. Vandenberg, pp. 519-45.
22 Vandenberg, pp. 500-506.
23 Ibid., p. 503.

thinking. Vandenberg felt the controversy over military assistance was useful in demonstrating his independence not only to an administration that had neglected bipartisan consultation but to Republican senators who had sometimes been suspicious of his participation in such consultation.

The arms assistance bill was the last important measure in which Vandenberg played a significant part. He was ill throughout the 1950 session and died in April, 1951, leaving a gap in Republican leadership that has never been filled. During the period from 1947 through 1949 he was more responsible than any other man for the degree of Republican support given to the major new foreign programs being introduced by the Truman administration. In a period when Republican isolationism was still strong and when partisan feeling on domestic issues ran high, Vandenberg's accomplishment was a massive one.

Vandenberg is famous as one of the leading architects of a successful bipartisan foreign policy. He recognized more fully than men like Connally and Taft the necessity of bipartisan consultation and cooperation, particularly in a period of divided government. Yet Vandenberg's power rested on a political base. His greatest influence was on Republican senators. The White House recognized him and worked with him primarily not because of his ability and his viewpoints but because he could command Republican votes. He never attained the breadth of Republican support in the Senate that Taft enjoyed, and his authority would have been endangered if Taft had chosen to challenge his right to be a party spokesman on foreign affairs. Yet Vandenberg drew strength in the Senate because of Republican support for him throughout the country. In 1947 and 1948 Vandenberg was frequently mentioned as a candidate for President. He was not an active candidate and believed that his vigorous advocacy of internationalism had destroyed his chances for the nomination. His position as an inactive candidate gave him maximum effectiveness in the Senate. He avoided the legislative traps that might have been set for an active candidate; yet many Republican senators were reluctant to disagree with the man who might become their party's candidate. The apostle of bipartisanship was able to achieve what he did because he was a skillful party leader.

SENATOR GEORGE AND DEMOCRATIC
LEADERSHIP ON THE COMMITTEE

Senator Walter F. George, chairman of the Foreign Relations
Committee in 1955 and 1956, had a reputation in the Senate as
a conservative, independent thinker—a reputation that increased
his influence in the field of foreign affairs. As William S.
White expressed it, "Few public men feel, in principle, a deeper pain
at the size of the public debt. In a word he is suitably 'safe'
in the fiscal sense—a circumstance that greatly forwards his influence in the Senate."[24] George had the respect of senators with
widely differing opinions, but particularly the southern conservatives, whose votes were most in doubt during the period of
George's chairmanship. Southern senators felt it politically safe
to support measures when George did, just as Taft's endorsement of a bill made many Republicans feel safe in voting for it.

George's internationalism was less firmly rooted than that of
most Democratic senators active in foreign policy roles in the
postwar period. He arrived in the Senate in 1922 as a vigorous
opponent of the League of Nations, and it required World War
II to convert him to internationalism. George's record from
1947 through 1954 was not uniform. He supported all major
foreign assistance measures except arms aid in 1949 and Point
Four in 1950. In both cases he was opposing, not the principle
of the programs, but their cost or the speed with which they
were being undertaken. He was an earnest and vocal supporter
of economy in the aid programs and one of those who urged
a speedy termination in the programs. Yet more often than not
he voted against amendments to reduce the amount of foreign
aid spending. His frequent indecisiveness probably reflected a
struggle between his own deep convictions about the need for
economy and his sense of responsibility for the success of our
foreign aid program.

Despite doubts about some aspects of the Vandenberg resolution and the North Atlantic Treaty, he voted for both. The
compromising stand that he took on collective security issues
seemed to reflect another conflict in his mind: that between the

[24] William S. White, "Senator George—Monumental, Determined," *New York
Times Magazine*, March 13, 1955, p. 42.

foreign responsibilities of the United States and the constitutional responsibilities of Congress. Senator George's most serious challenge to a policy of internationalism was likewise designed to prevent encroachments on the authority of Congress. His compromise substitute for the Bricker amendment had the primary purpose of requiring congressional approval to make executive agreements effective as internal law. While his proposal was designed to block the original Bricker amendment, which he considered dangerous, as the debate wore on, George developed a fatherly pride in his proposal, which embodied principles he believed important, and he began to fight for it. His plan was narrowly defeated.

This was the background of the man who, for two years as chairman, worked skillfully to enact the foreign programs of the Eisenhower administration. What made this cautious independent such a vigorous champion of foreign economic and military commitments? Any man who becomes chairman of the Foreign Relations Committee is subjected to influences that tend to make him a supporter of the administration. He comes into regular contact with officials of the administration and with the committee's staff, and he becomes responsible for presenting and defending foreign programs in the Senate. Moreover, the Eisenhower administration deliberately and earnestly sought to win George's loyalty. When the Democrats won control of the Eighty-fourth Congress, President Eisenhower was instrumental in persuading George to become chairman of the Foreign Relations Committee instead of the Finance Committee. Secretary of State Dulles developed the habit of visiting George's apartment for breakfast about once a week to discuss international problems, and Eisenhower telephoned George more often than he contacted other senators.[25] Since the administration lacked a Republican senator who was both powerful and completely dependable on issues of foreign policy, it was natural that it turned to George. But this did not occur until the Democrats had won a majority in Congress. The parallel with the Truman administration and Senator Vandenberg is obvious. Like Vandenberg, George was a powerful leader in foreign affairs because of his ability and experience, because his views were widely respected

25 *Ibid.*, pp. 12, 47.

in the Senate, because he was acknowledgd by members of his party as their spokesman, and because the administration recognized that it needed his assistance and consequently worked closely with him. During his two years as chairman, Senator George gave the foreign aid program more consistent support than he had in the past. In 1955 the great economizer told the Senate, "This is no time for us to begin to trim a little here and a little there," as he fought back attempts to reduce either military or economic aid.[26] In 1956 Senator George gave one of his most eloquent speeches in the Senate on behalf of the full foreign aid bill in order to prevent the destruction of this country's position as a world leader. During these two years the only reductions in foreign aid were made in committees or in the House, but not on the Senate floor.

The best example of George's skill in winning Democratic support for Eisenhower's program was his success in securing prompt and almost unanimous Senate adoption of the Formosa resolution and the Chinese Mutual Defense Treaty in 1955. Although both were measures that aroused deep misgivings among many Democrats, George made effective opposition impossible by skillfully presenting the issues and the risks involved in challenging the President during a time of crisis.

After three conferences with high administration officials, George called a meeting of the Democratic members of the Foreign Relations Committee on January 23, 1955, to discuss the Formosa resolution. The meeting revealed that many Democrats disliked the President's attempt to gain an advance political commitment of support for any action he might take to defend the offshore islands. Yet although George did not try to force the Democratic senators to give this support, the group agreed to do so. When Admiral Arthur W. Radford's testimony in committee alarmed a number of senators and led Wayne Morse to charge that the resolution would authorize "preventive war," George secured Eisenhower's commitment that only the President would order the armed forces into action in the area of the offshore islands. Making use of this statement, Senator George took the Senate floor, brushed aside all criticism of the President

[26] *New York Times,* June 1, 1955, p. 16.

for seeking congressional authority to act, asked· what alternative there was to approval of the presidential request, and demanded a prompt vote for the resolution without amendments. Although twelve Democrats voted for substitutes offered by Estes Kefauver and Herbert H. Lehman, the Formosa resolution was passed by a vote of 85-3 on January 28, 1955—just eight days after the administration had first discussed it with congressional leaders.

On October 19, 1954, before the Chinese Mutual Defense Treaty was signed, Secretary of State John Foster Dulles sent Assistant Secretary Walter S. Robertson, who had negotiated the treaty, to Georgia to consult with Senator George. Robertson gained George's approval and thereby made him a charter subscriber to the principles of the treaty and effectively foreclosed Democratic opposition. The Senate consented to ratification of the treaty by a vote of 65-6 after a minimum of debate.[27]

With a threatened attack by Communist China in the offing, one would not expect the Senate to reject the President's requests. George's major accomplishment lay in gaining the Senate's endorsement of both measures with speed and near unanimity. When the President asked for a somewhat similar broad grant of power in the Middle East two years later, Senate approval came much more slowly and with greater Democratic opposition. Only then did the full extent of George's achievement in 1955 become apparent.

Critics of Senator George charged that he became a mere puppet of the Eisenhower administration, which was able to use him effectively in stifling Democratic criticism of its foreign policy. The charge was made particularly with regard to the Formosan issue, where it had the greatest force. Douglass Cater, in an analysis of the Formosan debate in the Senate, concluded that George "must bear singular responsibility for failing to achieve that balance between advocacy and criticism which Vandenberg always sought. In these first endeavors, George, though reputedly a stubborn independent thinker, appeared amazingly amenable to Administration guidance." In contrast, "Vandenberg would not have allowed bipartisanship to serve as an excuse for

---

[27] This summary of George's role is based largely on a detailed account by the well-informed Washington correspondent Chalmers M. Roberts, in "Strong Man from the South," *Saturday Evening Post*, CCXXVII (June 25, 1955), 30, 109-12, and on a column by James Reston in the *New York Times*, April 5, 1955, p. 4.

restraining criticism by the 'loyal opposition,' which once more happened to be the Congressional majority."[28]

Senator George did not always yield to the administration so willingly. When he did resist, however, he revealed a regional bias toward financial conservatism and protectionist trade policy that was characteristic of many southern senators. For example, he resisted the administration's attempts to gain a long-term legislative commitment to foreign aid, arguing that insistence on this goal would damage bipartisan foreign policy. He also opposed the use of American funds on the Aswan Dam in Egypt because of the threat to cotton involved; his opposition contributed to the ultimate abandonment of American support for the dam. Though earlier he had usually supported reciprocal trade, in 1955 he insisted on including in the program a measure to protect textile manufacturers despite the objections of many Democrats in both houses. The influence of a regional bias upon George not only put him out of step with many of his Democratic colleagues both on the floor and in the Foreign Relations Committee but also revealed a deficiency in his creation of a responsible opposition policy.

The one occasion on which Senator George took the initiative to offer a constructive alternative in foreign affairs was his proposal in 1955 for a summit meeting. George's initiative reflected his own deep concern about growing international tension; it also represented Democratic thinking, though it did not result from any prolonged consultation between George and other Democratic senators. Senator George gave President Eisenhower greater flexibility to negotiate with both the Russian and Chinese Communists by taking a stand contrary to that of Senator Knowland and other Republican leaders. Though the administration reacted cautiously to George's suggestions, his initiative helped to pave the way for the *de facto* cease-fire in the Formosa Straits and the Geneva summit conference in July.[29]

The sources of George's authority in the Senate are not obscure. Though less effective than some leaders in behind-the-

[28] Douglass Cater, "Foreign Policy: Default of the Democrats," *Reporter*, XII (March 10, 1955), 21-23.

[29] For a description of George's activity in encouraging summit talks, see a column by Chalmers M. Roberts in the *Washington Post and Times Herald*, March 23, 1955.

scenes negotiations, George was preeminent as a debater in an age of vanishing oratory and spoke with judicious infrequency at crucial moments. More important, his vast experience and his conservative views commanded respect particularly among those senators less inclined to embrace internationalism. Furthermore, he was one of the most prominent leaders of the southern bloc, which has always been influential in the Senate. His influence, though greatest among southern Democrats, extended in some degree to most members of the Senate. He had a close working relationship with Lyndon Johnson, and he could speak for the Democratic party because no other Democrat in Congress seriously challenged his role as spokesman.

Despite his experience and the respect he commanded, it is noteworthy that George did not become recognized as the chief Democratic spokesman in foreign policy until Democratic control of Congress made him the chairman of the Foreign Relations Committee and precipitated the White House effort to make George a partner in bipartisanship. It would be a mistake to exaggerate George's influence in the Senate. His fervent speeches in behalf of foreign aid in 1955 and 1956 attracted the votes of fewer Democrats than had supported previous aid measures. It is difficult to determine whether he stemmed the tide of southern economic isolationism, but despite his unique qualifications as a southern leader, he did not succeed in reversing the tide. He could speak with greatest authority, as when he was urging a summit conference, on issues that would not come to a rollcall vote. He swung the greatest number of votes on the occasion, involving Formosa, when he was allied with a President demanding emergency support in a moment of crisis. George did not represent, but rather thwarted, those Democrats versed in foreign affairs who were both able and willing to provide constructive criticism of both the collective security and foreign aid programs presented by the administration. George, like Vandenberg, had the greatest success when he was rallying opposition party support for the President's program. He showed less skill than Vandenberg in the far more difficult task of developing a responsible challenge to those administration policies that caused misgivings in his party.

George's retirement at the end of the 1956 session left the

Democratic leadership of the Foreign Relations Committee in the hands of a small group of senators, no single one of whom was able to replace George as spokesman for the party. Theodore Francis Green, who was 89 when he succeeded George as chairman, was a veteran Democrat and an unswerving internationalist with years of personal experience in foreign affairs. Yet he labored under an obvious handicap of age and stepped down from the chairmanship after two years. An equally important liability was his failure over the years to seek a place of leadership, to speak out forcefully on international issues, and to carry the burden of defending measures through days of debate.

William Fulbright, a thoughtful and articulate senator, is experienced in foreign affairs and respected in the chamber for his knowledge of that field. There are several reasons why he did not immediately become the Democratic foreign policy leader. He has been an independent, somewhat aloof figure in the Senate, not particularly amenable to Lyndon Johnson's influence and not a part of the "inner circle" of party leadership. Perhaps because of Fulbright's critical attitude toward the Eisenhower administration, the President did not extend to him the full measure of recognition given to George through frequent personal consultation.[30]

Senator Fulbright had to share Democratic leadership in foreign affairs with several colleagues. Mike Mansfield, equally respected in the Senate, was a more skillful manipulator of votes and enjoyed a much closer working relationship with Lyndon Johnson, who chose him as party whip in 1957. Among the other Democrats on the committee were John F. Kennedy and Hubert Humphrey, both intelligent and articulate, both conscious of the need to make a record on foreign policy to assist their campaigns for the Presidency. These senators did not always speak with one voice, and even when they were in agreement, they did not speak for the whole party, which was becoming increasingly divided on foreign policy issues. Though the Democrats on the Foreign Relations Committee agreed, for example, on the need for shifting the emphasis of foreign aid away from military assistance and toward longrun development aid, they could not

[30] See Charles B. Seib and Alan L. Otten, "Fullbright: Arkansas Paradox," *Harper's*, CCXII (June, 1956), 60-66.

command unified Democratic support for this position, particularly in the House.[31]

THE COMMITTEE AS A POLITICAL INSTITUTION

The most effective leaders of the Foreign Relations Committee have been those who held a place of power and respect in their party; yet a chairman draws his authority in part from the committee itself. The Foreign Relations Committee has great prestige in the Senate. Membership on it has become increasingly popular, and consequently the caliber of its membership, particularly Democratic, is high.[32] In the postwar period the committee has been characterized by unusually united support for programs offered by both Democratic and Republican administrations.[33] Largely this unity has resulted from the members' particularly close familiarity with foreign affairs and the deliberate efforts of the committee's various chairmen.

The importance of unanimous reports by the committee was greatest in the early days of the Truman administration, when isolationist sentiment was stronger in the Senate. The committee unanimously approved Greek-Turkish aid, the European Recovery Program, the Vandenberg resolution, the North Atlantic Treaty, the Point Four Program, and—in a joint session with the Armed Services Committee—a compromise resolution on sending

[31] On September 10, 1958, for example, all of the Democratic members on the committee except Russell Long issued a statement, signed also by William Langer, urging the President to put greater stress on long-term economic aid to underdeveloped areas and less emphasis on military assistance programs. For an account of a more successful Democratic initiative in the field of foreign aid, the Monroney resolution urging that the administration study the creation of an International Developmental Association, see James A. Robinson, *The Monroney Resolution: Congressional Initiative in Foreign Policy Making* (Case Studies in Practical Politics; New York: Henry Holt and Co., 1963). For a thorough analysis of congressional initiatives in foreign policy, see James A. Robinson, *Congress and Foreign Policy-Making* (Homewood, Ill.: Dorsey Press, 1962), Chs. 1-4.

[32] Donald R. Matthews, pp. 149-50, has analyzed the change of senators from one committee assignment to another during the 1947-1957 period and has concluded from his figures that the Foreign Relations Committee was the most popular, having net gains from nearly all others and net losses to none.

[33] Matthews, pp. 166-69, concluded that during the eighty-fourth Congress the Foreign Relations Committee was the most united because its members had a higher degree of cohesion in floor votes on foreign policy matters than members of any other committee on matters in their field of specialization.

troops to Europe. Only one member of the Foreign Relations Committee, Senator George, opposed the military assistance bill in 1949, the only other major program of the Truman administration. The committee's unanimous approval of Point Four in 1950 was especially significant because this highly partisan measure passed the Senate by only one vote with the support of only eight Republicans, including three members of the committee. Measures to extend the foreign aid program during the Truman and Eisenhower administrations passed the committee either unanimously or, in later years, with only two or three dissenters. During the Eisenhower administration, the unanimous vote by the committee to confirm Charles Bohlen's nomination as ambassador to Moscow was a major factor in destroying the opposition to him. Walter George's success in winning the committee's approval of the Formosa resolution with only two dissenters helps to explain why that measure cleared the Senate so quickly.

The importance of united support by the committee for the administration's measures extended beyond voting by the members. Witnesses at hearings in behalf of administration programs were treated sympathetically by nearly all members of the committee, whose questions were usually designed to clarify a program, emphasize its advantages, or provide the witness with a chance to answer criticisms most effectively. Members of the committee were so sympathetic to the North Atlantic Treaty that two of its most vigorous opponents, Republican Senators Arthur V. Watkins and Forrest C. Donnell, sought and received reluctant permission from Chairman Connally to attend the meetings and question witnesses. Though Connally later felt that he had been mistaken in permitting Watkins and Donnell to sit with the committee, the conclusions of H. Bradford Westerfield seem to be more accurate: "Their unfriendly, probing questions helped to elucidate obscure sections of the pact and created greater confidence in the Senate that the Foreign Relations Committee was not simply rubber-stamping a project to which it had long since become committed by direct participation."[34] During the second Eisenhower administration, the Democratic committee members

34 Westerfield, p. 332.

began to play a more critical role in hearings, even on occasions when they were willing to support the measures under consideration.

In his study of the Japanese Peace Treaty, Bernard C. Cohen has emphasized the importance of united support by the Foreign Relations Committee. A bipartisan subcommittee carried the burden of the treaty, consulting regularly with John Foster Dulles (who was negotiating it), traveling widely throughout the Far East, and handling defense of the treaty on the Senate floor. Its members even negotiated with the Japanese premier on one occasion. The Foreign Relations Committee always acted as if the treaty was noncontroversial. The hearings were brief and little-publicized meetings at which members provided maximum assistance to the administration witnesses. When Senator Watkins offered a reservation that would have damaged the treaty, it was the subcommittee that negotiated an innocuous resolution on the subject.[35]

Not surprisingly, the committee was divided more often over the details of legislation than it was in voting on measures as a whole. Even so, there were relatively few questions on which the committee was sharply split; when this did occur, a partisan division often took place.

During the Truman administration there were several party votes in the Foreign Relations and Armed Services committees on Far Eastern issues, an area almost untouched by bipartisan experience. These votes included the earmarking of foreign aid funds for China in 1949 and the holding of secret hearings on General MacArthur's dismissal in 1951. Some aspects of the 1951 troops-for-Europe controversy produced party splits in the two committees, although there was unanimous agreement on a compromise resolution.

There were some partisan splits during the Eisenhower administration. An unusual one occurred when Eisenhower disagreed with Republican leaders in Congress on the terms of a resolution on the Yalta agreements. All but one Democrat on the Foreign Relations Committee voted to support the President, while all the Republicans voted against him. The Republicans on the Foreign Relations and Armed Services committees sup-

[35] Cohen, *The Political Process and Foreign Policy*, pp. 146-69.

ported the President on the Formosa resolution in 1955, but the Democrats were badly divided. The most serious partisan divisions in the committees during Eisenhower's term concerned the 1957 Middle East resolution. The Republicans stood solidly behind the President, while a majority of Democrats sought, with little success, to amend the resolution, and a narrow majority of Democrats voted against reporting it to the Senate.

What is the significance of unity or partisan conflict in the Foreign Relations Committee?[36] Do its members lead their colleagues in the Senate or simply reflect their views? A unified stand by the committee does appear to carry weight in the Senate. For senators recognize the claims of the specialist and therefore respect the opinions of committees—particularly when those committees have been able to reach agreement. From a partisan standpoint, since the senators normally look upon the members of their party on the Foreign Relations Committee as their party's leaders in this area, they are likely to provide voting support for the decisions taken by those leaders. The lines of party leadership may, however, lead outside the committee, especially in the case of the opposition party, which cannot look to the President for political leadership. At any rate, a division in the committee along party lines—notable since it is rare—increases the possibility of partisan conflict on the Senate floor.[37] As a rule, then, the stand of the Foreign Relations Committee on an issue is indicative of the stand of the whole Senate.

During the Truman administration the Republican contingent on the Foreign Relations Committee not only was ovewhelmingly internationalist but included two senators in addition to Vandenberg who commanded wide respect in this field: H. Alexander Smith and Henry Cabot Lodge. Vandenberg had been instrumental in gaining committee seats for both when a realignment of committees occurred in 1947.[38] The views and

[36] In a study of all Senate committees during the eighty-fourth Congress, Matthews, pp. 168-70, found a close correlation between the amount of agreement in a committee on a bill and its chances of passage in the Senate. Every motion which had the support of 80 percent or more members of the committee concerned passed the Senate.

[37] Cohen, pp. 203-204, has pointed out that during floor consideration of the Japanese Treaty, Democratic senators generally let Democrats on the Foreign Relations Committee speak for them in debate, but Republicans did not have such complete respect for their colleagues on the committee.

[38] Vandenberg, p. 333.

votes of Republicans on the committee had little influence on the shrinking band of Republican isolationists but did win sometimes a few and often many votes among the growing number of converts to internationalism. The 1950 election, which made another seat on the committee available to Republicans, touched off a struggle between old-guard and liberal groups in the party, which illustrates how the seniority principle can be manipulated by contending forces. Each side proposed a series of candidates of increasing seniority, until the liberal wing won with Charles H. Tobey, who was outranked in seniority only by senators who already were on the committee or did not desire to be.[39] At the start of the Eisenhower administration there was an influx of Republican party leaders—Taft, Ferguson, and Knowland—into the committee. As they left the Senate, one by one, the committee's influence among Republicans declined, since no senators of equal party stature replaced them. Hence, the unity among Republicans on the committee and the growing unity among Senate Republicans were not factors of cause and effect but were coincident results of a Republican administration and the near disappearance of isolationists from the Senate chamber.[40]

During the Truman administration the Democrats on the committee were internationalists, who maintained a nearly unanimous record of support for the President's program. The presence of a few Democratic isolationists on the committee would have been an obvious embarrassment and possibly a significant handicap to the President. Nevertheless, Democratic unity in the Senate resulted primarily from a combination of conviction and loyalty to the administration. The example set by Democrats on the committee was of lesser importance.

Until the Eisenhower administration, Democratic members of the committee were chosen largely on the basis of seniority. In 1949, for example, the Democrats were able to add five members to the committee, and the leadership chose—out of twelve who applied—the five with the greatest seniority. The year 1953

[39] Willard Shelton, "Civil War in the G.O.P.," *Nation*, CLXXII (Jan. 27, 1951), 75-76.

[40] For a more detailed account of personnel changes on the committee, see David N. Farnsworth, *The Senate Committee on Foreign Relations* (Illinois Studies in the Social Sciences, Vol. 49; Urbana: University of Illinois Press, 1961), pp. 16-31. This is a useful account of the committee and its role in major foreign policy issues during the period 1947-1956.

marked the beginning of Lyndon Johnson's policy of subordinating seniority to other factors in the choice of all committee members. At that time the Democrats selected two junior senators who were vigorous and independent internationalists—Hubert Humphrey and Mike Mansfield. Humphrey was chosen at the request of President Truman and Secretary of State Acheson.[41] Senator Johnson's new technique strengthened his hand as party leader, and he used it to provide the committee with Democratic membership of the highest caliber.[42] The Democratic contingent on the committee continued to be strongly internationalist, but the party showed no hesitancy in picking Russell Long in 1956, despite his record of opposition to foreign aid.

Although the internationalist Democrats on the committee held the line against reductions in President Eisenhower's foreign aid program, in the Senate itself there were significant defections among Democrats. In this respect the leadership of of committee Democrats appeared weaker. Most of the Democrats on the Foreign Relations Committee worked to revise the aid program in order to put more emphasis on long-term economic development, and several of them led the criticism of the "blank check" military authority that the President sought in the Far East and the Middle East. In these cases also, the Democrats in the Senate failed to follow those on the committee with consistent unity. After Senator George's departure, Democratic leadership on the Foreign Relations Committee proved unable to unite the party either in support of those administration proposals it favored or of the alternatives it offered to other administration programs.

OTHER COMMITTEES DEALING WITH FOREIGN POLICY

Two other committees that have frequently shared the responsibility for acting on international legislation are the Appropriations and the Armed Services committees. The former has had

[41] Charles E. Gilbert, "Problems of a Senator: A Study of Legislative Behavior" (Unpublished Ph.D. dissertation, Northwestern University, 1955), pp. 288-89.

[42] During the eightieth through the eighty-fourth Congresses the average new member of the Foreign Relations Committee, from either party, had a little over eight years seniority. Matthews, pp. 152-53.

to approve the annual appropriations for foreign aid after authorization of funds by the Foreign Relations Committee and the Senate. From 1949 through 1954 the Armed Services Committee studied and approved foreign assistance measures either in concert with the Foreign Relations Committee or immediately after its deliberations. It has also met jointly with the Foreign Relations Committee to consider collective security measures.

While the members of these committees tended to follow the lead of the Foreign Relations Committee, they usually supported foreign military and economic programs in the Senate with less unity and consistency than did members of the Foreign Relations Committee. Powerful leaders in both parties played important roles on both committees, and their influence helps to explain the degree of support provided by the committees for both administrations as well as the support given by the Senate to the committees' decisions.

On questions of foreign aid the Senate Appropriations Committee has usually taken a quite different stand from the House committee. During the early years of the Truman administration and throughout the Eisenhower administration, the Senate committee repeatedly restored large proportions of funds cut by the House committee, cuts far below the levels already authorized by Congress. Only in the later Truman years did the Senate committee make cuts equal to or exceeding those made in the House. Since information about voting in the Senate Appropriations Committee is scarce, any explanation of the committee's position must rest on speculation. A comparison of voting in the Senate by members serving on the committee during both administrations does not suggest that turnover in membership or changes in views increased the support for appropriation requests during the Eisenhower administration as compared with the later years of Truman. The proportion of senators devoted to economy remained rather consistent during both administrations.

The leadership of the Appropriations Committee seems to have been particularly decisive in creating its record on foreign aid.[43] During the Truman administration the ranking Democrat and

---

[43] The chairman and ranking members of the committee have a greater opportunity to influence foreign aid appropriations because these are considered by the whole committee rather than by a subcommittee as most appropriations are.

later chairman was Kenneth D. McKellar. McKellar was initially hostile to the Greek-Turkish aid program and the Marshall Plan. Though he subsequently voted consistently for foreign aid measures on the floor, he generally spoke and voted in the committee for reductions in funds. Because of his age and illness and perhaps because he represented a minority viewpoint among Democrats, McKellar did not seek to use his authority as chairman to curtail drastically foreign aid programs. Yet his reluctance may have been one reason why the committee's support for Truman's aid measures diminished. Senator Carl Hayden became ranking Democrat in 1953 and chairman in 1955. He consistently voted in the Senate to supply the funds requested for foreign aid by both Truman and Eisenhower. Since Hayden was regarded as one of the most influential men in the Senate, particularly in its inner councils, it seems accurate to give him some credit for the growing support provided by the committee to the Eisenhower administration. During both administrations, Hayden's steadfast endorsement of massive appropriations was a factor in providing Democratic votes in the Senate for foreign aid. In addition, Lyndon Johnson joined the committee in 1956 to provide an important link between it and the party leadership.

The Appropriations Committee in recent years has included an unusually high proportion of Republican party leaders. Styles Bridges was the ranking Republican and occasionally chairman throughout the period under study. Leverett Saltonstall was a member during the whole period, and Kenneth Wherry, Homer Ferguson, and William Knowland served until they left the Senate. During the Truman administration, particularly its later years, these leaders frequently criticized the administration of foreign aid and often voted for reductions in aid spending (though less frequently in the case of Saltonstall). Bridges, Saltonstall, Ferguson, and Knowland, all of whom served after 1952, together with Everett Dirksen who was on the committee from 1953 through 1958, provided strong support for most or all aspects of Eisenhower's aid program. Their efforts seem to have been largely responsible for the increasing generosity of the Appropriations Committee. In addition, they were in an excellent position to encourage Republican votes in the Senate for the appropriations agreed upon in the committee. As ranking Republican and as chairman of the committee in 1953-1954, Senator Bridges held a particularly crucial post. He was also a veteran party leader and became chairman of the Policy Committee in 1955.[44]

For several years after the addition of military assistance to the foreign aid program, the Armed Services Committee zealously guarded its right to share in consideration of the measure before floor action. It seldom made any changes in the foreign aid authorization and abandoned its claim in 1955. In the case of collective security commitments jointly reviewed by the Foreign Relations and the Armed Services committees, there was little difference in voting patterns of the two groups. Leadership again appears to be the key to understanding this committee. Senator Bridges and (from 1951) Senator Saltonstall were its ranking Republicans, and their consistent support of Eisenhower's collective security programs contributed to the unity of Republicans on the committee.

Democratic leadership on the committee was divided. Millard Tydings, ranking Democrat and then chairman through 1950, had a consistently internationalist record and shared responsibility with Tom Connally for managing the first two annual military assistance bills. Richard Russell, who succeeded Tydings as chairman, supported President Truman's collective security measures, worked closely with Connally on the troops-for-Europe resolution, and performed a major service as chairman of the MacArthur hearings. He voted for most of Truman's foreign aid programs but frequently backed amendments to reduce the cost. During the Eisenhower administration he became a strong critic of foreign aid on grounds of economy and voted against most of the aid measures. As long as his colleague from Georgia, Senator George, was in the Senate, Russell seemed unwilling to assume the leadership of the economy bloc. He did not try to use his position as chairman of the committee to delay or drastically curtail military assistance measures; in fact it was under his chairmanship in 1955 that the committee stopped reviewing such legislation. After George's retirement, Russell began to play a more important role, being most prominent during Senate con-

[44] See chapter 4 for a further analysis of Bridges' role.

sideration of the Middle East resolution. Russell strongly criticized this measure, and after his amendment to eliminate the
economic and military aid section of the measure was defeated,
he voted against the entire resolution. His opposition probably
had something to do with the fact that fourteen southerners voted
for his amendment and ten voted against the resolution. Russell's
power and prestige in the Senate made him a natural leader for
the growing tide of southern opposition to foreign economic programs.[45] The second-ranking Democratic member, Harry Byrd,
who supported economy and opposed foreign aid, provided powerful support for Russell. On the other hand during the Eisenhower administration, Senator Lyndon Johnson provided leadership on the committee for those Democrats who supported Republican as well as Democratic foreign programs.

One further aspect of foreign policy, reciprocal trade legislation, comes under the jurisdiction of the Finance Committee.
Democratic members of this committee during the period were
almost entirely sympathetic to reciprocal trade legislation. During the Truman administration two veterans in foreign affairs,
Walter George and Tom Connally, served as the top-ranking
Democrats on the committee and led the defense of the President's trade program. The Republicans on the committee, led
by Eugene Millikin and Robert A. Taft, consistently sought extensive revisions to provide more protection for American industry. Voting in the committee therefore closely followed party
lines, and there was a similar voting pattern in the Senate. During the Eisenhower administration, Harry Byrd, who became
chairman in 1955, continued to support reciprocal trade legislation, with only limited wavering among Democratic committee
members; however, the Democratic support for the committee's
decisions declined. Although there were no Republican leaders
on the committee after 1956, there was growing support among
Republicans on and off the committee for the Eisenhower reciprocal trade program. Throughout the period the Finance
Committee lacked the unity characteristic of the Foreign Relations Committee. When leadership was most evident on the
Finance Committee, it was sharply partisan.

[45] Russell is also the second-ranking Democrat on the Appropriations Committee.

The Senate Judiciary Committee, which seldom has a chance to exert any influence on foreign policy, did so in 1953 when it favorably reported the Bricker amendment by a vote of 9-5. In contrast to the membership of other committees involved with foreign affairs, a minority of the Judiciary Committee's members had records of support for American economic and military programs abroad.[46] Moreover, the small extreme-isolationist wing of the Republican party was strongly represented by William E. Jenner, Herman Welker, and William Langer, while there was only one member—Alexander Wiley—who was well versed in international affairs.[47] At that time the committee did not contain a single Democratic or Republican leader, nor is there any evidence that party leaders sought to prevent the committee's endorsement of the Bricker amendment. The Republican chairman and the ranking Democrat on the Judiciary Committee were William Langer and Pat McCarran, respectively, two senators notably unsusceptible to guidance and frequently out of step with a majority of their parties. Nevertheless, Senator Langer, a proponent of the Bricker amendment, voted in committee against reporting it because he thought further attempts should be made to draft a version acceptable to the administration. Instead the committee voted to revise the Bricker amendment and made it even more unacceptable to the administration. Had the committee defeated the entire amendment, it would never have reached the Senate floor. Had the committee softened the Bricker amendment or at least not made it stronger, the measure might have passed the Senate in the absence of the determined opposition that developed to the committee's version.[48]

---

[46] These were Democrats Thomas C. Hennings, Harley M. Kilgore, Estes Kefauver, and Republican Alexander Wiley, all of whom voted against the Bricker amendment, and Democrats Pat McCarran, James O. Eastland, and Republican Robert C. Hendrickson, who voted for it. William Langer also voted against it.

[47] One other member of the committee, however, Thomas C. Hennings, was an expert in constitutional law who skillfully led the forces in the Senate opposed to any amendment.

[48] Although the minority report of the Judiciary Committee recommended further consideration by the Foreign Relations Committee and several members of the latter committee favored such action, no steps were taken. Alexander Wiley, a signer of the minority report and chairman of the Foreign Relations Committee, publicly suggested that his group reconsider the measure but probably did not attempt to force the issue because the Judiciary Committee's jurisdiction over constitutional amendments was clearly established under Senate rules.

COMMITTEE LEADERSHIP

A high level of bipartisanship has characterized decisions of the Foreign Relations Committee and to a lesser extent the other committees dealing with foreign affairs. Nevertheless, in the absence of strong policy committees or caucuses, these committees and their chairmen are important sources of political leadership in the Senate. In foreign policy, personal leadership has come from committee members more often than from elective party leaders, but actually it might be more accurate to say that there is a partnership between the top party and committee leaders. For in committees along with such leaders as Arthur Vandenberg, Walter George, and Richard Russell have served elected party leaders like Robert Taft, William Knowland, and Lyndon Johnson.

Political leadership is most effective when there is unity of purpose among the top party and committee chiefs, such as the Democrats enjoyed during the Truman administration and the Republicans lacked in the early Eisenhower years. When the leadership is divided on questions of policy, influence becomes a matter of personal ability and of viewpoint rather than of party rank. Generally, a man of ability will not exercise commensurate power, however, unless he holds party or committee posts. While leadership in the Senate follows such a variety of patterns that generalization about it must be limited, on some issues certain senators will follow particular leaders. Most of the time they will follow members of their own party, particularly those holding party or committee posts.

The influence of senatorial leadership is heavily dependent on the role of the president. Senate leaders have commanded support most successfully from both the administration and the opposition parties when they spoke in behalf of the President's program. A senator, as the example of Knowland demonstrates, is least successful when he challenges the President of his own party. The experience of men as diverse as Taft and Fulbright shows the difficulties an opposition leader faces in persuading his party to support alternates to the President's foreign policies. Thus, a survey of political leadership is not complete without an inquiry into the techniques of presidential leadership in the Senate.

The conduct and care of international affairs is a special preserve of the President. One consequence of this situation is the more direct, personal involvement of the President in executive-legislative relations.

—HOLBERT N. CARROLL

The most important "pressure" on us in this office is Dwight David Eisenhower and his program. . . . It's not a matter of their calling us up or anything—we know what the White House wants and we don't have to be told.

—Republican senator's assistant
quoted by DONALD R. MATTHEWS

7

PRESIDENTIAL LEADERSHIP AND THE SENATE

DURING THE LAST QUARTER CENTURY THE PRESIDENT'S RESPONSIbility for initiating and promoting legislation has steadily grown, nowhere more than in the field of foreign affairs. The evidence in Chapters 2 and 3 shows that a President can normally depend on greater support for his foreign programs from senators in his own party than from those in the opposition. It remains necessary to demonstrate what presidential techniques are most valuable in augmenting partisan support and how these can be combined with the techniques needed to develop bipartisan support for the President's program.

There has been congressional resistance to the growth of presidential authority in foreign affairs, as is shown by the controversies over troops for Europe and the Bricker amendment. Sometimes, however, it has been difficult to distinguish between partisan conflicts and disputes between the two branches of government. Democratic senators, for example, may hold the middle ground in a conflict between a Democratic President and Republican senators. Those who criticize the growth of the President's responsibility in foreign affairs are fighting a rearguard action, for world events have forced Congress to recognize, however reluctantly, the necessity for the President's authority. Consequently the President has acquired important leverage for dealing with senators of both his own party and the opposition.

Other studies have emphasized that "the hard core of a president's support in the Senate comes from his own party," and that the initiatives of the President make possible a higher degree of unity in his party than the opposition is usually able to achieve.[1] There are reasons why this should be particularly true for foreign programs of the President. A senator belonging to the administration party usually wants to support those measures most critical to the prestige of the President and the success of the administration. In the postwar period a great proportion of these high-priority measures have dealt with foreign affairs. Willingness to support a program for economic aid or collective security is conditioned frequently on confidence in those who will administer the program; this confidence is often deeply rooted in partisan convictions. In addition to the factors that induce support for his party leader, a member of the administration party shares with other senators a strong disposition to grant what the President requests abroad, particularly in time of emergency.

The President can frequently generate bipartisan support because senators of both parties are reluctant to demonstrate serious disunity to either our allies or opponents abroad and are reluctant to undermine international commitments often already made by the President in public. Moreover, the opposition party, lacking the information, the staff, and the machinery to construct alternative foreign policies, has little choice except support of the

[1] Matthews, *U.S. Senators and Their World*, p. 145. Truman, *The Congressional Party*, pp. 289-90.

President. The reasons why the President often must seek bipartisan support, already discussed in Chapter 1, can be briefly summarized: The administration party has often had only a small majority or none at all in Congress; party unity has never been dependable; and some policies require extraordinary majorities to comply with the Constitution or to maximize their impact abroad.

THE PRESIDENT AND PARTY LEADERS

Presidential leadership may be divided into four categories: cooperation with party leaders in Congress, bipartisan consultation, private appeals to individual congressmen, and appeals to public opinion calculated to generate congressional support. For a variety of important reasons, the President must rely primarily on his party's leadership in dealing with Congress. David Truman has stated the case most cogently: "Relations with the leaders of the Congressional party can be supplemented, as they often have been, but no substitutes have appeared on which he can rely with equal confidence. To the degree that the mechanism of the Congressional party is relied upon, however, it must be taken as it is, with the leaders it has produced. For a President to attempt to act directly as the leader of the Congressional party almost certainly would be to destroy, for the time being, this valuable if variable, governing instrument."[2]

From time to time the President will find it necessary to consult committee leaders, especially in questions of foreign affairs. Yet, as Matthews points out, the President is concerned with a total program, while the committee leaders are specialists—knowledgeable, influential, and perhaps sympathetic concerning only a limited portion of the presidential program.[3] The President must deal with the generalists in Congress, usually the party leaders. He must cooperate closely with the party leaders in order to demonstrate his support for them, support that they need in order to promote his program most effectively.

Moreover, the President is forced to deal with party leaders

[2] Truman, p. 298.
[3] Matthews, p. 142.

by the pressure of time. As David Truman has said, "In the thundering crises that are the normal lot of Presidents in times when 'normalcy' exists only in the past, the clock provides no hours for the cultivation of rank-and-file legislators which direct leadership of the Congress would require."[4] Even in the relatively few years since Franklin Roosevelt's administration, the international burdens of the Presidency have cut deeply into the time available for legislative leadership. Roosevelt estimated that he averaged "three to four hours a day spent on congressional relations during the session."[5] Seldom could a President in the 1950s spare so much time to Congress. Yet even Roosevelt found his day too crowded for developing many contacts with the rank-and-file.[6]

There are other reasons why the President concentrates attention on the party leaders and occasionally on the committee leaders. These are the best informed men on Capitol Hill, the men most capable of judging the political climate in Congress and weighing the prospects for legislation, and these are men familiar enough with the President to express their judgments frankly. Finally, when the President directs his appeals for legislation through the party leaders, he avoids the possibility that personal appeals will lose their impact through overuse.[7]

The major instrument of cooperation between the President and congressional leaders of his party has been the weekly legislative conference. Started by Franklin Roosevelt, the conferences were continued by Truman and Eisenhower and have become an institution that no successor would likely abandon. Political scientists have often proposed that some larger executive-legislative cabinet be instituted. The "Big Four" meetings have proved their usefulness through durability, however, and their value lies in the flexibility and informality of the arrangement.

[4] Truman, p. 297.

[5] Arthur M. Schlesinger, Jr., *The Age of Roosevelt*, Vol. II: *The Coming of the New Deal* (Boston: Houghton Mifflin Co., 1958), p. 554.

[6] James M. Burns, *Roosevelt: The Lion and the Fox* (New York: Harcourt, Brace, and Co., 1956), pp. 348-50. Early in his first term President Eisenhower held a series of luncheons to which all members of the Senate and House were individually invited. These were completely social affairs designed to cultivate friendly relations with members of Congress, and it may be doubted that they served any significant purpose. Donovan, *Eisenhower*, p. 85.

[7] Truman, p. 298. Matthews, p. 142.

Committee leaders or other important members of Congress are sometimes included on an *ad hoc* basis, or separate large-scale conferences may be called to discuss major legislation, but the party leaders remain the regular core of presidential-congressional relations.[8] The success of these meetings depends on the candor with which legislative problems can be discussed and the mutual trust between the President and congressional leaders. There were reports that Senator Knowland sometimes used the meetings for lengthy speeches expounding his views, while Dirksen was more successful in explaining senatorial viewpoints and evaluating legislative prospects for the President.[9]

The success of presidential cooperation with party leaders obviously depends in large part on the skill and the viewpoints of these leaders. The President has no choice of Senate leaders; he must work with those elected by the senators in his party. It is true that Franklin Roosevelt played a quiet role in Alben Barkley's election as majority leader.[10] Eisenhower, however, instructed administration officials to refrain from expressing any views on a successor to Robert A. Taft.[11] If the senatorial party has chosen a leader who lacks the skills necessary for maximum effectiveness, there is little the President can do to remedy the situation. When the President disagrees sharply with the party leader in the Senate, as was often true with Eisenhower and Knowland, he is similarly handicapped. The President can try to compromise or can bypass him and work with other leading senators, but the risks of trying to force a party leader's removal are too great to make such a gamble worthwhile.

Since, with a few exceptions, the details of presidential-congressional conferences are not made public, the success of presidential endeavors must be judged by results. The success of

8 When the President's party controls Congress, the "Big Four" usually consist of the Vice President, the Speaker of the House, and the majority floor leaders in both houses. When the opposition party controls Congress, the minority floor leaders in both houses and the minority whip in the House attend along with the Vice President. Of course, other congressional leaders may be included rather regularly.

9 *Time,* LXXIII (June 8, 1959), 15-18.

10 Burns, *Roosevelt,* pp. 309-10.

11 Donovan, p. 112. Note, however, Eisenhower's role in first discouraging and later permitting Charles Halleck's efforts to succeed Joe Martin as minority leader in the House. *Time,* LXXIII (June 8, 1959), 17.

President Truman's foreign programs in Congress and the outward appearances of his relations with Democratic congressional leaders suggest that these relations were smooth. Democratic leaders in the Senate were all men in sympathy with the President's foreign program. Seldom were they forced to report to the White House Democratic divisions on foreign policy sufficiently great to endanger the legislative program. Despite occasional lapses in coordination, the Truman administration's record was a remarkable demonstration of skillful and harmonious relations between the President and senatorial leaders.

The greater friction between President Eisenhower and his senatorial leaders resulted not only from the firmness of Senator Knowland's dissents but from serious divisions among Republican senators during the early years of the administration. White House conferences were not sufficient to eliminate the open opposition of Knowland and Bridges to those parts of the aid program applying to countries like India and Yugoslavia. The differences between the President and Taft and other Republican leaders on the terms of the Yalta resolution were clearly revealed and the likelihood of open conflict became apparent at two White House legislative conferences, one before and one after the President's formal request to Congress. Later in 1953, when Senate Republican leaders, particularly Knowland, planned to offer an appropriations rider that would cut off all United States funds for the U.N. if Communist China were admitted, Eisenhower persuaded them to agree upon a resolution simply expressing opposition to the admission of Communist China.[12]

There were occasions when Republican congressional leaders persuaded President Eisenhower to make substantial modifications in his foreign programs. This was true in 1954, when he first sought a three-year extension of the reciprocal trade program and then agreed to a one-year extension. It was true again in 1958 when he yielded to the demands of Knowland and Bridges and abandoned his support for an amendment facilitating foreign aid to certain Communist countries. Despite instances to the contrary, the regular legislative conferences at the White House seem to have played a part in the steady growth

12 Donovan, pp. 148-53, 48-49, 133-36.

of Republican support for most aspects of Eisenhower's foreign program.

The best example of extended efforts to compromise a serious difference between the administration and Republican senators is the Bricker amendment, one of the most seriously divisive issues encountered by the party during Eisenhower's administration. The Republican leaders recognized the dangers of disunity, sought persistently to bridge the gap, and appeared successful in uniting the party behind a compromise until Senator Walter George's alternative produced a new division.

The President had at first not been familiar with the technicalities of the measure and only gradually began to commit himself against it in the early months of 1953. When Eisenhower realized that the Status of Forces Treaty, with which he was familiar, would be barred by the Bricker amendment, his opposition to the latter sharpened; however, the administration was itself divided on the amendment. Secretary of State Dulles, after first suggesting that a substitute rather than a mere revision of Bricker's proposal be sought, came increasingly to believe that an effective compromise was impossible and that the Bricker amendment could and should be defeated. Vice President Nixon and Attorney General Brownell, on the other hand, favored continued efforts toward a compromise, for fear that an outright defeat of the amendment would seriously split the Republican party. President Eisenhower agreed with the views of Nixon and Brownell. Republicans in the Senate likewise favored finding a compromise that would not divide the party.[13]

As a result, the administration engaged in repeated negotiations with Republican senatorial leaders, with Senator John W. Bricker, and eventually with Democratic Senators Walter F. George and Lyndon Johnson, meetings in which the President often participated. These talks led to the Knowland compromise, which the President publicly endorsed, and a year later to the Knowland-Ferguson compromise, which the Republican senatorial leaders said was acceptable to the administration. Neither was finally enacted. The administration's prolonged efforts at compromise may have encouraged some Republicans to vote against the more stringent versions of the Bricker amend-

13 *Ibid.*, pp. 231-38.

ment, but they may also have reduced the resistance of those senators in both parties who opposed any amendment.

BIPARTISAN CONSULTATION

Bipartisanship is a term with many meanings.[14] It is defined here simply as consultation between the administration and leaders of the opposition party in Congress. Primarily we are concerned with those instances in which the President has sought to win maximum support for a foreign program by directing consultations with congressional leaders in advance of presenting the program to Congress. The need for such consultation is greatest when the opposition party controls Congress or when foreign policy legislation, for either constitutional or political reasons, requires an extraordinary majority.

Though the advantages of bipartisan consultation are often so great as to make it a necessity, there are also disadvantages from the viewpoint of the administration. It is sometimes difficult to find an opposition leader who not only is willing to work closely with the administration but also commands broad support in his own party.[15] Senators with the viewpoint and the stature of Arthur Vandenberg or Walter George are not always available. Both during and after Vandenberg's period of active leadership, the Democratic administration was perplexed about how much effort should be made to include Senator Taft in consultations. The administration also runs the risk that senators critical of its policies will use the information gained through advance consultation as ammunition for attacks on these policies. If the administration practices "real" consultation and invites suggestions for change before the framing of a policy has been completed, it must decide how to handle proposed changes that it considers unwise. Yet the opposition is more likely to be critical when consultation degenerates into a briefing on already completed policy. A practical argument against bipartisan consultation is that high officials in the administration and senators both are often too busy to engage in the con-

---

[14] See Westerfield, *Foreign Policy and Party Politics*, pp. 12-13. Crabb, *Bipartisan Foreign Policy*, pp. 156-72.

[15] Dean Acheson, *A Citizen Looks at Congress* (New York: Harper & Brothers, 1957), p. 72.

tinuing consultation that might be the most productive.[16] The administration therefore has tended to use bipartisan consultation only when forced to, usually to conciliate an opposition majority in Congress.

The Vandenberg resolution, which passed the Senate in 1948, was the result of prolonged talks between Senator Vandenberg and Under Secretary of State Robert A. Lovett. For three or four weeks the two met at frequent intervals to draft the resolution, with assistance from the State Department and Foreign Relations Committee staffs. Late in the drafting stage, the members of that committee and John Foster Dulles were consulted. The result was a resolution that satisfied the administration's needs but was drafted largely by Vandenberg with an eye to what the Senate would accept. The resolution passed the Senate with only four dissenting votes.[17] The "unusual and happy" relations between Lovett and Vandenberg, two close friends, illustrates the importance of personal factors in successful consultation between the two branches. "Their work together," in Dean Acheson's words, "produced what neither could have accomplished separately."[18]

The Japanese Peace Treaty presents an unusual example of bipartisan cooperation because the treaty's negotiator, John Foster Dulles, was a Republican serving in a Democratic administration. Dulles' performance was a model of consultation. In addition to numerous informal contacts with key senators, during negotiations Dulles held nine sessions with the Subcommittee on Far Eastern Affairs and one with the full Foreign Relations Committee. He always met with the senators soon after returning from his trips abroad. By this technique of participation he was in effect, committing the members to support the treaty. He also kept in touch with Taft, Millikin, and other important Republican leaders, and even consulted the House Foreign Affairs Committee, though it had no jurisdiction over treaties. He incorporated some suggestions from senators

---

[16] Acheson, *ibid.*, p. 65, has estimated that as Secretary of State he spent about one-sixth of his working hours in Washington testifying before congressional committees, meeting with congressional leaders, and preparing for such meetings.

[17] Vandenberg, *The Private Papers of Senator Vandenberg*, pp. 404-408.

[18] Acheson, *A Citizen Looks at Congress*, p. 73.

in the text of the treaty; certain financial and military provisions of the treaty, for example, were clearly designed to satisfy Republican viewpoints. He cooperated with members of the subcommittee in obtaining formal public assurance from the Japanese premier that Japan would not recognize or conduct treaty negotiations with Communist China.

Dulles' skill and persistence in bipartisan consultation were certainly instrumental in obtaining senatorial support for the Japanese treaty with a minimum of opposition. Dulles had full authority to act for the President, and in this case presidential participation in consultations was unnecessary. In fact, on one occasion, Truman through ignorance hindered the treaty's progress with a public statement implying that the Senate would probably move slowly in approving the treaty when in fact it was the Defense Department that was urging delay in ratification while it sought quick Japanese agreement for stationing American troops in Japan.[19]

The drafting of the North Atlantic Treaty provides an example of bipartisan consultation that is important because it shows what intensive collaboration is possible. The preliminary talks on NATO among Western nations began in July, 1948, and led to an agreed statement of policy by the working group in September. There was a lull in the negotiations during the American electoral campaign and while the various governments were reaching a decision to negotiate a formal treaty. Work on drafting the pact was resumed in early December and was nearly completed by the end of January.[20]

Frequent consultations with senators apparently began in December, and Lovett kept in daily telephone contact with Connally and Vandenberg. Some senators had seen a draft of the pact by mid January. When Marshall and Lovett resigned and Dean Acheson became Secretary of State in early January, however, liaison with members of the committee was interrupted. Senator Tom Connally has said that Acheson did not consult the Foreign Relations Committee until Connally insisted on it in early February. At that time, Connally and

---

[19] Cohen, *The Political Process and Foreign Policy*, pp. 145-69, 235-50.
[20] Harry S. Truman, *Memoirs*, Vol. II: *Years of Trial and Hope* (Garden City, N.Y.: Doubleday and Co., 1956), pp. 247-50. Stephen K. Bailey and Howard D. Samuel, *Congress at Work* (New York: Henry Holt and Co., 1952), p. 387.

Vandenberg had at least two discussions with Acheson. On February 18 and March 8, Acheson held long meetings with the full committee; its members gave informal approval to the treaty at the second meeting. The agreed text was released on March 18 and the treaty was signed on April 4.[21]

The senators had a hand in rewriting part of Article 5 of the treaty, which provided for action by other NATO members in case of an armed attack on any member. The draft offered by the European countries said that each nation would "take military and other action forthwith." Lovett, sensitive to senatorial thinking, suggested changing the conjunction: "take military or other action forthwith." Vandenberg and Connally suggested simply the words, "take action forthwith," and Acheson proposed this language to the other nations. The senators on the committee then decided that the Senate would accept firmer wording. Connally proposed the statement that each nation would take "such measures as it may deem necessary." The committee as a whole then agreed upon the principle of the final language, that each nation would take "such action as it deems necessary, including the use of armed force." The committee also succeeded in adding to Article 11 of the pact the statement, "This treaty shall be ratified and its provisions carried out by the Parties in accordance with their respective constitutional processes."[22]

These detailed changes were important for two reasons: They facilitated ratification by meeting the particular anxieties of many senators, and the committee's members who helped to draft them gained a sense of responsibility for ratification. The negotiations were completely bipartisan; in this case, Vandenberg and Connally seem to have shown an equal sensitivity to senatorial opinion.

Other instances of successful bipartisanship were the consultations between the Eisenhower administration and Senator George about the Chinese Mutual Defense Treaty and the Formosa resolution and those between the Truman administration and Senator Vandenberg about the Marshall Plan. Though

[21] Bailey and Samuel, pp. 387-89. Connally, *My Name is Tom Connally*, pp. 332-33. *New York Times*, January 13, 1949, p. 8.
[22] Vandenberg, p. 476. Report of the Committee on Foreign Relations on Exec. L, Exec. Report 8, 81st Cong., 1st sess., p. 3.

in each case the discussions undoubtedly resulted in greater Senate backing of the measures, they otherwise did not exhibit any noteworthy feature of bipartisanship. The quickness with which the Greek-Turkish situation developed did not allow any extensive discussion of possible measures; nevertheless, two meetings between administration and senatorial leaders were held a few days before the aid program to Greece was presented to Congress, and the briefings by Truman, Marshall, and Acheson made a great impression upon the congressional leaders. Here again, consultation, even though hurried, materially improved Senate reception of the program.[23]

There are numerous reasons why bipartisan cooperation has often broken down. The Point Four Program, like the Marshall Plan, was introduced without any significant advance consultation—it was a part of President Truman's 1949 inaugural address. Not only was the program suddenly thrust upon Congress, it was later handled ineptly. Before the measure reached the floor of Congress, there was some consultation with Saltonstall and Herter, which led to the addition of provisions to encourage private investment in underdeveloped countries. Yet the administration failed to consult Senator Taft and other important Republican leaders, and failed to keep Democratic leaders informed about the compromise it had worked out with Saltonstall and Herter.

A problem of transition may have hindered bipartisan consultation with regard to the Middle East resolution in 1957. The close relations between the administration and the chairman of the Foreign Relations Committee ended when Senator George retired at the end of the 1956 session. The administration evidently felt that his successor, Theodore F. Green, either lacked comparable influence or would not be sympathetic to partnership with the administration. In any case, senators first learned about the proposed Middle East resolution through the press. On January 1 the administration held a bipartisan briefing on the proposal, but congressional leaders later complained that the proposal was presented on a take-it-or-leave-it basis that provided no opportunity for suggestions. Only later, when the ques-

---

[23] Truman, *Memoirs*, II, 99-105. Joseph M. Jones, *The Fifteen Weeks* (New York: Viking Press, 1955), pp. 3-8, 75-77, 129-42, 168-69.

tion of U.N. sanctions against Israel became involved, were legislative leaders invited to a meeting with the President that satisfied the Democrats' definition of "consultation." Surprisingly, the administration failed to consult Senator George in advance on the substance of the proposal and to seek his advice on its handling in Congress. Though George had retired, he was just assuming a new post in the State Department as a special consultant on NATO problems and might easily have been used to smooth the way for the Middle East resolution. After the Senate began consideration of the resolution, George carefully avoided any action that might be construed as an effort to influence senatorial views. Earlier and more thorough consultation with Democratic leaders might well have paved the way for speedier passage of the resolution with fewer dissenting votes.

President Eisenhower regularly held bipartisan congressional meetings prior to the introduction of his annual foreign aid measures. Apparently these meetings did not assist significantly in gaining passage of the programs. For the most part they were no more than briefing sessions; the congressional leaders had little opportunity to offer suggestions or propose shifts in emphasis of the program. Democratic leaders, for example, were never able to make an effective presentation of their case for greater emphasis on economic aid to underdeveloped areas. Advance briefings on the continuation of existing programs do not seem to be a very effective means of presidential leadership.

By and large it is true to say that prior bipartisan consultation has been limited to certain foreign policies requiring legislative authorization. It has had little real applicability to diplomatic or military decisions outside the legislative sphere. When President Truman sent American forces to repel the invasion of South Korea, congressional leaders of both parties were informed only after the decision had been made.[24] President Eisenhower informed bipartisan congressional leaders that he planned to send troops to Lebanon shortly before carrying out his decision.[25] In neither case did the leaders have any alternative but acquiescence.

In 1954, during the prolonged debate in the administration over American intervention in the Indochina war, congressional

24 Truman, *Memoirs*, II, 333-43.
25 Fletcher Knebel, "Day of Decision," *Look*, XXII (Sept. 16, 1958), 17-19.

leaders were consulted privately. When Secretary of State Dulles, in a major speech on March 29, urged "united action" by the Western powers to prevent Communist conquest of Indochina, some Democratic leaders complained that they had not been consulted by the administration. On April 3, however, a bipartisan group of eight congressional leaders were given a direct voice in administration policy. Secretary Dulles and Admiral Arthur W. Radford met secretly with the leaders to seek their views on a joint congressional resolution to permit the use of naval and air forces in Indochina. The plan then was to use American carrier-based planes in an air assault designed to save the besieged French fortress of Dien Bien Phu in Indochina. Congressional questioning brought out that the proposal did not have the support of other members of the Joint Chiefs of Staff and that the other Western powers had not been consulted. The congressional leaders advised Dulles to get support from our allies before seeking congressional authorization. In succeeding weeks Secretary Dulles sought but failed to achieve British support for military intervention; in the wake of this failure the Geneva conference met to plan a partition of Indochina. In retrospect, the decision to consult congressional leaders seems to have saved the administration from the bitter congressional debate that might have greeted a request for a resolution authorizing unilateral action. But the consultation had the effect of forcing on the administration negotiations with the British that eventually doomed the plan for intervention. Subsequent to the April 3 meeting, State or Defense officials met with congressional leaders on numerous occasions to keep them informed on administration thinking, but no further specific proposals on Indochina emerged.[26]

Bipartisan consultation has been undertaken with limited objectives in recent years, for it only becomes important to the administration when the voting support of opposition members in Congress is necessary. Where bipartisanship was too little or too late, it was usually the result of carelessness or overconfidence on the part of the administration. On other occasions the administration was handicapped because no single leader or small group of opposition senators was able to speak for the party on foreign policy. It would be reckless for the administration to make concessions to the opposition party that would cost it equivalent or substantial support in its own party. Usually, however, the techniques of bipartisanship do not contravene those necessary to retain the support of the administration party. Rather they are likely to strengthen support from those members of that party who may share some of the doubts of the opposition about any proposed policy. In sum, bipartisan consultation, wisely employed, appears to be one of the strongest presidential weapons for winning congressional support for foreign programs.

PRIVATE APPEALS TO SENATORS

In behind-the-scenes efforts to gain senatorial votes for foreign policy measures, the State Department and related agencies have been far more active than the White House. They have borne the day-to-day responsibility for presenting the administration's case to Congress both in formal hearings and in informal discussions.[27] Although most of the work is done at lower levels, the men who have served as Secretary of State or who have administered the foreign aid program have engaged in personal lobbying for their programs. The influence of these efforts should not be underestimated. Certainly senators are more likely to vote for those programs about which they feel well informed.[28] In terms of political influence, however, the State Department is weak; it lacks the powerful constituents of the Agriculture Department, for example. If a political appeal is to be made by the administration to senators, it must come from the White House.

When approaching congressmen, the President relies mostly on members of the White House staff. Personal appeals by the President are limited not only by the other demands on his time but by the danger of senatorial resentment if such high-

---

[27] According to Acheson, *A Citizen Looks at Congress*, p. 61: "The center and focus of legislative-executive relations lie in the congressional committees and in the method of their operation."

[28] For an analysis of this relationship, see Robinson, *Congress and Foreign Policy-Making*, Chs. 5 and 6. This is an excellent analysis of the nature and consequences of legislative-executive liaison on foreign policy.

level pressure is often applied on a member, particularly one who is known to be in disagreement with the President. A personal call from the President is not effective if it becomes a common occurrence.

The growth of presidential responsibility for a legislative program has led to the appearance of legislative specialists on the White House staff. Naturally the work of these staff members is little publicized. In addition to conveying the President's views on legislative matters, staff members may be able to promise White House favors of one type or another to members of Congress. They serve further as a source of information on the sentiments on Capitol Hill. White House staff members work closely with the legislative liaison officers of the various departments to avoid duplication of effort. In the final analysis, however, no special assistant in the White House can make an appeal or exert pressure equal to that of the President.

Some of the President's efforts to influence particular committees in Congress are more public than private. When the Senate Appropriations Committee or a conference committee is considering the restoration of foreign aid funds, for example, a publicized letter from the President to the membership has become almost a routine device of presidential leadership. A more direct and presumably more effective practice is to invite a committee to the White House for a presidential briefing or exhortation on pending legislation. Both Truman and Eisenhower on numerous occasions gave such briefings on foreign aid measures. At such a meeting the President may stress some aspect of his program that he considers particularly important or feels is in great jeopardy in Congress. When a foreign aid measure is being discussed by a conference committee, the President has occasionally telephoned key members of the committee to emphasize some particularly crucial aspect of the bill. These various efforts, usually directed to a group and frequently bipartisan in nature, test the persuasive powers of a President, but not his political power.

When the President tries to exert political pressure on a senator, he will normally concentrate on members of his own party, and his appeal will be direct, personal, and private. The extent and effectiveness of such direct private appeals cannot be measured precisely. During interviews in the preparation of this study, several senators were asked if they had ever been personally requested by the President or other White House officials to support a foreign policy measure. Over half of them answered negatively. One Democratic senator said that during twenty-one years in Congress his vote had been requested only once by a President and once by a White House official—both times on domestic issues. Two other veteran Democratic senators said that their support had been sought by the White House only once or twice, and then on domestic issues. In all, five Democratic and four Republican senators denied having received any White House requests for support on foreign policy. Several of these mentioned that high officials of the administration had occasionally asked their support. Five Republicans and one Democrat said there had been requests from the White House and, in some cases, from the President for voting support.

President Truman apparently did not frequently contact senators personally to seek their backing for foreign programs. Truman's effectiveness in recruiting support for his policies was limited by his personal coolness toward a number of Republicans, southern Democrats, and even some northern Democrats. For this reason, his calls were most likely to be made to a rather small group of senators with whom he was on close terms. Since these were usually senators already sympathetic toward his programs, his appeals were usually intended to gain more active support rather than to change these senators' votes.

President Eisenhower's personal popularity in Congress was higher than Truman's, yet he appears to have been slow in fully exploiting his congressional standing to gain voting support for his programs. During the 1953 session of Congress, when Senator Taft was still alive, the President hesitated to compete with him in mobilizing senatorial voting support. In contrast to Truman, Eisenhower apparently did not believe at first that presidential intervention was wise or proper.

Eisenhower's willingness to play a direct personal role in the search for votes seems to have increased during the course of his administration. Yet when he was asked at a press conference in 1956 whether he would exert pressure on Congress in behalf of his foreign aid program, Eisenhower said, "Well, I have never really understood thoroughly this expression 'pressure on Congress.' "[29] During a press conference in January, 1958, he explained that he did not offer support in elections or threaten to withhold it as a means of winning congressional backing for his programs. He described the methods that he did use: "I do every possible thing I can in the way of consultation, communication, both in Congress, within the Congress, with people outside of Government, to persuade them of the soundness of the view that I have put before the Congress for, in my opinion, the welfare of the United States. That I will continue to urge and argue far more behind the scenes than in front, but, nevertheless, I will argue for it as long as I have strength to do it."[30]

Personal appeals by the President or by members of his staff do not appear to have frequently been important in winning votes on foreign policy issues. One reason is that the sanctions which a President can profitably invoke are limited. Patronage is a question on which knowledgeable persons tend to be uncommunicative. One well-informed member of Truman's staff told the writer that the use of patronage to bargain for votes on specific bills was unwise because it created congressional resentment. He believed that the administration was more likely to gain voting support by consulting congressmen regularly on patronage questions than by linking patronage to individual legislative proposals. In the area of private consultation, more can probably be achieved by represetnatives of those government agencies who can argue the merits of the case than by those members of the administration who can exert political pressure.

PUBLIC PRESIDENTIAL APPEALS

When the President speaks, he commands attention throughout the country and the world. He can make effective use of various forums: a joint session of Congress, broadcasts and telecasts, speeches to organized groups, and press conferences. Through his public statements the President can influence the course taken by Congress in two ways. When he publicly announces a new foreign policy that requires legislative implementation, the United

[29] *New York Times*, Jan. 26, 1956, p. 12.
[30] *Ibid.*, Jan. 16, 1958, p. 14.

States becomes committed to that course in the eyes of the world. Members of Congress who want to disavow his stand face a responsibility heavier than most of them wish to bear. Secondly, the President can generate public support for a program and motivate constituents to put pressure on members of Congress.

Several of this nation's most important foreign programs have been launched publicly by the administration in such a fashion as to make congressional rejection most difficult. President Truman proposed Greek-Turkish aid to Congress in a dramatic speech which publicly committed the United States to that policy. The Secretary of State's speech launching the Marshall Plan had a similar effect on world opinion. This country's commitment to NATO was more gradual and was undertaken in closer consultation with senatorial leaders; yet on the day when the Brussels pact was signed, President Truman told Congress and the world that the United States would support the movement for collective defense in Western Europe. President Eisenhower's public requests for passage of the Formosa resolution in 1955 and the Middle East resolution in 1957 committed this country to policies that Congress did not dare to disavow.

These public statements by the President, tantamount to commitments on foreign policy, have usually been made after some bipartisan consultation with congressional leaders but before congressional sentiment on the issue was clearly formed. By adopting the tactic of public commitment, the President is taking a risk. He substantially increases the pressure on Congress to support his policy, while he maximizes the potential damage to national prestige should Congress reject it. In recent years the gamble has worked; Congress has not defeated any of these major programs, and on some occasions—notably the Formosa resolution—the fact of a public presidential commitment has contributed significantly to voting support.

Creating public pressure on Congress, like private appeals to senators, is a device limited both by the press of time and by the danger of diminishing returns from overuse. A President cannot expect the American people to deluge Congress with approving letters if he is making weekly appeals for his legislative policy. Judicious use of the public appeal by a popular President can produce important consequences in Congress.

President Truman did not make maximum use of public appeals on behalf of his foreign programs. He was not a highly effective speaker, and at times his popularity was at such a low ebb that there was little basis for any appeal. The burden of public explanation was often carried by his subordinates. As public support for the foreign aid program appeared to be waning late in his administration, the President did make an intensified effort to explain it to the nation. When he sent his aid program to Congress in 1952, for example, he described the need for it in a radio and television address and supplemented this with three speeches. Yet during the prolonged controversy in 1951 over sending troops to Europe, Truman never used the radio and television facilities to explain his case to the public; he relied entirely on press conference statements.

President Eisenhower was more persistent and imaginative in his appeals for his foreign policy, particularly in regard to foreign aid. As public apathy grew, Eisenhower increasingly spoke out for the program, both in press conferences and on radio and television. It was a frequent theme of press conferences, and in 1957 he called a special news conference for the sole purpose of requesting restoration of foreign aid funds cut by the House Appropriations Committee. He warned that the cut might necessitate a special session of Congress, but the House did not restore the funds. During the controversy over the Bricker amendment in 1953 and 1954, President Eisenhower presented his viewpoint to the public in seven press conferences and public statements but did not engage in public speeches, perhaps because he believed the issue was too complex for broad public understanding.

In general it can be said that no President has fully exploited the opportunities for generating public support for his foreign programs, that no President has fully realized his potential influence on the public mind when international issues are under discussion. The President occupies the preeminent position in foreign affairs and his word carries the greatest weight with the public in this area. But his difficulty comes with avoiding further wearying of a public already weary of repeated crises.

THE POTENTIALS OF PRESIDENTIAL LEADERSHIP

The successful President will use the various devices of leadership as the occasion demands. It is useful to distinguish between those techniques designed to secure partisan support and those that are essentially nonpartisan. Fortunately, these techniques are not necessarily opposed to one another. There is no evidence in specific cases that a President's efforts to secure the cooperation of senators in the opposition party have been handicapped by simultaneous efforts to create party unity.

The best examples of effective presidential techniques are bipartisan ones. There are circumstances in which advance bipartisan consultation is not only important but essential to the success of a legislative program. There are other occasions in which a public statement by the President has been effective in committing the nation to a policy in advance of congressional action or in creating strong public support for a policy. Early consultation followed shortly by a public presidential commitment is probably the strongest guarantee of congressional cooperation. These techniques are most valuable when the President is launching a bold new program such as the Marshall Plan or is moving with speed to meet a crisis such as that created by Communist pressure in the area of Formosa.[31] The President's greatest problem with regard to foreign policy, however, is not in meeting crises; it is in assuring adequate, sustained support in Congress for continuing and expanding existing programs. As Richard Neustadt has said, "We may have priced ourselves out of the market for 'productive' crises on the pattern Roosevelt knew—productive in the sense of strengthening his chances for sustained support *within* the system."[32] Advance consultation does not seem to aid a continuing program as it does a new measure, nor does the technique of public appeal carry weight when the question is on the dangers of attaching crippling amendments to a reciprocal trade bill. At present there seems

[31] Robert Dahl has pointed out that the President, who has superior facilities for influencing the congressional and public view of world events, not only can emphasize a foreign crisis, as the Truman administration did in Europe, but can play down a crisis, as the same administration did with regard to China. *Congress and Foreign Policy* (New York: Harcourt, Brace, and Co., 1950), pp. 103-108.

[32] Richard E. Neustadt, *Presidential Power* (New York: John Wiley and Sons, 1960), p. 186.

for the President no simple solution to the problem of gaining congressional support for his continuing foreign programs. The analysis of foreign policy rollcalls shows that the President has enjoyed bipartisan support for most new programs of importance, but that members of his party have provided greater support for existing programs. To maximize this kind of support, the President must develop further his role as a partisan leader in foreign policy. No President today has time to do all those things that are important to the successful performance of his manifold duties. He should take on additional burdens only if they have a clear priority over tasks he already performs. Though a President might win votes for his programs if he devoted more time to personal persuasion of senators and representatives, such a time-consuming effort is difficult to justify. Likewise a President might win votes by skillful handling of patronage matters, but this weapon is not effective enough to justify greater personal use by the President. Most of the responsibilities the President has delegated to his leaders in Congress and to his staff he cannot personally reassume. The arguments for relying primarily on party leadership in dealing with Congress are persuasive.

To effect such party loyalty the President does not need added sanctions so much as a willingness to assert his prerogatives boldly. His strongest potential sanction is one that has been little used. The President can require substantial support for his major foreign programs as the price of campaign support for members of his party seeking reelection. The public recognizes the President's preeminence in foreign policy and gives priority to foreign policy qualifications when it chooses a President, and it is more than likely that the voting public would heed the President's judgment concerning the relative contribution of various congressional candidates to his foreign programs.

The unhappy truth is that the prevailing public opinion has been destructively wrong at the critical junctures. . . . They [the people] have compelled the governments, which usually knew what would have been wiser, or was necessary, or was more expedient, to be too late with too little, or too long with too much, too pacifist in peace and too bellicose in war, too neutralist or appeasing in negotiation or too intransigent. Mass opinion has acquired mounting power in this century. It has shown itself to be a dangerous master of decisions when the stakes are life and death.

—WALTER LIPPMANN

I see no reason why each senator should not run on his own foreign policy.
—Senator RORERT A. TAFT, discussing the 1942 election

8

PUBLIC OPINION

A SENATOR MAY BE CONVINCED BY A PRESIDENTIAL ADDRESS that some new foreign program is imperative, he may be persuaded by the Foreign Relations Committee that the program is wise, and he may be receptive to the majority leader's pleas for party unity in support of the program. Yet he may read his mail, visit his constituents, study a public opinion poll, and vote no. No one realizes better than a senator what different concepts of foreign policy are held by the citizens on Main Street and the elected officials on either end of Pennsylvania Avenue. The foreign policies considered essential by the administration in our day usually carry risks and a price tag that will not be popular with the voters. The contemporary problem of conducting foreign policy in a democracy centers on the difficulties of generating public understanding of international necessities and preserving ultimate public control over policy without placing the administration in a straitjacket. The senator is the middleman in this situation.

The concern about the effect of public opinion on foreign policy in this country is based on a recognition that international problems are growing more complex while the average citizen remains woefully uninformed about events and problems beyond our nation's shores. A consistent finding of the public opinion polls is that unless the national leaders and the press have carried on a major educational campaign concerning some issue, a substantial proportion of the population will be totally unaware that the issue exists, while only a small fraction will have any coherent understanding of its nature. This unawareness continues despite great improvements in the reporting of foreign affairs. But the problems of today are new and bewildering; they involve countries nonexistent and people unknown a few years ago. Disarmament, once a question of sinking equal proportions of battleships, today involves nuclear equations shrouded in technological complexity and governmental secrecy. The challenge of the sixties is a new and difficult one for the American public. President Kennedy described it in his inaugural address (1961) "not as a call to bear arms, though arms we need —not as a call to battle, though embattled we are—but a call to bear the burden of a long twilight struggle year in and year out."

Walter Lippmann and others have argued that the American public, ill-informed and parochial in its outlook, creates an increasing pressure on its leaders to make the wrong decisions in foreign policy.[1] On the other hand, the public is especially dependent on its leaders for information and guidance when foreign problems arise. We need to understand better how the public thinks about foreign affairs, how and when public viewpoints influence the thinking of senators.

Actually, public opinion is not one thing but many, and is not to be covered by simple generalizations. Bernard C. Cohen has distinguished usefully between two forms of public opinion:

[1] See Walter Lippmann, *Essays in the Public Philosophy* (Boston: Little, Brown and Co., 1955), Chs. 1, 2, 3, 5.

"The first is the background or climate of opinion which, by creating in the policy-maker an impression of a public attitude or attitudes, or by becoming part of the environment and cultural milieu that help to shape his own thinking, may consciously affect his official behavior. . . . The second type of public opinion is made up of the active and articulate expressions on policy of specific individuals and organized groups, including the media of communication. These are the identifiable voices that interpret the mood and the strivings of different segments of the general public in terms that have some operational meaning for the policy-makers in government."[2] Though the climate of opinion may have an important effect on the senator's range of choice, he is particularly concerned with assessing the second category, the articulate expressions of groups and individuals. Roger Hilsman has concluded that senators are subject to less organized pressure on foreign policy than on most important domestic issues.[3] Nevertheless, there are some types of foreign issues on which the pressure of articulate opinion, organized or unorganized, is likely to be felt by senators. A senator may realize that his constituents know nothing about a pending treaty, while they are organized in angry opposition to a reduction in tariffs or brood quietly about the cost of foreign aid. The senator is naturally most interested in those opinions of constituents that are intense and of long enough duration to affect voting habits.

MEASURING CONSTITUENT OPINION

A senator faces a serious problem in trying to gauge constituent opinion on any issue. Since he is interested in the intensity of opinions, a simple yes-and-no poll may be misleading. Moreover, national polls do not necessarily represent opinion in his home state, and for him to conduct a private poll requires expert knowledge and considerable expense. The senator reads local newspapers with interest but often without knowing whether their editorials influence or reflect constituent opinion, or whether they do neither. The activity of lobbyists may be a sign that groups in his state are concerned about an issue, but the senator

2 Cohen, *The Political Process and Foreign Policy*, p. 29.
3 Roger Hilsman, "Congressional-Executive Relations and the Foreign Policy Consensus," *American Political Science Review*, LII (Sept., 1958), 727-28.

still must determine how large a group is involved and how accurately a lobbyist reflects their views. The fact that senators frequently rely more on mail than on other indications of constituent thinking, as Donald Matthews points out, often simply means there is a shortage of other reliable guides.[4] Mail has serious disadvantages as a mirror of opinion. It may come from pressure groups;[5] it may come from an articulate minority; it may come simply from the fact that the opponents of some measures seem more inclined to write than the supporters.[6] In addition to providing a guide to constituent thinking, letters do measure intensity of feeling. Those persons who take the trouble to write on an issue are more likely than the average citizen to become familiar with the senator's stand on that issue and to remember it on election day. On visits to his home state, a senator can better judge the intensity of opinion.

There is no sure or simple way to measure how much senators have been influenced either by the general climate of opinion on international issues or by groups advocating specific foreign policies. It is possible to describe what the polls have shown about the climate of opinion on major foreign policy issues, and to gauge roughly the influence that the President has had on this opinion. It is also possible to provide some examples of more specific constituent pressures on senators. The average citizen looks to the President for knowledge and leadership more on foreign affairs than on domestic questions. The greater the emergency and the bolder the policy, the greater the President's potential influence. The public, perhaps unprepared for the emergency, unaware of alternatives, and ignorant of the ulti-

[4] Matthews, U.S. Senators and Their World, pp. 219-24. Matthews' book contains an excellent discussion of senators' relationship to constituents.

[5] An example of an interest group's extraordinary success in organizing pressures on senators occurred during the 1935 controversy over United States membership in the World Court. A radio speech by Father Charles E. Coughlin denouncing the World Court led to an estimated 40,000 telegrams to senators in the two days before the vote was taken; this constituent pressure was credited with playing a large role in the defeat of the measure. Grassmuck, Sectional Biases in Congress on Foreign Policy, pp. 85-87.

[6] Dahl, Congress and Foreign Policy, pp. 33-38, has provided vivid examples of the frequent contrasts between letters from constituents and the attitudes revealed in polls. In 1939 congressional mail ran more than five-to-one against repeal of the arms embargo, but a poll showed almost 60 percent of the public favored repeal. The next year 90 percent of the mail opposed a selective service measure, while polls indicated 70 percent support for it.

mate cost or risks, is likely to respond initially with approval to a presidential program, but its support may wane as the program becomes an established one.

PUBLIC ACCEPTANCE OF FOREIGN AID

Because of its long duration, the foreign aid program provides a good test of constituent influence. In 1947 and 1948 the internationalist leaders of both parties were notably successful in creating a public awareness of the nation's growing responsibilities for foreign assistance. President Truman launched the Greek-Turkish aid program dramatically in 1947 before a joint session of Congress. The Marshall Plan was undertaken with less urgency but with a constant stream of high-level publicity. Consequently the polls showed that in March, 1947, an unusually high proportion of people (82 percent) had heard of the Greek-Turkish program, while there was a steady growth of familiarity with the Marshall Plan to nearly the same level by November, 1948. Information did not necessarily mean support. A majority favored aid to Greece and Turkey, but there was a preference for turning the whole program over to the United Nations. Initial opposition to the Marshall Plan gave way to strong support (about 3-1) as understanding about it grew, though the majority was smaller among those who realized how costly it would be. The initial public reaction to a military aid program for Western Europe, early in 1949, was nearly as favorable as the attitude toward economic aid. Later in the year, as Republican leaders attacked the administration's military aid bill, the majority shrank.[7]

The Point Four Program of aid to underdeveloped areas never benefited from such effective promotion by the administration or so much bipartisan support as the Marshall Plan had. As a consequence, the polls showed that in mid-1950 less than a quarter of the voters had heard of the program and very few

[7] *Public Opinion Quarterly*, XI (Summer, 1947), 285-86, (Fall, 1947), 495, (Winter, 1947-1948), 675-76; XII (Spring, 1948), 172-73, (Summer, 1948), 365-67; XIII (Fall, 1949), 549, (Winter, 1949-1950), 725. The polls cited in this chapter are primarily those of the American Institute of Public Opinion (Gallup Poll). Those found in the *Public Opinion Quarterly* during the period through 1951 are cited. Others were on file at the Roper Public Opinion Research Center at Williams College.

had any real understanding of it.[8] By contrast, the public supported the 1957 Middle East aid program (particularly economic aid), a measure to which President Eisenhower had given an air of urgency. In recent years the polls indicated rather steady support for foreign aid. The polls did not reflect the upsurge of opposition, to foreign aid that many senators thought was occurring, but polls usually do not measure the intensity of opposition. Moreover, the polls showed vast ignorance about just how much was being spent for foreign aid.

In so far as polls are accurate indicators, the extensive publicity efforts for major new programs in 1947 and 1948 appear to have created a favorable climate for foreign aid. There seems to be a clear relation between the degree of support which major political leaders give to aid programs and the degree of support which the public gives. To put this relationship in different terms, the climate of opinion has not usually created pressures on senators that contradicted the views of political leadership in Washington. In recent years, however, when there has been broad agreement in Washington about the general nature and scope of an aid program—though not about many of its features—there has probably been less public understanding and support, though the polls do not indicate any sharp decline.

An analysis of senatorial mail would provide another picture of constituent influence on senators. Senator Tom Connally's mail is perhaps not typical, but it shows an interesting trend of opinion during the early years of foreign aid. Connally received over 200 letters on the Greek-Turkish aid program, a slight majority of them from opponents, who were concerned about the risks of war, the disadvantages of bypassing the United Nations, and the imperfections of the Greek and Turkish governments. He received a somewhat greater number of letters in 1947 and 1948 on the Marshall Plan. Though the early letters on the Marshall Plan reflected reluctance and uncertainty, the later ones indicated a strong majority enthusiastically in support. Public interest and controversy about foreign aid died quickly after 1948. There were only some 35 letters on the military assistance program of 1949, a majority favorable, while correspondence on the Point Four Program was almost nonexistent.

8 *Public Opinion Quarterly*, XIV (Fall, 1950), 600.

After the first two or three years, Connally's mail on foreign aid dealt almost exclusively with legislative details of economic concern to the writers, notably agricultural surpluses and the use of American shipping.[9]

Interviews with senators and their assistants in 1956 and 1957 concerning their mail showed that most of them thought constituent opposition to foreign aid was rising and that positive interest was waning. Two assistants, for example, said that for a year they had not seen a letter in support of foreign aid except from organized groups. At that time, aid to Yugoslavia was particularly unpopular with constituents. In many cases the mail on foreign aid in recent years may have been so light as to be completely unrepresentative.[10] Senator Barkley, for example, received fifteen letters on foreign aid in 1955, all but one favorable and mostly focused on the need for contributing to the U.N. technical assistance program. The following year he received seventeen letters, all but one urging abolition or reduction in the aid program. There is no reason to believe that sentiment in Kentucky changed that drastically or that either year's mail was typical of views in the state.[11]

Pressure group activity on foreign aid bills has been relatively light, less than on reciprocal trade measures, for example. Most of the major labor, farm, and business organizations have given consistent support to the various aid measures, and church groups have endorsed economic aid programs, particularly for underdeveloped areas. These endorsements have contributed to the general climate of support for foreign aid; consistent and vigorous opposition by one of these major groups might have created considerable difficulties for the aid programs. On the other hand, it is doubtful that the endorsements of these groups have created substantial "pressures" on senators, in the sense

[9] The letters received by Senator Connally are among a massive assortment of files from his office stored in the Manuscripts Division of the Library of Congress. Though the files may not be complete, they probably at least provide a good sample of his correspondence.

[10] In 1956 William S. White concluded "on the authority of Senatorial contacts with the various small publics representing the various states, that the people were a bit tired and a bit bored with foreign aid, and possibly a bit hostile to it, too." "The Nation's Mood—And the Issues," *New York Times Magazine*, July 15, 1956, p. 20.

[11] Senator Barkley's papers are stored at the library of the University of Kentucky. The files of correspondence for the period covered appear complete, though not all mail may have been saved.

that unions put pressure on a senator concerning labor legislation or oil companies exert pressure concerning oil depletion allowances. In other words, senators have probably estimated that these groups are usually not vitally concerned about the passage or defeat of foreign aid bills or—more to the point— amendments increasing or decreasing the size of aid programs. The most vigorous pressure group activity has related to specific features of the programs. Agricultural groups have been instrumental in the development of legislation designed to dispose of agricultural surpluses through the foreign aid program. Congress has generally been more enthusiastic than the State Department about these programs. The major farm groups have recognized the dangers of burdening the aid program with a disproportionate emphasis on farm surpluses, however, and have refused to support some proposals with minimum foreign benefits. During the early years of the Marshall Plan one of the most serious problems of its administrators was the heavy pressure of shipping interests on Congress that resulted in legislation requiring a high proportion of foreign aid shipments to be carried in American ships. At various times such diverse groups as machine-tool manufacturers, flour millers, and coal exporters have sought specific benefits under the foreign aid program.[12] The various groups seeking particular benefits have often concentrated on congressional committees. The average senator has probably seldom heard from pressure groups seeking particular foreign aid benefits except in the area of agriculture.[13]

THE EXPANSION OF AMERICAN COMMITMENTS

Apparently there was a similar pattern of constituent opinion on the question of military commitments to Western Europe. The

[12] The activities of pressure groups with regard to foreign aid are discussed in Holbert N. Carroll, *The House of Representatives and Foreign Affairs* (Pittsburgh: University of Pittsburgh Press, 1958), pp. 54-56, 67-72, 125-27, 250-54, 304-305. See also William A. Brown, Jr., and Redvers Opie, *American Foreign Assistance* (Washington: Brookings Institution, 1953), pp. 166-71.

[13] Note, however, the judgment of Thomas L. Hughes that a growing proportion of a congressman's errand-running duties involves matters of contracts and personnel in the foreign field. Hughes believes that "this is the most important kind of Congressional penetration of Executive responsibility." This casework may stimulate a congressman's interest in and perhaps criticism of an agency operating abroad. "Foreign Policy on Capitol Hill," *Reporter*, XX (April 30, 1959), 29.

polls showed that in early 1948 there was a small majority in favor of American support for NATO, while in 1949 the margin of support grew to 4-1.[14] The press reported both before and after the Senate's debate on ratification that the public appeared to be apathetic, ill-informed, but generally in favor of NATO. Apparently this was not an issue on which constituent pressures were strongly felt by senators, while the climate of opinion was clearly favorable. Some of the major pressure groups gave general support to the North Atlantic Treaty, while some church groups and organizations devoted to promoting the United Nations expressed reservations about it. Neither seems to have had much effect.

Polls taken in 1951 showed that a majority of respondents, some of them with reservations, favored sending more troops to Europe. These opinion surveys indicated, however, that two-thirds of those polled believed Congress should have the right to determine how many, if any, troops should be sent.[15] Several senators at the time stated that some of their constituents, either by letters or by answers to questionnaires, had shown a strong preference for congressional rather than presidential control over the dispatch of troops.[16] This issue does not appear, however, to have evoked strong constituent pressures on senators.

Bernard C. Cohen has thoroughly explored the influences of public opinion on the Japanese Peace Treaty. The climate of opinion toward Japan in the 1950s was "permissive and tolerant, giving policy-makers wide latitude in their search for internationally acceptable policy substance. Popular restraints on their freedom to decide in concrete terms how Japan should be treated were few."[17] There was a public belief, shared by American military leaders, that our troops should be kept in Japan, and there was strong public as well as senatorial insistence that Japan not trade with Communist China. A poll in October, 1951, showed that 52 percent of those interviewed favored the treaty, 3 percent opposed it, while 45 percent had no opinion or had never heard of it.[18]

14 *Public Opinion Quarterly*, XII (Summer, 1948), 353, (Fall, 1948), 549; XIII (Spring, 1949), 163-64. (Summer, 1949), 351, (Fall, 1949), 549.

15 *Ibid.*, XV (Summer, 1951), 382-84.

16 *Congressional Record*, March 30, 1951, p. 3029.

17 Cohen, p. 57.

18 *Ibid.*, pp. 57-61.

Among the pressure groups, the treaty was supported by the major business, labor, church, and veterans groups that had endorsed other important foreign programs. Opposition came from fringe ideological groups, pacifists, patriotic organizations, and archconservative-isolationist groups. Cohen has pointed out that the administration and Congress received conflicting impressions about pressure group activities. The groups supporting the treaty directed many of their communications to the administration, often with specific comments about details of the treaty. The groups in opposition concentrated their efforts almost exclusively on Congress, and their comments were general and ideological. Senators received little mail on the subject; Senator Everett Dirksen, for example, had about a dozen letters on the treaty though he had discussed it in state radio broadcasts. Consequently the mail from a small group of opponents was completely unrepresentative, and senators seem to have recognized it as such and discounted it. The single pressure group with a major economic interest in the treaty was the fishing industry on the West Coast. This group enlisted the aid of Senator William Knowland of California and other members of Congress. With congressional assistance it was able to negotiate a compromise through the State Department that led to a separate fisheries treaty.[19]

When President Eisenhower sought approval of programs for expanding military commitments, there was sufficient public support, or sometimes public apathy, to permit the Senate to act without fear of constituent reaction. The President's rather vague request for authority to act in the Formosa Straits generated some public support but little understanding. In March, 1955, 32 percent of those polled were willing to have this country guarantee the Quemoy and Matsu islands, 21 percent were not, 24 percent were undecided, and 23 percent had not heard of the problem; only 10 percent proved to have accurate information about the islands.

The Middle East resolution illustrated the frequent contradiction between senatorial mail and opinion polls. In February, 1957, the *New York Times* reported that the mail of senators on the Foreign Relations Committee was running more than eight

19 *Ibid.*, pp. 62-109, 253-77.

to one against President Eisenhower's proposal for a Middle East resolution. The mail was relatively heavy and appeared to be unorganized. The critical letters started to arrive in large numbers after Democratic senators began their public criticism of the Eisenhower proposal.[20] On the other hand, a public opinion poll at the time showed that over two-thirds of the voters were willing to send economic aid to Middle Eastern countries threatened by Communist attack, while half were willing to send both arms and American troops. On neither the Middle Eastern nor the Formosa issue does there appear to have been strong public support for the action sought by the President. Neither was there strong opposition, and senators evidently did not believe the critical mail on the Middle East resolution was representative. The congressional debates on these issues do not suggest serious concern by senators about the attitude of their constituents.

THE ISSUES THAT GENERATE PRESSURE

These security commitments did not arouse public opinion because they did not in fact lead to the involvement of American troops in foreign wars. The Korean war overshadowed all other foreign policy issues in the public mind because Americans were losing their lives on a foreign battlefield. President Truman's original decision to defend South Korea had wide public support; in August, 1950, two-thirds of those polled favored the action and only one-fifth thought it was a mistake. By January, 1951, after the Chinese Communists had entered the war, half the voters thought the decision to defend Korea was a mistake and two-thirds of the voters thought the United States should pull its forces out of Korea.[21] As the stalemate in Korea continued, the administration remained unable to convince a majority that its limited-war policy was wise. The bitterness engendered by the grim deadlock in Korea poisoned bipartisan relations, damaged other foreign programs, and, after it became an issue in the 1952 election, forced an end to the war itself.

The Korean war did not present the Senate with legislative

[20] *New York Times,* Feb. 1, 1957, p. 3.
[21] *Public Opinion Quarterly,* XV (Spring, 1951), 170, (Summer, 1951), 386.

choices; senators could not effectively dictate strategy through the power of the purse. Senators realized that the war was unpopular, and the dismissal of General Douglas MacArthur brought criticism of the administration into focus. The crowds that greeted MacArthur on his return, the reaction of newspapers, and the weight of congressional mail all testified to the unpopularity of the administration's policies. The senatorial hearings on the Far Eastern controversy may have clarified the issues, but they did not tip the popular scales in favor of the administration. Though the event served to impress constituent sentiment on senators, their mail proved once again to be an inaccurate guide. The mail was so overwhelmingly pro-MacArthur and anti-Truman that most senators, though recognizing that the voters were deeply concerned, decided that a disproportionate number of critics were writing.[22] The Korean war illustrates the force of public opinion and the difficulty any administration faces in carrying on an unpopular war. Neither the public nor Congress could force the administration to follow MacArthur's policies, but public sentiment eventually made necessary the Korean truce.

Except for the Korean war, the issues of American economic and military commitments abroad have not usually provoked sufficient public concern to produce pressure on senators. In sharp contrast is the question of reciprocal trade. Though the basic principle of reciprocal trade probably has as broad public acceptance as foreign aid does, the demands for amendments to protect specific industries are much more intensive than most criticisms of foreign aid. The benefits of reciprocal trade are general, but its burdens are specific. Senators whose constituents are particularly affected by foreign competition probably face more pressure on the tariff question than on any other foreign issue except war.

The polls indicate that in the postwar period there has been a climate of opinion favorable to a low tariff policy, though the sentiment for higher tariffs has been increasing. The proportion of those polled who favor higher tariffs was 14 percent in January, 1947, 13 percent in June, 1953, 26 percent in January, 1955, and 30 percent in June, 1959. The polls also suggest

---

[22] *New York Times*, April 13, 1951, p. 7; April 22, 1951, sec. iv, p. 7.

that the level of information about tariffs and the workings of the reciprocal trade program remains low. A favorable climate of opinion is of little help to a senator if significant numbers of his constituents are unemployed and believe that foreign competition is to blame for their plight. The senator, always most concerned with that type of opinion which is expressed by organized and articulate groups, finds a maximum amount of organized pressure on the issue of reciprocal trade.

The role of pressure groups in congressional disputes over the tariff has been discussed by other writers.[23] It is possible here only to cite some examples. In recent years the objective of specific interests has been to win special exemptions through amendments in the law or to accomplish changes in administrative procedures designed to help the domestic producers. Textile manufacturers both in New England and the South have sought protection from Japanese textiles. The manufacturers of bicycles, watches, pottery, glassware, and chemical and electrical products are among those claiming that foreign industrial competition has been damaging. While many farmers favor a low tariff policy to encourage agricultural exports, there has been a growing demand for protection of certain domestic products such as cherries, sugar, dairy products, wool, and fur products. Perhaps the strongest pressure for protection has come from coal mining, petroleum, and natural gas interests, all of which compete with imported residual oil, and from the producers of other mineral products, such as lead, zinc, and copper. In states with a substantial proportion of persons engaged in these areas of production—notably southern and western states—the pressure on senators is obvious.[24] The reader of the *Congressional Record* will find that senators are frank to describe which economic groups in their states have forced them to endorse amendments designed to give general or specific protection to domestic producers.

Chapters 2 and 3 demonstrated the relationship between state economic interests and the voting records of senators on recip-

[23] See E. E. Schattschneider, *Politics, Pressures and the Tariff* (New York: Prentice-Hall, 1935).

[24] Richard A. Watson, "The Tariff Revolution: A Study of Shifting Party Attitudes," *Journal of Politics*, XVIII (Nov., 1956), 678-701.

rocal trade legislation. In some cases a senator appears particularly sensitive to the plight of a relatively minor economic interest in his state. Some of the southern senators trying to limit Japanese textile imports come from states that in recent years have exported cotton to Japan worth considerably more than the textiles imported. Douglass Cater has cited an extreme case of protectionist sensitivity: a New York congressman who voted against the reciprocal trade program because a birdcage manufacturer in his district employing fifty persons was hurt by foreign competition, though the docks in his district handle over a billion dollars' worth of goods annually.[25]

A senator's mail on reciprocal trade legislation is likely to be larger and is more often organized than mail on other foreign questions. Lewis A. Dexter, who studied the 1955 reciprocal trade bill, found that nearly all senators received substantial mail on this issue, though they often received little on foreign aid. The mail appeared to be organized, much of it by a relatively few firms in such industries as electrical equipment, chemicals, coal, oil, and textiles. Protectionist mail outnumbered that supporting reciprocal trade by at least ten to one, with most of the latter inspired by the League of Women Voters.[26]

Alben Barkley's mail in 1955 illustrates how reciprocal trade overshadowed other foreign questions. That year he received 34 letters on the Bricker amendment, 15 on foreign aid, 19 on the Formosa resolution, and over 400 on reciprocal trade legislation. A sample of his mail on the trade question indicated that three-quarters of those writing were opposed to the trade bill or wanted specific exemptions in it. Nearly all of these mentioned specific industries affected by foreign competition. A substantial proportion of the letters clearly resulted from organized efforts. For example, there were many "personal" letters from workers in a textile plant; with little variety in wording they said, "My job is in danger because of low-priced Japanese textiles."

In view of the heavy pressure that many senators experience

---

[25] Douglass Cater, "The Southern Textile Tale: Out of Whole Cloth," *Reporter*, XII (June 2, 1955), 29-32. Cater's article is an excellent description of the organized campaign by textile interests concerning the trade bill.

[26] Lewis Anthony Dexter, "What Do Congressmen Hear: The Mail," *Public Opinion Quarterly*, XX (Spring, 1956), 16-27.

from groups seeking tariff benefits, it is perhaps surprising that the reciprocal trade program has been renewed periodically with relatively few special exemptions and with considerable discretionary authority to the administration to lower tariffs. The fact that senators represent a larger constituency than representatives reduces the concentration of pressure on them from a few interests and probably explains why the trade bill has usually passed with less difficulty in the Senate than in the House. It is surprising, in a sense, that there are not more "logrolling" operations among senators, each seeking special protection for a particular industry. In fact, only major industries like textiles and coal have been able to win some form of specific exemption. Most senators appear to respect the arguments for reciprocal trade advanced by the administration and vote for the legislation after making efforts of varying intensity to win protection for their state's industry.

If there has been a single foreign policy issue on which the climate of opinion could be described as apathetic, it was the Bricker amendment. A poll in October, 1953, showed that only 19 percent of those questioned had heard of it; 9 percent favored it, 7 percent were opposed, and 3 percent had no opinion. By January, 1954, 28 percent of those polled had heard of it, but only 13 percent could give even a partially correct description; of these, 4 percent favored it, 7 percent were opposed, and 2 percent were undecided.[27]

In this case, however, the pressure groups working in behalf of the Bricker amendment presented their views so persistently and were so effective in generating a letterwriting campaign that many senators appear to have overestimated constituent interest and support for the proposal. The campaign for it was spearheaded by the American Bar Association and its Committee on Peace and Law through the United Nations. It had the support of various groups of businessmen and doctors and some women's and veterans' organizations. The debate over the Status of Forces Treaty intensified support for the Bricker amendment.[28]

Numerous senators and senatorial assistants who were inter-

[27] *Congressional Record*, Jan. 22, 1954, p. 672; Jan. 27, 1954, pp. 860-61.
[28] See Edward M. Bershtein, "The 'Bricker' Movement to Amend the Constitution" (Unpublished Ph.D. dissertation, University of Chicago, 1955).

viewed by the writer commented on the large amount of mail received during the debate, and most reported that the mail was heavily in favor of the Bricker amendment.[29] A number of senators apparently believed (largely on the basis of mail) that there was considerable risk in opposing all versions of the Bricker amendment. Certainly one reason why advocates of the Bricker amendment dominated the senatorial mailbag was that the President had not presented his case against the Bricker amendment effectively and persistently enough to arouse much public support for his stand. The President appears to have erred just as much as the Senate in overestimating public support for the measure.[30] For these various reasons the Senate was peculiarly sensitive to constituents on one of the most complicated, least understood, and least genuinely popular foreign policy issues of the postwar period.

There is substantial evidence in the polls and in senatorial mail that aside from the Korean war, there has been relatively little constituent pressure on most senators with regard to foreign policy. On many issues the public has been apathetic; on others the administration has presented the case for its program vigorously enough to develop substantial public support. Organized pressure groups have been active in trying to influence the details of legislation, but they have brought substantial pressure to bear on senators only with regard to reciprocal trade legislation and the Bricker amendment.

FOREIGN POLICY IN ELECTION CAMPAIGNS

The influence of constituents on foreign policy may be measured indirectly through a study of senatorial election campaigns. Our premise is that when one or the other candidate raises a question of foreign policy during a senatorial campaign, it usually indicates that this is a matter of concern to the voters. Obviously the candidate may misjudge public interest, but during a campaign he is close to the voters, and if he continues to

[29] The mail received in Senator Hubert Humphrey's office strongly favored the Bricker amendment and was the third heaviest volume of mail on any issue during the 1952-1954 period. Gilbert, "Problems of a Senator," pp. 232-33.
[30] Donovan, *Eisenhower*, p. 238.

emphasize an issue, it is usually because many voters are responding favorably. Since domestic issues, local questions, and personalities as a rule dominate senatorial election campaigns, those international issues that occasionally rise to prominence in a campaign have an increased significance as indicating public response.[31] In addition, whether a candidate supports, opposes, or ignores the stand on foreign policy taken by his national party reveals his judgment of public opinion in his state. A campaign may also provide clues concerning the President's influence in the state.[32]

The 1948 election was the first opportunity the voters had to pass judgment on the major postwar economic and military commitments of the Truman administration. Since both major presidential candidates approved these programs, foreign policy controversies might be expected to develop primarily in the congressional and particularly senatorial campaigns.[33] And, significantly for a study of the Senate, at that time there were still a number of senators who were isolationists and were therefore opposed to the nation's becoming immersed in the affairs of Europe and Asia.[34]

[31] Hughes, p. 29, points out, however, that a candidate may inject foreign policy into a campaign for another purpose, "as a device for blunting the attack of his opponents on domestic policy." He believes that candidates are making increasing use of foreign policy, often in an irresponsible way, because this issue "lends itself to grandiose expressions of sentiment that are helpful to the campaigning congressman's momentary reputation and are not easily susceptible to convincing counterargument or meaningful repudiation."

[32] The writer has not tried to survey in detail all the senatorial election campaigns of recent years but has concentrated on about thirty. These were relatively close contests in which the known views of one or both candidates indicated that foreign policy was a probable issue. This survey is based primarily on a detailed study of one or two newspapers in each of the states involved. Every issue of the paper was checked for a period of four to eight weeks. This was supplemented by interviews with some of the senators involved and correspondence with some reporters who had covered the campaigns. Briefer information about a number of additional senatorial campaigns was obtained from the New York Times and national magazines.

[33] The presidential campaign is covered well in Westerfield, Foreign Policy and Party Politics, pp. 306-24. Henry Wallace and the Progressive party, of course, sought to make foreign policy a major campaign issue in 1948 but drew little public response.

[34] The term "isolationist" is used in this chapter and elsewhere in the book, not in a polemic sense, but as a concise and convenient way of describing senators who usually voted against the major programs under which this nation assumed increased international responsibilities. The supporters of most or all such programs are called "internationalists."

As it turned out, the 1948 election dealt a serious blow to isolationism in the Senate. There were eleven Republicans and three Democrats with terms expiring in 1948 who had voted against either Greek-Turkish aid or the Marshall Plan. Only three of them won reelection; seven were defeated, and four did not seek reelection. Yet an analysis of the campaigns does not suggest that their isolationist records were frequently a cause of their downfall. Only one of the four who retired—Albert W. Hawkes of New Jersey—retired because of his record; party leaders were reported to have cast him aside because of his isolationism and conservatism. One of those who was reelected, Kenneth S. Wherry of Nebraska, won in a strongly Republican state with an isolationist record, while another, Edwin C. Johnson of Colorado, won despite the fact that his opponents in both the primary and general election labeled him an isolationist.[35] The seven isolationists who were defeated in 1948 were all Republicans.[36] In only two cases did their Democratic opponents make extensive use of the foreign policy issue. Paul Douglas believed that his repeated attacks on Senator C. Wayland Brooks of Illinois as an opponent of the bipartisan foreign policy did in fact win some Republican votes. It is less likely that Hubert Humphrey's charges of isolation contributed materially to the defeat of Senator Joseph H. Ball of Minnesota, whose record was a mixture of internationalism and isolationism.

There appear to be several reasons why foreign aid was not a major issue in the 1948 senatorial campaigns. By that time the issue had already become less controversial. Public opposition to aid programs was declining, but it was probably still strongest in several of the states, such as Nebraska, Iowa, Idaho, and Colorado, where isolationist senators were running. Their opponents were often dubious that an internationalist stand would produce votes. Isolationist senators or candidates in many states had even more reason to doubt that their views on foreign policy

[35] The third who won reelection, Democrat James E. Murray of Montana, had a generally internationalist record despite his vote against Greek-Turkish aid.
[36] They were: C. Wayland Brooks of Illinois, Joseph H. Ball of Minnesota, Chapman Revercomb of West Virginia, C. Douglass Buck of Delaware, Henry C. Dworshak of Idaho, Edward V. Robinson of Wyoming, and George A. Wilson of Iowa.

would be popular; frequently they minimized the issue. A final and important reason why the issue was subordinated is that it did not play a part in the presidential campaign (except as Henry Wallace raised it).

In subsequent elections there were only a few occasions when Democratic candidates sought to make an effective issue out of the isolationism of Republican senators; the issue seldom appeared to affect the outcome. In 1950 Senator Scott Lucas attacked his Republican opponent, Everett Dirksen, as a "bumbling, fumbling, confused isolationist," but Lucas was defeated and, as majority leader, may have been hurt by some of Dirksen's criticism of the Truman foreign policy. Republicans Homer Capehart of Indiana and Henry C. Dworshak of Idaho are examples of senators who won reelection in 1950 despite Democratic criticisms of their votes against foreign aid. In Ohio it was Senator Taft who took the initiative in raising foreign policy issues, against the advice of some supporters who feared the "isolationist" tag. He reiterated and expanded his many criticisms of the Truman administration, ranging from the failure to rearm Germany to appeasement in Asia. But his Democratic opponent lacked the necessary experience to join the debate, and the election never became a referendum on foreign policy. In 1952 Democratic candidates seldom emphasized foreign policy in their campaigns. Senators like William E. Jenner of Indiana and John W. Bricker of Ohio ran successfully for reelection with little criticism of their isolationist record. In Missouri, however, Stuart Symington defeated Republican Senator James P. Kem in a campaign that emphasized the charge that Kem was "the most isolationist senator of them all."

In most of the 1950 and 1952 elections candidates of both parties appeared to believe that the issues of foreign aid and military commitments did not concern the voters enough to be valuable campaign issues. There were internationalists like Symington and Lucas and isolationists like Jenner and Bricker who stressed them, but often the candidates seemed to lack confidence that there was a preponderance of public support for their views. A more important factor was that in 1950 and especially in 1952 these issues were overshadowed by the Korean war. During the 1950 campaign most Republican candidates criticized the Truman administration for originally withdrawing American troops from South Korea, excluding that country from our defense perimeter, and failing to maintain a strong enough military establishment. There was little criticism, however, of Truman's decision to defend South Korea. As the United Nations counteroffensive gained momentum during the fall, Republican candidates made less use of the Korean issue. Although the news of Chinese troops in Korea late in October raised doubts about American policy in Korea, the full implications of Chinese entry did not become apparent until after the election, when United Nations troops were forced to retreat and the war eventually became stalemated. Had the election occurred two or three months later, the Korean war would have been the dominant issue, and more Democrats probably would have lost their seats.

In 1952 the Korean war was the single most important issue in the presidential campaign; polls showed that three-quarters of the voters thought the Republicans would end the war more quickly than the Democrats would. Republican candidates for the Senate took their cue from General Eisenhower, who put increasing stress on the issue as the campaign developed and eventually promised that he would go to Korea and seek an early end to the war. The Korean war intensified the issues of Communists in government, stimulated inflation, and eclipsed the Democratic boast of prosperity.[37] There was probably not a single Republican senatorial candidate, internationalist or isolationist, who did not make the Korean war a significant campaign issue.

The 1952 campaign demonstrated two things. First, and most obvious, a war like that in Korea which had become unpopular was a far more potent issue than questions of foreign aid, military

[37] Louis Harris, *Is There a Republican Majority?* (New York: Harper & Brothers, 1954), pp. 22-26, 31-32, 43, 178. Harris discussed polls conducted by Elmo Roper in 1952. These also showed that the percentage of persons describing the Korean war as an important issue rose from 30 in June to 53 in late October. Lubell, *Revolt of the Moderates*, pp. 39-43, 118, 265-66, reported his interviews showed: "In 1952 the public's thinking was dominated by the bloody stalemate in Korea. On that issue the popular mood was to demand a decision —to get the war over with one way or another." He believed the Korean war motivated the voters' switch to Eisenhower well in advance of the latter's promise to go to Korea.

treaties, or isolationist voting records. Second, the fact that this was a dominant theme of the presidential campaign gave it particular importance in all the senatorial contests. Senatorial campaigns had a unifying foreign policy theme in 1952 that had been lacking in 1948, when Truman and Dewey had no important differences on foreign policy.

THE PRESIDENT AND SENATORIAL CAMPAIGNS

Foreign policy was a unifying theme for Republican senatorial candidates in 1952 because even those whose voting record and views conflicted with Eisenhower's could join him in urging an end to the war. The campaign tactics of those Republicans who differed greatly with Eisenhower's internationalist views but who usually ignored or discounted these differences demonstrated how completely a presidential candidate can dominate the campaign.

A particularly interesting example is Senator William Jenner of Indiana, whose voting record was one of the most isolationist in Congress and who was seeking reelection in a state where Taft had been more popular than Eisenhower and where isolationist sentiment was relatively strong. Despite these factors, Jenner repeatedly asserted that his record was "very little different" from that of Eisenhower, whose endorsement he claimed to have. Jenner repeated but did not emphasize his opposition to NATO and foreign aid. Senator Kem of Missouri, under attack as an isolationist by Stuart Symington, said little about his foreign policy views because he recognized how much he differed with Eisenhower and believed that this difference would hurt him at the polls. Senator Bricker, on the other hand, took the offensive on foreign policy questions with little apparent worry about his disagreements with Eisenhower. Democratic opponents frequently criticized these and other Republicans for being out of step with the Republican presidential candidate.

In subsequent elections other Republicans were embarrassed by their differences with the President on foreign policy. An example is Joseph T. Meek, who opposed Illinois Democratic Senator Paul Douglas in 1954. Early in the campaign Meek left no doubt about his opposition to "foreign giveaway programs" and his support for the Bricker amendment. In an exchange of letters late in July, however, he pledged support for the Eisenhower administration and received the President's endorsement. Thereafter Meek's statements on foreign policy were more cautious and less frequent, though he did not entirely abandon the expression of isolationist viewpoints. Douglas believed that the isolationist reputation helped to defeat Meek. The same year, Senator Guy Cordon of Oregon said little in his campaign about a voting record on foreign policy that frequently conflicted with Eisenhower's. He did emphasize that he had only voted for the less extreme versions of the Bricker amendment. His Democratic opponent, Richard Neuberger, attributed his narrow victory in part to the differences between Cordon and the President on foreign policy.

The role of the Bricker amendment as an issue in the 1954 campaign sheds light on presidential-senatorial relations. Despite the concern of many senators over constituent reaction to this issue, there is no good evidence that any senator was seriously hurt at the polls in 1954 because he voted against the Bricker amendment. Republican Senator Homer Ferguson, who lost his bid for reelection in Michigan, has attributed his defeat to his vote against the Bricker amendment, arguing that his stand caused Republicans to abstain from voting in the senatorial race. This estimate is not borne out, however, by other political observers or by a cursory examination of the Michigan election returns.[38] On the other hand, Republicans such as Meek and Cordon were on the defensive because they disagreed with Eisenhower.

Loyal defense of the Eisenhower administration's foreign policy and particularly a firm stand against the Bricker amendment proved to be serious handicaps, however, for Alexander Wiley, the senior Republican on the Foreign Relations Committee, who sought reelection in Wisconsin in 1956. Foreign policy dominated the Republican contest that preceded the state

[38] Approximately 43,000 more votes were cast in the gubernatorial than in the senatorial election. In order to have won, Ferguson would have had to receive virtually all of these 43,000 votes—a prospect made more unlikely by the fact that Ferguson actually led his gubernatorial running mate, in percentage terms.

convention in late May. At a series of caucuses, Senator Wiley's three competitors for the Republican nomination—former Representative Charles J. Kersten, Mark Catlin, Jr., and Howard H. Boyle, Jr.—repeatedly attacked Wiley's record on foreign affairs. While all three of Wiley's original competitors represented an extreme isolationist point of view, the Republican convention nominated a compromise candidate, Representative Glenn R. Davis, who—although more moderate—had a record of opposition to foreign aid. During the primary campaign following the convention, he urged a reduction in foreign aid and the passage of a constitutional amendment based on the principles of the Bricker amendment. He devoted comparatively little attention to foreign policy, however, and emphasized his strong support for Eisenhower's domestic policy. The campaign became less vitriolic, less a test of foreign policy, and more an informal handshaking campaign, which both Wiley and Davis seemed to prefer.

Wiley was nominated with a margin of approximately 10,000 votes. The narrowness of his victory can be seen in the 20,000 votes polled by the third candidate, an isolationist, who obviously drew votes from Davis. Doubtless, Wiley's fervent internationalism and particularly his opposition to the Bricker amendment were important factors undermining Republican support for him in Wisconsin. He realized that isolationist sentiment was strong among Republicans, avoided discussing foreign policy, and argued that his voting record had been dictated by loyalty to Eisenhower. Davis' tactics indicated, however, that he did not consider extreme isolationism and hostility to the Eisenhower administration politically advantageous in the primary. The circumstances of the campaign suggest that Wiley's victory did not prove whether a majority of Wisconsin Republicans endorsed Eisenhower's foreign policies.

The views and records of senators were of declining importance as election issues during the campaigns of the Eisenhower administration. Republican candidates usually refrained from attacking Democratic senators for supporting Eisenhower's foreign programs. Despite growing Democratic criticism of some aspects of these policies, Democratic candidates usually did not make them a campaign issue. The international issues of 1956 and 1960 did not involve voting records. In 1956 Republican senators echoed the national party theme that the Eisenhower administration had preserved peace and was best able to steer the nation through the crises that emerged at the last minute involving the Suez and Hungary.[39] In 1960 senatorial candidates repeated the Kennedy-Nixon debates over declining national prestige and the preservation of peace.

ISOLATIONISM AS AN ISSUE IN SOUTHERN PRIMARIES

The clearest recent examples of foreign policy as a campaign issue have been in southern Democratic primaries. The South is one of the regions where senators have sensed growing opposition to the foreign trade program as well as to foreign aid. Southern candidates, furthermore, were bound by no sense of loyalty to the administration, as were Republican candidates. Foreign policy became a major issue in Georgia months before the 1956 primary in which Walter F. George, chairman of the Foreign Relations Committee, was expected to seek renomination. His prospective opponent, former Governor Herman Talmadge, started his campaign early and, among other issues, stressed his support for the Bricker amendment and his opposition to foreign aid, the Point Four Program, and particularly those forms of aid that would intensify foreign competition with Georgia's textiles and agricultural products. He argued that the aid program was lavish compared to the inadequate federal aid given to Georgia farmers. Although he did not recommend abolishing foreign military assistance, he expressed doubts about its value. Talmadge avoided personal attacks on Senator George but obviously was criticizing programs with which George was closely identified. Unwilling to carry the burden of a prolonged campaign against a strong opponent, George withdrew from the race before the primary. Thereafter, Talmadge continued to

[39] The studies of the Survey Research Center showed that in 1956, in contrast to 1952, Democratic voters were no more likely than Republicans to give internationalist responses to questions on foreign policy. This probably resulted from the internationalist policies of the Eisenhower administration, and it illustrates "the role played by the parties in lending structure to mass public opinion." A. Campbell and others, *The American Voter* (New York: John Wiley and Sons, 1960), pp. 198-200.

take an isolationist line, which his remaining opponent, M. E. Thompson, occasionally criticized.[40] Since George withdrew from the race, it is difficult to estimate the effectiveness of Talmadge's isolationist arguments, but Talmadge was familiar with public opinion in the state and presumably had reason to believe that the issue was a strong one. One close observer of Georgia politics has suggested, however, that Talmadge criticized foreign aid primarily to win campaign funds from the Georgia textile interests, which were strongly opposed to the aid program. There were other factors that contributed to Talmadge's strength: his gubernatorial record, comparative youth, his name, and strong rural support. The foreign policy issue in Georgia stood out primarily as a symptom of a trend in southern politics.

The trend has not gathered momentum rapidly in the South— in part because veteran southern senators do not often face serious primary competition. Estes Kefauver and Albert Gore of Tennessee have both been under attack in Democratic primaries because of their votes for the aid and trade programs. Whatever the effectiveness of isolationism as an issue in Tennessee, it has not prevented the reelection of Kefauver and Gore. In 1954 Kefauver's opponent in the primary, Pat Sutton, described Kefauver as an "internationalist" and a "one-worlder" and defined the major campaign issue as "internationalism as opposed to Americanism." His specific criticisms were directed against foreign aid and the United Nations. Kefauver largely ignored foreign affairs during the campaign. In the 1960 campaign Kefauver emphasized foreign policy more; his opponent, Judge Andrew Taylor, while saying less about it, leveled his criticism primarily at the foreign trade program. In 1958 Senator Gore was criticized in the primary because of his voting record on foreign policy. His opponent, former Governor Prentice Cooper, attacked both the aid and trade policies as "a do-gooder, one-world, global give-away program." Gore met the challenge head on. He vigorously defended the foreign trade program,

[40] Cabell Phillips, " 'Hummon'—Chip Off the Talmadge Block," *New York Times Magazine*, May 20, 1956, pp. 12, 68-69. George McMillan, ". . . So Goes the South," *Collier's*, CXXXVII (June 8, 1956), 42-47. Douglass Cater, "Regression vs. Conservatism in Georgia," *Reporter*, XIII (Oct. 20, 1955), 13-16. Issues of the *Atlanta Constitution*.

reminding Tennessee audiences that it was established by their native son, Cordell Hull, and emphasizing the stake that both cotton farmers and manufacturers in Tennessee have in foreign trade.[41]

It is too early to evaluate whether isolationism is strong enough in the South to become an effective campaign issue; it has yet to be decisive in a southern primary. Most of the southern senators who have remained loyal to internationalist principles either have been able to defend this position in campaigns or have found defense unnecessary. It may be that southern isolationist candidates will find the issue even less effective with a Democrat in the White House. Southern isolationists on domestic issues are generally segregationists and often fiscal conservatives as well. In the South, then, questions of foreign policy have been lost beneath more urgent domestic problems.

THE IMPLICATIONS

The senator is relatively free from constituent pressure on most issues of foreign policy. His mail and his other guides to opinion usually show that the voters have little interest in most foreign problems because they do not believe these questions affect them directly. An issue like the Korean war will stir deep public concern because of its direct effect on the average citizen, while an issue like the tariff, with its specialized economic impact, will produce some pressure on the senator, often through organized groups. The relationship between senator and constituent cannot be understood without reference to a third factor, the influence of the President.

More than anyone else, the President determines both the climate of public opinion on foreign issues and the extent and nature of public pressure on a senator. Through bold action in an emergency or through persistent efforts to explain the facts of international life to the citizens, the President can—on occasion—mobilize public support so strong that the senator becomes conscious of it and may hesitate to vote against presidential pro-

---

[41] David Halberstam, "The 'Silent Ones' Speak up in Tennessee," *Reporter*, XXIII (Sept. 1, 1960), 28-30. *Washington Post and Times Herald*, Aug. 6, 1958, p. A12.

grams. If the President fails to develop or maintain public understanding of his policies, the result may be public apathy or resistance. In the case of foreign aid, some senators believe the public is apathetic while others feel it is growing hostile. If the public is apathetic, the senator may have a free hand; in the case of the Bricker amendment, however, public apathy and ignorance permitted a small pressure group to create a distorted image of national opinion, and the President's efforts did not supply a sufficient cushion of public support to protect those senators sympathetic to the President. The Korean war demonstrated that massive opposition can develop when the President has been unable to create public understanding of his policy. The policy of limited war in Korea was by its nature difficult to explain to a public accustomed to the idea of unconditional surrender. Respect for presidential authority and knowledge in foreign affairs was great enough, however, that the Republican leaders in Congress needed a man of General MacArthur's stature to take the initiative in seeking public support for an alternative policy. The most serious handicap faced by the opposition party in Congress is its inability to compete with the President in foreign policy, for no opposition leader can speak with comparable authority.

Senatorial election campaigns in recent years confirm these conclusions. Except for the Korean war and the associated issue of which party could best keep the peace, foreign policy has seldom been a major issue in postwar election campaigns. Though a significant number of isolationists lost at the polls in the early postwar years, there is little reason to believe that isolationism was the prime reason for their defeat. When the voters did give weight to foreign policy questions, they usually paid little attention to the voting records of individual senators on specific issues. Instead, they sometimes chose a senator because of what his party and its presidential candidate stood for.[42]

[42] The results of public opinion research show what a small proportion of voters are familiar with political issues and perceive interparty differences on these issues. What we know about the American voter supports the conclusion that he would seldom be familiar with senatorial voting records and would more likely judge a senator by the success or failure of the administration in general areas of foreign policy, such as maintaining peace. It is also reasonable to suppose that the issue of a senator's loyalty to his President might be easier for voters to understand than the details of a voting record. See Campbell, Chs. 8, 9, and 10.

In choosing a President, the voters have been paying increasing attention to his views on foreign policy and particularly his ability to handle grave questions of war and peace. In every election since 1940 (except 1948), this has been the outstanding factor in the voters' minds. It is likely that the split-ticket voting that predominated during the Eisenhower era occurred largely because many voters had confidence in Eisenhower as a foreign policy leader but preferred the domestic program of the Democratic party. The voters recognized the President's primary responsibility for the conduct of foreign relations, while relegating to Congress the responsibility for domestic affairs.

For these reasons, it would be a mistake to exaggerate the number of votes won or lost by senators because of the voters' attitude toward the administration's foreign policy. Nevertheless, a senator's political future may sometimes be greatly affected by the administration's success or failure. There is no doubt that Democratic candidates suffered in 1950 and 1952 because many voters believed the Truman administration had failed first to maintain peace and then to win the war in Asia. Republican candidates benefited in later years because Eisenhower had kept the peace.

While a senator may be helpless if his party's President is unpopular, he does not profit automatically if the voters approve of his President. He may benefit if he has been a loyal supporter of the President's policies; if not, he may lose votes. There are not enough examples to establish proof in any sense, but the recent history of campaigns suggests that Republican voters in some states expected Republican senators to give Eisenhower more consistent backing for his foreign programs than on domestic issues. This may be one explanation of the growing support given by Republican senators to Eisenhower's foreign policy as the administration progressed.

Though the evidence is fragmentary, it is important because it casts a new light on the President's leadership of his party in the Senate. If voters in at least some states expect a senator to support the President of his party on foreign policy matters, the President can afford to use the promise of support or the threat of withholding it as a weapon of leadership. President Eisenhower did not in fact use this tactic, though his popularity was great enough so that he could have. Eisenhower carefully avoided intervention in Republican contests for senatorial nominations. In 1958 he told a press conference: "I have always refused in advance of any primary or of any selection of Republican candidate [sic] for any office to intervene in any way."[43] Franklin Roosevelt's 1938 experience in trying to purge conservative Democratic senators by backing their opponents in primaries seems to have made a lasting impact on American politicians. It should not be considered conclusive proof, however, that a President could never dislodge a senator who consistently opposed his views. There would be greater justification and chance of success if the President found some means to support a loyal senator of his party who was facing stiff primary opposition. In the case of Alexander Wiley's 1956 primary, the President deliberately sidestepped this opportunity to strengthen his own political hand.

In general elections the President has greater opportunity to use his endorsement as a tool of leadership. Particularly since his time for campaigning is limited, the President can endorse his loyal supporters with enthusiasm and demonstrate his support by campaigning in their states, while giving only a perfunctory endorsement or completely ignoring those senators or candidates in his party who have frequently differed with him. Eisenhower abstained from this technique also. In 1952, for example, he endorsed isolationist Senator William Jenner in an Indianapolis speech and stressed his respect for independent-minded Republicans, though in Missouri his endorsement for another isolationist Republican, James Kem, was more perfunctory. In 1954, when he made a whirlwind trip on one of the last days of the campaign to help out several Republican senatorial candidates, he sent publicized telegrams to all the other Republicans campaigning for the Senate, including several strong isolationists, asserting that their election was of equal importance.[44]

In 1958 it began to appear that the President intended to use his endorsement as a method of developing support for his major programs. At a January press conference he denied that he intended to follow this tactic. At a March press conference, however, Eisenhower emphasized that he would not support

---

[43] *New York Times*, March 27, 1958, p. 18.
[44] *Ibid.*, Oct. 29, 1954, pp. 1, 16, 17.

candidates who were in disagreement with him on such major issues as national security, foreign aid, and economy in government. In May he added the issue of reciprocal trade as a test of candidates' loyalty.[45] In the 1958 elections there were six Republican senators seeking reelection with records that could clearly be called internationalist, while seven others had strongly isolationist voting records.[46] The President did not make it clear to the voters that he was endorsing some but not others. Though he did not make any speeches in the states where isolationist senators were running, he spoke in only one of the states with an internationalist Republican candidate. Vice President Richard Nixon, who played a much more active role in the campaign, did not seem to make any clear distinction between the two types of Republicans. Had the President really desired to put to the test the theory that his endorsement was worth votes, he might have campaigned intensively for such senators as Edward Thye of Minnesota, William Purtell of Connecticut, and J. Glenn Beall of Maryland. The risks of such a policy are clear, however; Eisenhower's prestige and authority in the party might have been diminished if he had campaigned vigorously for selected candidates in a year when the Democrats were capturing numerous seats in the Senate.

Until the President is willing to test his influence on the voting public, the issue will remain in doubt. Nevertheless, it seems reasonable that if a President made foreign policy issues the major criteria of loyalty, he might be able to demonstrate that such loyalty is an asset and disloyalty a liability for senators in his own party seeking reelection.

[45] *Ibid.*, Jan. 16, 1958, p. 14; March 6, 1958, p. 12; May 7, 1958, pp. 1, 20.
[46] The internationalists were: William A. Purtell of Connecticut, Frederick G. Payne of Maine, J. Glenn Beall of Maryland, Charles E. Potter of Michigan, Edward J. Thye of Minnesota, and Arthur V. Watkins of Utah. The isolationists were: Barry M. Goldwater of Arizona, John J. Williams of Delaware, Roman L. Hruska of Nebraska, George W. Malone of Nevada, William Langer of North Dakota, John W. Bricker of Ohio, and Frank A. Barrett of Wyoming. The two Republicans from West Virginia, Chapman Revercomb and John D. Hoblitzell, served too briefly and had too mixed a voting record to classify.

The great gaping hole in the structure of responsibility is the empty place left by the American party system. Without responsible parties, Congress cannot be responsible; and unless Congress is responsible, it has slight claim to enforce responsibility on the President.—ROBERT A. DAHL

9
THE ROLE OF PARTIES IN THE FOREIGN POLICY PROCESS

CAN THE AMERICAN PARTIES CONTRIBUTE A GREATER MEASURE of rationality and responsibility to the policymaking process in foreign affairs? The problem is a twofold one. The President needs more help from his party for the initiation and particularly for the continuation of foreign programs. These programs require the dependable support of a party majority; they must not be subject to the vicissitudes of shifting coalitions in Congress. The opposition party faces a greater problem. Lacking a President, it needs machinery to devise and publicize agreed-on alternatives in foreign policy. Even if the opposition can seldom offer complete alternatives, it has a responsibility for constructive criticism.

What is the prospect for a greater party role in the Senate? The rollcalls during the Truman and Eisenhower administrations show what a significant role party has played in the recent past. The President has normally been able to depend on more support from senators of his own party than from opposition senators. Often the majority in his own party for his programs has been a lopsided one and has included senators who harbored serious doubts about the programs. On the other hand, the opposition party has been frequently divided; though its members owe no loyalty to the President's party, many feel he deserves support in foreign affairs. The geographic patterns of voting suggest that senators opposing the administration's programs often believe they are either expressing constituent views of isolationism or fiscal conservatism or are defending local economic interests. Senators with such views will naturally resist efforts at party unity when the party's position conflicts with theirs.

With a large measure of party unity on foreign policy, what changes in party leadership and institutions are feasible? Experience suggests that stronger parties will come from strong and skillful leaders more than from a new institutional framework. The position of majority leader has grown in importance chiefly as a result of Lyndon Johnson's vigorous control. The problem is to assure that men of high ability have the chance to assume leadership in the Senate and to suggest institutional techniques these leaders might use.

The senatorial parties have usually shown more skill and less regard to seniority in choosing party leaders than in other choices. Lyndon Johnson was selected by the Democrats as floor leader in 1953 after only four years in the Senate. Taft, as chairman of the Policy Committee and later as floor leader, was the natural Republican choice. The parties, however, have not always chosen so well. Ernest MacFarland lacked vigor as Democratic floor leader, while Kenneth Wherry as Republican leader did not represent his party's views in foreign policy. The Republicans have sometimes chosen a party whip who appeared seriously out of step with the views of the floor leader. The Democrats, in particular, have sometimes promoted the party whip to be floor leader with little discussion; if the floor leader is given wide discretion in choosing the whip, as Lyndon Johnson had, this gives the party a minimum of actual choice in picking its leader. Though the incumbents are normally subject to reelection by party caucus every two years, this practice has not forced them to be more responsible to the party. It is not realistic to expect rank-and-file senators to challenge an incumbent's leadership in most cases, nor would this promote party unity. Yet, if there were modern precedent in the Senate for such action, it might minimize the danger that leaders would grow unrepresentative of the party.

Since the President has such a stake in the senatorial leadership of his party, it does not seem unreasonable to suggest that he should play some informal role in the choice of these leaders. This too is a matter of tradition but it is also an area where presidential influence has been felt in the past. While the President may have some influence over the initial choice of party leaders, he is less likely to succeed in encouraging a change in leadership. Any strong effort by President Eisenhower to remove Senator Knowland as floor leader would have run into opposition not only from Republican senators who shared Knowland's views but from those who were jealous of senatorial prerogatives. The most the President might successfully do would be to give informal approval to a change initiated in the Senate; this appears to have been the extent of Eisenhower's participation when Charles Halleck replaced Joe Martin as Republican leader of the House.

The most serious barrier faced by able senators seeking positions of leadership is undoubtedly the seniority principle in committees. The issue of seniority is one on which reformers in quest of a stronger party system and practicing politicians familiar with the Senate usually clash. The reformers insist that committee chairmen who owe their position to seniority are able to flaunt every effort at increased party unity. The politicians argue that the seniority system minimizes intraparty conflict and serves the vested interests of most senators. The sanctity of the seniority rule did not prevent Lyndon Johnson, a most practical politician, from making one important breach in the principle in 1953, when he decided to use other criteria in making the intial appointments of senators to committees and to guarantee each Democrat at least one major committee assignment.

The rule that the senior member of the majority party becomes chairman of his committee is undoubtedly more important, more disruptive of party unity, and more difficult to break. It should not be assumed, however, that this principle must stand unchanged, nor should it be assumed that the only alternative is to ignore seniority completely in picking a chairman. The principle of appointing experienced men to responsible positions is too reasonable to need defense. Yet experience needs to be combined with capability. The seniority principle can promote such obviously qualified men as George and Vandenberg on the Foreign Relations Committee. At other times, however, on the same committee it has advanced men like Theodore F. Green, aging and infirm at 89, Alexander Wiley, who lacked party stature, and, during World War I, William J. Stone, an isolationist senator who completely opposed Woodrow Wilson's foreign policy.[1]

Deep-seated customs in the Senate are changed only gradually. The best chance of modifying the seniority rule will come when that rule makes eligible for the chairmanship of a committee some senator who is fundamentally in disagreement with most members of his party on issues directly relevant to that committee. Such an opportunity for change did come in 1956, when Senator James Eastland of Mississippi inherited chairmanship of the Judiciary Committee, with its jurisdiction over civil rights measures and judicial nominees. On that occasion the Senate followed the seniority rule, but it need not always do so. From a few exceptions to the rule might easily grow a practice of choosing from among the two or three senior men on a committee the senator who is most able and whose viewpoints are representative of his party. Ideal standards of party unity would require that recalcitrant committee chairmen be subject to removal by the party. This is not realistic in the forseeable future, nor is it a practical necessity for stronger party organization; in fact, the resulting periodic controversies might well be disruptive of party unity.

If the rules and customs of the Senate can be improved to facilitate the emergence of strong leaders, there is less need for

---

[1] Stone retained his post as chairman despite an effort in 1917 to remove him and despite an unsuccessful attempt to expel him from the Senate for treason. George H. Haynes, *The Senate of the United States* (Boston: Houghton Mifflin Co., 1938), I, 297-98.

building elaborate institutions of party leadership. Existing institutions may be adapted to present needs. A staff of skilled assistants now exists and, with the increase of details to be considered, has become a necessity. The policy committee, while it has varied with leaders and circumstances, has the greatest potential of any institutions that have been tried, providing that its limitations as well as its possibilities are realized. It cannot effectively compel unity in the party, and often it cannot usefully promulgate a party policy; but it can serve as an agent of compromise, and it can devise tactics and offer legislative proposals to exploit any substantial party unity. It cannot make the floor leader accountable to the party, though it can provide him with valuable advice and with judgment on the temper of senatorial opinion. To operate most successfully, the policy committee must represent regions and viewpoints in the party and include the most influential senators and chairmen or ranking members of a few major committees.

By contrast, the opportunities for greater use of the caucus in the Senate appear relatively small. The familiar arguments against the caucus have considerable weight: It is impotent, unwieldly, time-consuming, and disruptive of unity. Although there may be occasions when they serve the purposes of the party leadership, regular or frequent caucuses would seem to be a liability.

THE PRESIDENT AS PARTY LEADER

Skillful leadership and effective organization in the administration party in the Senate are important, but the ultimate leader of foreign policy must be the President. He must develop programs and means of supporting them in the Senate. On most important matters the President will usually attempt to secure bipartisan support and at the same time assert his party leadership. He can develop programs through advance consultation with leaders of both parties, a public announcement committing this country to the program, and an educational campaign to stimulate approval from at least the enlightened public. Senators and the public alike respond to these initiatives because they recognize that the President has superior access to information, holds the responsibility for developing policies, and—particularly in times of crisis—needs united support to make these policies effective. Both Presidents Truman and Eisenhower used these techniques well on most occasions. A review of the postwar period suggests that when foreign crises arise, the President has ample resources for inducing the necessary degree of congressional support.

It is for the less dramatic responsibility of continuing and expanding an existing foreign program that the President must rely particularly on party support. As W. Y. Elliott has said, "Party discipline is, therefore, necessary to maintain the coherence and continuity of foreign policy through adequate legislative support. It is also essential in winning popular support by seeing to it that the Administration's policy is defended by effective political spokesmanship."[2] When there is sentiment in Congress for paring a half billion dollars from the foreign aid program or for limiting the President's authority under the reciprocal trade act, the President usually must rely primarily on his own party to hold the line for his policy. Elliott points out that party responsibility also assures "the stable nucleus of support for issues that to the average voter or Congressman may seem unimportant or peripheral to foreign policy, but that in reality are central to it."[3] In the early postwar period, there were a multitude of foreign crises in which the President could rely on broad, bipartisan support. In later years, the success of foreign policy has depended increasingly on the continuity of support for established programs. We have learned that the nation's foreign responsibility is a long-term undertaking, not fulfilled simply by signing a pact, issuing a congressional resolution, or granting stopgap aid to an ally in distress. We have also come to recognize that there is no clear separation between foreign and domestic problems.

This trend suggests that the President is increasingly dependent on partisan support for most of his foreign programs. This may even be true if his party lacks a congressional majority. Since his time is severely limited, the President must rely upon the leaders in the Senate to consolidate partisan support. The

---

[2] Elliott, *United States Foreign Policy*, pp. 135-36.
[3] *Ibid.*, p. 135.

skillful use of patronage and support for legislation of interest to particular senators is a device occasionally valuable if used with caution, but here again he must rely largely upon subordinates for the actual detailed work. Probably the single most effective tactic for the President is a forthright public stand on foreign policy. As leader of the party, the President has at his disposal relatively few sanctions but is its primary spokesman. When a President makes full use of the authority resident in him as leader of foreign policy and his party's chief spokesman, constituents may begin to expect members of Congress in the President's party to give him support. There is some evidence of such a trend in recent senatorial elections. Neustadt has said, "Assured support [for the President] will not be found in Congress unless contemplation of their own electorates keeps a majority of members constantly aligned with him."[4] As a further step in forging party unity, the President might well consider the judicious use of endorsement and nonendorsement of candidates in primaries and elections, using the criterion of foreign policy voting records. Members of the President's party in Congress can frequently vote against him on domestic issues because their stand serves the interests of their district or state. In relatively few cases does foreign policy have such a directly adverse effect on constituents as to dictate congressional opposition. The President should be able to demand loyalty from his party on foreign policy and make this prerequisite to his endorsement without alienating those members of the opposition who frequently support his policy. In the years ahead, the President will be frequently advocating foreign policies that are demanding, expensive, and potentially unpopular. He has the resources, if used imaginatively, to win continuing legislative support for these policies.

DILEMMA OF THE OPPOSITION

If the administration already has the resources and techniques available for foreign policy leadership, the opposition party does not. It may be argued that the dangers resulting from opposition failure are less serious than those resulting from deadlock or

[4] Neustadt, *Presidential Power*, pp. 186-87.

erosion of the administration's policies in Congress. Some observers differ, however. They point to the dangers of a presidential *fait accompli* and the increasing risks that nuclear war might result from an ill-advised step taken by the President without congressional approval. They argue that with increasing presidential authority to shape the course of foreign policy, the opposition has a growing responsibility to criticize mistakes of policy and to focus attention on neglected problems abroad.[5]

The difficulties faced by the opposition party in devising a foreign policy are formidable. It has no leader or group of leaders with a staff or sources of information equal to the President's or with widely recognized responsibilities for foreign policy. The opposition is handicapped if it tries to develop foreign policy issues for use in election campaigns. The public is seldom interested in foreign policy unless it is some overwhelming problem comparable to the Korean war. Some foreign problems fade in importance before the next election is held, and others are too subtle for campaign purposes. In the 1960 campaign, for example, Senator Kennedy made an issue out of declining American prestige but made no serious effort to discuss the need for a foreign aid program aimed more at underdeveloped and uncommitted countries—though this had been a theme of some Democratic senators. There can be serious risks in making foreign policy a major election issue. As a consequence, the victory of one party might cast doubt on American commitments abroad; whatever the outcome, the campaign alone might make this country appear to be an unstable ally. Unless the administration's foreign policy is thoroughly unpopular, the opposition party may hesitate to challenge the policy vigorously in an election campaign.

A fundamental difficulty the opposition party faces is that of developing alternative policies. As one writer has said, "In the framing of foreign policy the only real possibility of an integrated program of policy and action lies with the chief executive."[6] The opposition party may easily develop comprehen-

---

[5] See, for example, Thomas L. Hughes. "Foreign Policy on Capitol Hill," *Reporter*, XX (April 30, 1959), 28-31; Arthur N. Holcombe, *Our More Perfect Union* (Cambridge: Harvard University Press, 1950), pp. 280-83, 424-29.

[6] Malcolm Moos. *Politics, Presidents and Coattails* (Baltimore: Johns Hopkins Press, 1952), p. 160.

sive legislation for federal aid to education or labor reform, but in the foreign field it often lacks the information necessary for action. In some cases the opposition is restrained from offering an alternative program because the President has already so deeply committed the nation to one course that a different one could not succeed. The administration party has a leader in the President; while his colleagues may disagree with him, none are able to challenge his leadership successfully. The opposition party usually has no single spokesman (except during presidential campaigns). Some of the strongest leaders are often outside Congress and consequently lack immediate and direct policy-forming responsibilities. For these reasons the opposition is seldom able to unite behind a single policy and, even when successful, lacks a leader able to present such a policy as authoritatively as the President presents his.

If the opposition party is sometimes able to agree on an alternative program, it is usually unable to get it enacted. Presidential vetoes are seldom overriden, and the chances are least if foreign policy is involved. If Congress avoids a veto by enacting a new program as part of broader legislation, the President can delay implementing it, as President Truman did in the case of aid programs for Spain and Nationalist China. Many foreign programs are dependent less on legislation than on methods of administration and diplomatic initiatives over which Congress has no direct control. In Roger Hilsman's words: "Although Congress could almost always find a way of denying support to a particular policy and dictate policy in the sense of paralyzing it, one must doubt whether it can force the Executive to accept a positive alternative in foreign policy by the exercise of its formal powers. It has no way of making an Executive follow a different policy, and there are always tempting, if devious, routes by which the Executive can follow its own policy no matter how many obstacles Congress puts in the way."[7]

If the opposition party is to have any role beyond mere acquiescence, it must, in Senator Vandenberg's words, add its trademarks to the President's policy. The opposition can be alert for aspects of proposed legislation that it considers unwise or dangerous, it can seek to clarify vagueness or contradictions

[7] Hilsman, "Congressional-Executive Relations and the Foreign Policy Consensus," *American Political Science Review*, LII (Sept., 1958), 730.

in policies, it can try to raise or lower the financial costs of programs, and it can attempt to make foreign commitments compatible with domestic programs or the interests of American citizens. Many of the changes sought by the opposition may be of considerable importance, but they are likely to fall short of radically different policies. Even if the President has a majority in Congress, one disciplined enough to provide the votes for his policy, he will not necessarily ignore the arguments of the opposition. There will be times when a broader, bipartisan base of congressional support is important enough to justify yielding to some of the opposition demands. If the President has a dependable majority, he is free to make the choice. There is no contradiction between the need for an administration party united enough to carry out the President's desires and the need for a vigorous and cohesive opposition party; if the first is achieved, the second becomes even more necessary.

There are occasions on which a single opposition leader can force the administration to reconsider or modify its proposals by the strength and wisdom of his criticisms. Too often, however, the opposition is ineffective because it speaks with different and contradictory voices or because its spokesman has little effective party support. What are the methods available for giving the opposition a more unified voice? All that has been said in this chapter about the practices and institutions of the Senate applies to the opposition party, which must promote men of ability to party and committee leadership, give them maximum flexibility of leadership, and develop institutions such as the policy committee to greater usefulness.

Because of its handicaps in dealing with foreign affairs, the opposition party must utilize all of its resources, and some of these lie outside of Congress. During the Eisenhower administration, for example, the Democrats leaned heavily on Adlai Stevenson and on men with diplomatic experience such as Dean Acheson, Averell Harriman, and Chester Bowles. These men played as big a role as the congressional leaders in developing an "opposition foreign policy," and these were among the men chosen to carry out a new policy under the Kennedy administration. In foreign affairs, perhaps more than in domestic problems, the opposition leadership must come largely from sources outside of Congress. Since it is Congress that must do the voting, there needs to be some liaison and cooperation between these two elements in the opposition party. Chairman Paul Butler devised the Advisory Council for the Democratic party. It gave the noncongressional Democrats a useful vehicle for expressing their views on both foreign and domestic issues. Its weakness was that congressional leaders, for very natural reasons, did not want to serve on it and be under any resulting obligation to accept its lead. Consequently, there was often a wide gap between the goals of the council and the strategy of Democratic leaders in Congress, though this difference affected domestic more than foreign policy.

The Advisory Council and most Democratic leaders outside Congress frequently urged greater emphasis on aid to underdeveloped areas than the Eisenhower administration was willing to give. Though this view was shared by some Democratic senators, there was not sufficient Democratic party unity in Congress to accomplish a change in the Eisenhower program or even to make a clear party record on this issue. During the debate over Formosa and the offshore islands, congressional leaders rejected a criticism of the administration's policy prepared in consultation with Dean Acheson and other Democratic foreign policy leaders and circulated by the Democratic National Committee. Adlai Stevenson spoke out in criticism of the administration's policy after Democrats in Congress had approved the Formosa resolution and the Chinese Mutual Defense Treaty. During the 1957 Middle Eastern debate, former President Truman urged prompt approval of the resolution sought by President Eisenhower, but the Democrats followed Dean Acheson's advice and added Democratic "trademarks" to the resolution. On this issue the public image of the Democratic stand was blurred because critics of the administration's policy acted from a wide variety of motives and sought a variety of alternatives. Democratic disunity on international issues was not merely a result of mechanical difficulties in coordination. Acheson and Stevenson, for example, differed considerably in their attitudes toward handling the challenges of international Communism. Most national leaders of the party believed in long-term aid and trade policies unacceptable to many Democrats in Congress who were sensitive to constituent opinions.

Today there are equally serious divisions in Republican ranks.

Though the isolationist attitudes of the 1930s and 1940s are nearly dead, there is a wide range of opinion concerning the scope and the purposes of American commitments abroad. Those Republicans who had international responsibilities in the Eisenhower administration have an outlook different from that of many members of Congress. Republicans in Congress who supported international programs largely because of loyalty to and confidence in the Eisenhower administration will probably become increasingly critical of expensive international commitments.

Lacking the President as a unifying force, the opposition party is likely to be divided on foreign policy, but it must constantly seek unity if it is to influence the administration's policy or even establish a record for itself. The use of some device like the advisory council seems to be in order. If opposition leaders in Congress are reluctant to serve on it, means can be found for consultation between the leadership of such a council and the congressional leaders. Perhaps such a council should rely more on private consultation than on public manifestoes to coordinate policy. There is no point in underestimating the opposition party's difficulties, but if that party is to carry out its own responsibilities, it must improve the political machinery both in Congress and between the congressional and national party leadership.

PARTIES AND POLICY

The successful conduct of foreign policy depends on many factors—such as able and experienced officials, adequate congressional staffs, and a steady flow of information to Congress—which have no relation to parties. A foreign policy that is soundly conceived and frankly presented to Congress stands a better chance of approval than an inadequate policy, even though the latter is buttressed by strong party discipline and elaborate consultation.

Political parties are not a cure-all but a resource in making policy which has not yet been fully exploited. Both parties can play a more effective role in policymaking without damaging the possibilities of bipartisan cooperation. Holbert N. Carroll, a careful student of the congressional policymaking process, believes that the potential of parties has barely been tapped: "The political parties can be used as effective agencies for the development of consensus within a party, between the parties, and with the executive branch, both with regard to particular policies and over broad policy areas. Of all agencies of the Congress, parties alone bear some responsibility for what the Congress does or fails to do. Party resources also can, and have, been used to elevate the quality of the congressional response in foreign policy and to instill a sense of discipline and responsibility upon the parts of the Congress and among the members. In this regard, it is not sufficiently appreciated that a member of Congress normally enjoys a free hand, unhampered by constituency pressures, in dealing with foreign policy. To the degree that party pressures are applied in these circumstances, the parties are filling a vacuum."[8] Party discipline can be more effective in foreign than in domestic policy because it is here that constituent pressures are usually at a minimum. When foreign policy does become an election issue, a skillful President can make his program—and a senator's support of it—an issue in senatorial campaigns. The opposition is seldom likely to make foreign policy the dominant theme of its campaign, but it can clarify its views more successfully for the voter.

Party organization in the Senate grows by trial and error from senatorial experience. It will vary to suit the needs of individual leaders, and no scheme of itself will produce a perfectly disciplined party. In the Senate it is most important to insure that the ablest men—preferably those with experience in foreign policy—may take places where their capabilities and influence may have the widest range. Skillful leaders in turn should devise practices and institutions that can strengthen party responsibility. For parties with greater responsibility offer the best hope of maintaining a balance in making foreign policy between President and Congress. Responsible political parties would give careful scrutiny to policies advanced by the President and would provide him with the best assurance of the votes to carry them out. The experiences of the past fifteen years amply demonstrate the need for such a scrutiny and such an assurance.

[8] Holbert N. Carroll, "Congressional Politics and Foreign Policy in the 1960's" (Paper presented at the annual meeting of the American Political Science Association, New York, Sept. 8, 1960), pp. 13-14.

INDEX